The Rape of Our Neighborhoods

And How Communities Are Resisting Take-overs by Colleges, Hospitals, Churches, Businesses, and Public Agencies

by William Worthy

William Morrow and Company, Inc.
New York   1976

Grateful acknowledgment is made to the following for permission to reprint special material: William Johnston, Catharine L. Motley, *The Boston Globe,* Rev. Daniel Berrigan, Joseph Porzio, Rev. E. Marshall Bevins, Andrew Hacker.

Printed in the United States of America.

1 2 3 4 5   80 79 78 77 76

Library of Congress Cataloging in Publication Data

Worthy, William (date)
    The rape of our neighborhoods.

    Includes bibliographical references and index.
    1. Urban renewal—United States—Citizen participation.
2. Community power. 3. Institutional investments—Social aspects—United States. 4. Citizens' associations—United States. I. Title.
HT175.W67   309.2′62′0973   76-2678
ISBN 0-688-00318-4

BOOK DESIGN: H. ROBERTS

To Dee Dee Kapes Hiebert,
for whom the battle has been fought

(Duty arises from our potential control over the course
of events.   —ALFRED NORTH WHITEHEAD)

Acknowledgments

The founder of the American Civil Liberties Union, Roger Baldwin—himself approaching a vigorous ninety years of age—tells of an elderly aunt whose energy and joie de vivre astounded everyone. When asked for her secret of longevity and élan, she would reply: "I've always kept an unpopular cause or two at hand."

This book could not have been written without the inspiration, past and present, derived from all who are driven to resist wrongs and to uphold human dignity. First and foremost, thanks go to my late parents and to their contemporary hero, crusading Boston editor William Monroe Trotter. They shared with him the antisegregation barricades during my formative years.

More recently, thanks are due to my sister Myrtle, who fed the cats and did the shopping when manuscript deadlines drew uncomfortably close.

Because the news industry is traditionally addicted to titles and positions when it comes to interviewing spokespersons for a cause, many of my fellow tenants have never gotten in front of a radio mike or a TV camera and have never read their names in the morning-after news

7

reports. To correct this omission, I list their names here on an honor role: Mrs. Beatrice McDermott (who moved in as a bride in 1917); Stanley Rafal; the Seda family; Frank Groseclose; Julius Masturzi; Claudio Mello; Charles Mancini; Mrs. Rafaela Cruz (hostess to our tenant meetings); Mrs. Rose DeQuattro; Mrs. Berta Norton; Bobby Lee (an exceptionally hard worker for the Tenants Committee); Juan Deligne; Antoinette Farese; Irene Wastock (the one among us who had a genius for layouts and leaflet designs). They are living testimony that even Manhattanites can become good neighbors and can practice mutual aid.

At a time when politicians and government agencies are in low repute, honesty compels a tribute to several unsung—and necessarily unnamed—lower-rung officials in the New York City housing bureaucracy. On a number of occasions, out of a sense of outrage, they went out of their way to provide us with behind-the-scenes information and to see that the Housing Code was enforced.

In our immediate neighborhood, such members of Community Board 6 as Clara Reiss, Vicky Spiegel and the late Peter Detmold influenced the Board to take strong positions against the unwarranted institutional expansionism and against the harassing relocation companies. In the next block, it was neighbor Raymond Rubinow who lent a supportive hand and who coined the apt phrase "medical imperialism."

As the newspaper of record, the *Gramercy Herald* became the sine qua non for our sustained confrontation with Columbus Hospital. Despite an energy-draining struggle to survive, the *Herald* has evolved into a model community newspaper—the communication media of the future.

Supplementing the *Herald* has been a small army

of reporters from New York area dailies and from radio and television stations and the networks. Though not all were sympathetic to the tenant cause, we rarely had any complaint about inaccuracy or slanting in their news stories.

Whenever funds for legal fees and other large expenses ran low, "Ping" and Carol Ferry and the Metropolitan Applied Research Center under Dr. Kenneth Clark and Dr. Hylan Lewis were always generously responsive.

Mike Meyer is one of those rare persons who manages to keep all self-righteousness out of a life of almost total dedication. He has been a patient and insightful reader of the early manuscript pages as well as of the final draft.

For fear of the answer, I haven't dared to ask Bob Levine, Deborah Geltman and Jim Finkenstaedt at William Morrow and Company if they've ever before taken on an author so stubborn about accepting suggestions to tone down the language of righteous indignation. Once I've slept on their advice, more often than not I have found their editorial judgments to be correct.

Omitted from these acknowledgments are neighborhood and citywide tenant supporters whose names and contributions dot the text.

Dee Dee Kapes Hiebert, since Bates College days my severest critic and confidante, won many of the battles over revision of the manuscript. To return a compliment she paid a long time ago, she has always been around when I needed her during the research, the writing, and the birth pangs of what is clearly a controversial book.

Preface
by Kenneth B. Clark

As far as I know, no profound historian or social philosopher has yet argued that the essential determinant of civilization is that small number of human beings who persist, in the face of overwhelming odds, in demanding, fighting for, and, if necessary, giving their lives for justice and morality. This is probably too simple a point for erudite scholars to build or reinforce their reputations upon.

As I have watched the ongoing struggles for social, economic, and racial justice in the United States and throughout the world, I have come to the conclusion that the common element in every civilized society—that important difference between subtle or flagrant forms of barbarism among human beings and the continuing struggle for decency—is a critical minority of individuals who are compelled to argue that human beings are capable of functioning on a higher level of social responsibility. These persistent individuals insist that the prevailing definitions of what is realistic and of what the controllers of power mandate and defend are not acceptable in a just society. They challenge the existing norms of behavior. They dem-

11

onstrate the contradictions between the verbal and the religious ideals of their society on the one hand and the rewarded day-to-day practices on the other. They are rarely, if ever, popular. They are frequently ridiculed or ignored or, at times, even sacrificed. In spite of these risks, of which they must be aware, they seem incapable of changing their roles.

As I have watched the role of William Worthy over the past thirty years, as I have seen him involved in one important issue after another, I have seen him insist upon social, economic, and racial justice without ever resorting to the easy devices of emotional rhetoric and the simplifications of the demagogue. He has insisted upon the inextricability of reason and morality as the only acceptable weapons in the struggle for social justice.

As the American Vietnam protest developed and became the basis for persistent demonstrations, I was obsessed with the thought that, many years before these demonstrations, the lonely voice of William Worthy was crying out in protest unheard. His objections to the French and American tragic Vietnam adventures were not based upon the later realization that the people of Southeast Asia could not be defeated by the military might of an industrialized nation. William Worthy objected because he was concerned then, as later, with the critical moral issue of the inherent barbarity of man when he seeks to enforce his will upon his fellow man by sheer power and violence.

With this background of direct observation of one of civilization's unusual human beings, I reacted with adolescent enthusiasm to the knowledge that William Worthy was bringing his unique moral concerns back to the neighborhoods. Because of his quiet and calm personality, I could not afford the luxury of directly expressing my personal enthusiasm. I could not embrace him, saying,

"Thanks, thanks, thanks for coming back home and helping us educate our own people to rise above the consequences of selfishness and avarice which threaten to destroy our cities." I merely said to him, "I am glad that you are back."

The Rape of Our Neighborhoods is one of the concrete indications that William Worthy is back and that he has brought back to our cities and to America those qualities of total commitment and concern for powerless human beings. Again, quietly, he refuses to understand or to function in terms of the personal risks inherently involved in defying immoral and amoral power.

In this book he has used, in one chapter, a single personal incident to demonstrate what a truly concerned person must do if our civilization is to continue. Indeed, *The Rape of Our Neighborhoods* has implications which reach far beyond this specific community conflict: it is a microcosm of the larger process of the struggle for justice, morality, and decency throughout the world. These goals are not obtained by verbalization even when repeated most piously. They come when individual human beings believe so strongly in these goals as to involve other human beings in working for them, in organizing for them, and in continuing the struggle despite the ever-present chances of failure and futility. The goals of justice and morality will eventually be obtained when the functional empathy and compassion of individuals go beyond parlor discussions, beyond academic philosophical seminars or the ritualized sermons in the permitted oases of colleges and churches. These goals will be obtained when they are infused into a community's consciousness and become part of the day-to-day lives of the human beings who are being victimized. This is not easy. It has never been easy. It may never be easy.

As I close this introduction to *The Rape of Our Neighborhoods,* I find that I must repeat the thought stated in the beginning. The foundation of any civilization must be the continuing struggle for justice and morality. Every civilized society must have that critical minority of individuals who, for a variety of known and unknown reasons, must assume the inevitable risks and conflicts associated with being a part of this struggle. A society is in serious danger of sinking into barbarism when the individuals who should or could be involved in this struggle are so totally defeated, intimidated, silenced, or destroyed that the practical people of power are able to exert total control. Then, instead of conflicts or confrontations, there is merely the quiet acceptance of injustice. When this victory of "law and order" immorality occurs, mankind is not only the victim of social barbarism, but all possibilities of a civilization are destroyed.

The Bill Worthys of our society provide the moral fuel necessary to prevent the flickering conscience of our society from going out.

Introduction
by Nat Hentoff

Bill Worthy is a stubborn man, one of the reasons he's such a first-class journalist. He allows no force, individual or institutional, to throw him off a story. In that respect, by the way, Bill made journalistic history in the late 1950's when he traveled to mainland China while the United States State Department fulminated at his "disobedience." Bill got the story, which he had every right to do, came on back home and proceeded, as usual, to keep on going his own way.

I was impressed at the China venture, but I wasn't surprised. I had known of Bill Worthy for some years before that. We come from the same neighborhood, the same street actually—Howland Street in Roxbury, part of Boston. We also went to the same school, Boston Latin, which, despite its name, primarily taught, as Bill was saying recently, the precise use of English.

Coming up, some years behind Bill, I would read his reporting in the black press, and then the white press too, and I'd clip a lot of it because his stories were so firmly founded on facts. I also admired the attitude of the man writing. It was something like that of I. F.

Stone: a reporter's first responsibility to his readers is not to get conned by those he's writing about. Both Izzy Stone and Bill Worthy are men of often fierce passion, but when they're on a story, they keep a cold eye on everything going on, from all sides.

In this book, Bill Worthy has been on a story that may turn out to be the most durably influential he's written so far. According to a certain amount of current conventional wisdom, there is pervasive apathy across the land, even the "generation gap" having been sealed by a mutually shared sense of impotence. Yet, as Bill's book demonstrates—and as just about any local reporter anywhere in the country will tell you—there are community risings and auguries of risings. And there will be more.

The deflating but essential lessons of the 60's have finally been absorbed. Charles Reich to the contrary, there are no instant, magical routes to redistribution of power in this country. Righteousness alone is no more effective than handing a visiting FBI man a copy of the Bill of Rights. The only defense against illegitimate power is knowing how to organize and how to organize well. And that's what this book is about. (In addition to the fact that it's a hell of a good, true yarn.)

On the one hand, the book focuses on a particularly arresting, small-scale but vital urban Armageddon (with sidetrips to other pivotal clashes elsewhere in the country); on the other hand, it begins to suggest some nonjive, long-range answers to how power, institutional power, can be leashed and made accountable.

But for any of this to happen, those who choose no longer to play victim have to get themselves together. And getting to a state of thorough cohesiveness can require an awful lot of patience on the part of those whose consciousness of the odds is more sanguine than is the case with people who have been more effectively conditioned into hopelessness over the years. For instance, one of the most telling sentences in Bill Worthy's book is:

"Without exaggeration, it took at least one full year, with approaches from many different angles, to convince even tenants who desperately wished to keep their apartments that Columbus Hospital in fact did not have that absolute power of eviction, and that tenant rights could be effectively asserted over property rights."

It can be very difficult to convince even those with the most to lose that they *can* fight back, and that's why this book is so valuable for that kind of raising of consciousness from sullen impotency to therapeutically angry, effective action. I would think that every community organization, actual and putative, in the country ought to have this narrative-manual right next to the phone book.

In a prolonged campaign—and all campaigns of this sort ought to be mounted with the expectation that they may take as long as the Wars of the Roses—there is usually more ministering to do, besides convincing those of little faith that the enemy is not omnipotent. Here too Worthy is usefully precise—"ministering unto others can mean everything from paying the utility bills of elderly tenants who don't have checking accounts, to replacing light bulbs for women who can't climb ladders, to accepting parcels from mailmen and then climbing five flights of stairs to deliver them, to many other forms of mutual aid for which New York apartment dwellers are not particularly noted." And not only New York apartment dwellers. In most parts of the United States, certainly including suburbs as well as cities, a sense of communality is so attenuated by now as to be nearly extinct.

In the 60's, there was much sloganeering and,

17

for that matter, bragging about a soaring renewal of communality. But in that decade too, collectively egalitarian sharing of struggles and other concerns was usually brief and shallow. However, the kind of steadily, doggedly evolving mutual aid of which Bill Worthy tells in this book can become a deeply rooted experience with eventual effects on growing numbers of the populace that may change more than a neighborhood. Only from roots that are real, not just drawn on posters, can anything lasting grow.

There are, in the book, many other realistic guides to beleaguered and perplexed targets of institutional fox hunts, but I want to focus further on the potential impact of this volume as it reaches its heterogeneous but essentially linkable audiences.

First, as noted, the book is for the wide range of community groups already organized or about to be organized to defend their homes or their parks or other values and valuables from a loomingly encroaching institutional force which appears to be as invulnerable as a dread mythological figure. It is, alas, reasonable to expect that many of these community groups will be largely ignorant of how to skewer the mythological figure. And obviously, the less clear they are as to what has to be done, the more likely they are to be devoured.

However, as Bill Worthy emphasizes, "It's not necessary to reinvent the wheel." The key building blocks for resistance are in this book and can be adapted to all kinds of particular terrains and adversaries. (Eventually, as Bill Worthy suggests, it would also be wise to have a national clearing house of strategies and war news from resisting communities.)

Another target group for this book, Bill points

18

out, "are college students beset by ever higher tuition fees in institutions that are seldom short of money to expand needlessly." He also underlines the need for urban planners to absorb this volume. In some cases, moreover, the book will make it impossible for them not to admit to themselves which side they're on, a shock of recognition which may reintroduce them to their consciences, personal and social.

Worthy makes a further enlivening suggestion. A good many, not all, of the young activists of the 60's have subsided into careerism and personalism because to them there appear to be no more sharply clear "cosmic" causes around which to do battle. But they're being myopic. "They have not yet seen," Worthy says, "as I failed to see until 1970, the relevance and the importance of organizing for a better world around gut neighborhood issues, however 'narrow' and 'parochial' they may appear to be at first glance."

Bill himself wrote a letter to a newspaper about his awakening to where to start organizing for a better world. It appeared in the April 16, 1971, issue of the *Gramercy Herald* (a neighborhood weekly mentioned frequently and with honor during the book), and it told how the incursion of Columbus Hospital into his neighborhood had made him become familiar, for the first time, with the defenseless and exploited on his very own street.

The war in Vietnam was still going on when this letter was written, and Bill noted that "as wild and overstated as it may sound initially, I have gradually come to the conclusion that, in terms of remaking the United States into a peaceful and humane society, where defenseless people are not trampled on, it is just as im-

19

portant to stop the imperialistic type expansion of institutions in this and other communities as it is to stop our aggressive warfare in Vietnam."

That was quite a public acknowledgment for a widely traveled, antiwar journalist to make in 1971. And as of the writing of this book, of course, we are still far from a state of peace at home in terms of the institutional violence—and resistance to it—analyzed here by Bill Worthy. He was right in 1971, and he's right now. A society that does not abuse and manipulate its own citizens is less likely to help manipulate and abuse the citizens of another country—Chile, let us say.

Whoever has read this book, in any case, has learned a lot about the logistics of American urban political warfare—and the battles described herein are indeed political battles. Politics is how we live with each other, who has power over whom, and if it is illegitimate, how can it be taken away? And in such urban warfare, a primary key to making counter-power work is the press. Particularly the neighborhood press. Writing of a Boston battle (Fenway v. Massachusetts Historical Society), Bill Worthy says of a no-charge community monthly with a circulation of "only" 5,000 that "in terms of the Fenway's ability to keep itself together, putting out [this] eight-page offset tabloid every four weeks is just as important as storming City Hall."

A community newspaper, obviously, will give more regular coverage to the kinds of campaigns Worthy is writing about than will a big city paper or television. Not that the latter should be ignored. And in this regard, both concerning the community and the metropolitan press, Worthy has provided in the body of the book and in an appendix the most accurate and incisively useful dissection of how best to work with the press that I have

20

yet seen. It too can easily be adapted to different local situations, and I expect that, as this book gets around, a lot of us who work for newspapers are going to get many more difficult-to-resist calls from diverse community organizers than has been the case up to now.

The press (and television) being so vital to the reclamation of power over their own lives by the citizenry, journalists themselves ought to become knowledgeable about this book. It is Bill's urgent hope that "newspaper and magazine editors, as well as assignment and city editors on radio and TV news desks" will study what has been written here in order to "gain a better understanding of their professional obligation to cover neighborhood struggles on an ongoing basis."

I would add, in this context, that the idea is not that they become partisan—though some, by temperament, will so become—but rather that they tell the story and keep on it. As in the Columbus Hospital imbroglio which is the main theme of this narrative, the facts, once revealed and accurately placed in context, will illuminate culpability and then move other supportive political forces around the city into play.

It is also important, since this kind of story—legion though it is throughout the country—is not in the forefront of journalism studies, that, as Bill Worthy also suggests, this book be assigned to journalism students who "will be in a position over the years to bring such stories, block by block, to the public's attention in a meaningful way and with real impact."

In sum, Mr. Worthy has written what can be called a true interdisciplinary work—its audience ranging from citizens about to organize themselves to apprentice journalists. It also may be a kind of prophetic work if Bill proves correct in his Jeffersonian faith that once the citizenry knows what to do to restore itself to democratic power—first of all, in its own neighborhoods—it can change, as he puts it, the quality of the country. The political quality, the environmental quality, the quality— in which change is most sorely needed—of daily life.

It is a heady prospect, but Bill, a pragmatist, deals in specific strategies, not visions, and he is thinking, realistically, on a national as well as local basis. As, for example:

"By and large, each local battle against one particular tentacle of the octopus is and has to be won locally. Nonetheless, for mutual support and reinforcement, all community preservation organizations ideally should be hooked into a nationwide federation. Those formal links would help every embattled citizen perceive that it's all one fight against the same octopus. . . ."

And that kind of perception can also lead to a second American Revolution.

Bill Worthy, as he writes, never would have conceived of putting more than five years of his life into a "microscopic community battlefront." But it happened, it was his apartment that was under siege, and he had no choice but to organize and become organized. And now, because Bill has written this book about his own embattled microcosm (with which more and more Americans, out of their own experiences of assault, identify), his odyssey on his own block is going to have a good deal more impact over the years than his much, much, longer journey to China nearly two decades ago.

Of such short steps is history sometimes made.

chapter 1

Will King of the Asheville (N.C.) Housing Authority told me everybody was "very pleased" with this demolition area. "It's a beginning point to salvage the downtown area."

"In other words, you had to destroy it in order to save it?"

"Yes," he said.

—from "Goodbye, Asheville" by Perry Deane Young (a native who returned recently to the man-made ruins of Thomas Wolfe's hometown), *Harper's*, March, 1975.

Were the bewildered and the manipulated victims of institutional rape to convene nationwide to figure out how it all happened to them, their embarrassment at having been had would be just as acute as that of a lone raped woman at a desolate police lineup.

Like the common street rapist who so often gets off scot-free, institutional rapists deny all responsibility, even when caught *in flagrante delicto* (as lawyers describe open-and-shut cases). On the contrary, they not infrequently end up blaming the victims—for having "succumbed" to lures, offers, and propositions (in the case of physical rape), or for having genuflected in response to "generous offers" to "relocate."

The street rapist's machismo and his conquests-boasting mentality are matched by the wolfish drives and designs of unneighborly institutions, to whom new and shiny edifices represent "manhood" and "arrival" and conquests. By contrast, the victims who are tricked, cajoled, and coerced into giving up hearth and home tend to fall into three broad categories: (1) the easily corrupted, who are instantly and totally blinded by any "large" cash offer, no matter how quickly the money is predestined to run out; (2) the gutless, who subliminally are eternal candidates to be walked over, misused, and then tossed aside; and (3) those with the will to resist who understandably feel impotent, because they have little or no conception of what it takes to fight back.

More often than not, the rugged individualists in the first category are badly skinned, and it doesn't take them long to realize it. "Relocated" to overpriced and substandard tenements in run-down neighborhoods, they devolve into a mood of self-flagellation for letting their greed set them up to be taken. It's all the more painful for not being able to blame anyone but themselves. Almost uniformly, when the bribe was first dangled before their glistening eyes, they scoffed at neighborly warnings that taxes, moving expenses, and then higher rents would eat up the money in a painfully short time. Before the rude awakening, this group rejects any commitment to community preservation.

In upward aspirations, those in Category 2 also identify with money and with power at the top—which accounts for their wavering and their unreliability. Their love of "easy [relocation] money" and sudden "wealth" may not be quite so feverish, and to some extent they stop and weigh the consequences of being uprooted. Principles of loyalty to a stable community do not enter the equation. If there could be a guaranteed quick win over the encroaching institution, they would tend to go along with their neighbors, if only out of distaste for the bother of moving.

But, by definition, a fight by the powerless against an expanding institution is neither a pushover nor a short, clean, bloodless one-battle war. In the course of such a war, the weak links on the community side can occasionally be strengthened by contact with spunky neighbors. For this reason, they should not be written off at the outset as hopeless, however exasperating their vacillations may be. At the same time, it is folly to overrate their potential in a grinding, wearing struggle. Of all those involved, they do the smallest amount of work, pay the least dues, attend the fewest meetings. Yet their commonest complaint is that they are "tired" and unable to take the "uncertainty" over the war's outcome, even after it has become clear that the particular institution is powerless against a we-won't-move consensus. Not really respecting themselves, they command no respect from others on either side of the barricades.

It is for the seemingly impotent, in Category 3, that this book, with its varied examples of successful community resistance, is written. The strong are never absolutely strong, wrote Simone Weil in 1940 when France fell. "[N]or are the weak absolutely weak, but neither is aware of this." The powerful, she added, seem to "walk through a non-resistant element." And then "suddenly things cease to obey them." That "suddenness" is what disconcerts and panics an institution long accustomed to having its unchallenged way, and it is what leads institutional officials into irrational and self-defeating dead ends.

Completely at random, pick the name of any sacrosanct institution that seeks to build and expand on sites where people dwell or earn their living. Whether it's

(a) fair Harvard ever encroaching into the next-door blue-collar Riverside-Cambridgeport community ("Harvardization"), or

(b) world-famous Columbia-Presbyterian Medical Center upping patient charges and simultaneously ripping up four hundred inhabited apartments in tax-paying buildings, after appropriate hounding of the tenants, or

(c) the Massachusetts Port Authority, hell-bent for bringing in the SST and for building new airport runways at the expense of long-tormented East Bostonians, or

(d) less-than-prestigious Middle American colleges buying up surrounding real estate while raising tuition and reducing student aid,

whatever name you pull out of the hat, that institution's threatened neighbors and their counterparts elsewhere bear an identical cross, at least when the battle is first joined: a blind and a nagging worry about the future.

Blind, nagging and ulcer-producing, because expansionist institutions invariably operate in the murkiest and most adamant secrecy. They never level with their neighbors until either the heat from negative publicity becomes unbearable, or the community threatens the source of their funds. If there has been a single exception of an institution coming clean from Day One and baring all its expansionist projections, immediate and long-range, diligent research over a five-year period has failed to uncover it. That's not the nature of the beast.

Because of all the work that necessarily goes into large-scale fund-raising and into planning, no institutional

26

expansion that I've ever heard about occurs on an overnight crash basis. As a consequence of this time lag between projections and actual money in the bank, there is always ample opportunity to invite the community into the planning process. For public-service institutions, that presumably would be the normal human impulse—unless, of course, those planning the encroachment have a guilty awareness that it cannot be justified and defended. What finally happens where a community refuses to bow to an institution's bulldozer is that enraged and long-deceived neighbors eventually run out of patience, pick up a variety of battering rams—lawsuits, merciless and unremitting publicity, disruptive demonstrations, implicit or explicit threats of violence—and angrily break down the closed, bolted and darkened doors.

Behind all the locks, chains and moats the neighbors discover their secretly planned future: a planner's models for fancy new structures and blueprints for convenience parking lots to replace beloved if mortgaged homes; an absentee architect's rendering of cosmetic plazas where small shops have long stood; schemes to take over and build on segments of parks and to obliterate whole streets that happen to stand in the way of "progress"; and elaborate angelic-sounding proposals—usually to tax-supported agencies—for large chunks of money to implement the grand institutional design. The money proposals are more carefully guarded than anything else, because the public agencies—and even private foundations—can be quite vulnerable to community pressure if it is skillfully mobilized at an early stage.

Hovering over the extracted secrets, with a backs-to-the-wall stance, stand the administrators and the "public-spirited" trustees caught red-handed in their myriad untruths, and therefore all the more frightened at

27

having to confront previously passive but now outraged neighbors. As if by instinct, the next line of defense becomes a predictable (and institutionally interchangeable) mixture of sweet evasiveness, alternating with harsh new arrogance, bad-faith negotiating traps strung out interminably, and ingeniously phrased Nixon-type "explanations" whose total falsity unravels only in stages and phases.

It isn't necessary for every threatened community to go through this baptism by fire. Those who insist on being naïve, however, are certain to get burned and devitalized by politicians, by "impartial" judges, and by "mediators" drawn in by the institution. From community groups that have swerved from that mined road in time, more than enough information is available to forewarn would-be victims.

When inflation of institutional egos is at stake, as well as the building of a showplace edifice designed to attract lush federal and foundation grants, any community that seeks to stop the expansion will find itself in a state of siege for a while.

What might be called the full treatment includes the carrots of "relocation" bribes, as well as the stick of not-so-subtle threats, harassment, and violence. Any innocent belief that nonprofit institutions "don't do things like that" is akin to yesteryear's popular illusion that "our" government had no motives to lie to us, no occasion to overthrow legitimate governments, and no incentive to plot political assassinations at home and abroad.

Fortune, said Louis Pasteur, favors the prepared mind, and misfortune can be brought on by the gullible. *Everything* has to be examined and questioned, including all our comfortable old assumptions about professional eleemosynary institutions. For groups out to defend a community from this type of rape, a soft line keyed to outdated

28

assumptions is a guarantee of defeat—so much so that it makes more sense to negotiate a surrender at the start than to waste time pursuing a sweet and "reasonable" approach. Nice guys and gals don't best un-nice institutions. But with the right combination of sharp political insight and staying power, of tough tactics and hard-nosed strategy, of cold intelligence and passionate spirit, victory by communities is not only possible, it is entirely likely.

In the good old days, a cry of "We Won't Move" was, for the most part, in most places, unthinkable. Politically and psychologically, it would have been the equivalent of railing at the Salvation Army, or of thumbing one's nose at the flag. Free of any stigma for disrupting the lives of defenseless people, institutions that wished to expand expanded. No questions were asked. Legal or political challenges would have seemed quixotic, because of insufficient popular pressures. In moods of resigned helplessness, the victims sighed, shrugged their shoulders, and quietly stole away. "Renewal" and "relocation" are as old as the republic—appropriate handmaidens for the national mania for "growth" and "progress." From all I've been able to ascertain, the payment of fees just to cover the bare costs of moving is a relatively new act of grace—a direct and very prudent response to all the recent resistance.

Nothing so clearly dramatizes the change in the popular mood of submissiveness as does the long-stalled fate of the Kennedy Presidential Library and Museum. A decade after 20 million individuals enthusiastically contributed millions of dollars—much of it in small amounts—the entire project was still in the talking and debating stage, thanks to an effective Cambridge, Massachusetts, community coalition of elite Brahmins (strictly *ad hoc* activists) and everything-to-lose blue-collar residents. The

29

shadow-casting revelations of John Kennedy's early role in an unpopular Asian war and, later, the transcending trauma of Watergate made it possible to challenge this holiest of all the monuments proposed for deceased Presidents.

On the surface, institutional self-righteousness and the will to plunge ahead and to damn all dissenters remain intact. But doubts abound about the feasibility of overriding loudly expressed popular wishes. Even as institutions discuss and refine their plans to barge ahead, they are often testing community waters, in wary efforts to foresee any resistance. In Boston, for example, the Little City Hall manager in the area of Northeastern University has observed that the school has expanded into the "soft spots" of the community. "They seem to want to go where there is the least resistance," he remarked.

In 1969, the leaders of a multi-issue student strike at Harvard wrote:

> In the past, when Harvard or MIT tried to take land for building, the tenants started kicking up a fuss. This is called bad "public relations"— i.e., someone was fighting back. One way to prevent this is to buy land, raise the rents, and then rent to your own students. The displaced tenants blame the students, and the students don't fight because they move out each year and therefore don't care if the building is torn down in their wake.

These days, anyone acting in flagrantly bad faith can easily miscalculate the flash point of an aggrieved community and can misread the temper of the people. In the middle of October 1974, in New York City, several Bayside civic associations were threatening to block nearby highways and to take Queensborough Community College (a municipal institution) to court unless the student parking problem was alleviated.

"We have had it, just had it," said the president of the Oakland Hills Community Association. The college had submitted a $10,000 traffic consultants' report to the local Community Planning Board, which the board had rejected by a 19–3 vote, calling it "insufficient and inadequate."

One reason for the rejection was that the report failed to deal with expansion of the college. Even a proposal by the college to meet with the planning board was rejected by board members. "We have been meeting for more than five years on this," said the association president, "and the communications have gotten so bad that we now feel the only way we can get something done is to block the highways and take the city to court."

The civic groups announced they were passing the hat among Baysiders for a legal fund to pay for the court fight.

When a shoe pinches long enough and painfully enough, even a lethargic person may decide to do something about it. "Overnight" he can become transformed into a tiger, all the more carnivorous for having let obviously dishonest operators deny him self-respect. White middle-class suburbanites with not an ounce of fight in their trampled and fearful souls can finally be pushed to "extremist" measures by the cumulative effect of years of hanky-panky dealings. In 1964, when a group of militants in CORE (the Congress of Racial Equality) announced plans to snarl traffic over issues of civil rights, the wrath of New York City—political, journalistic, law-enforcement, white liberal—descended on them in a chorus of how-dare-you denunciations. A decade later, the same mass-circulation morning tabloid that led the outcry against the CORE proposal—the conservative New York *Daily News*—seemed unperturbed when reporting that respectable burghers had decided to resort to the same disruptive tactics in Bayside.

The pattern is both historical and universal. The New York homeowners suing a public college and taking to the streets have their counterparts abroad. When push comes to shove, when faced with serious threats to family, to livelihood and to pursuit of even minimal happiness, people everywhere become more disposed toward imaginative organizers, who frequently surface in timely though unpredictable fashion. Strategies that promise to save the day suddenly win careful consideration, even if openly "radical." In France, there has been mass support for 103 peasants in the Plaine du Larzac who have resisted the planned expansion of a military base from 3,000 to 18,000 hectares (one hectare equals 2.47 acres)—at the expense of land used for centuries for sheep grazing and grain growing. Lanza del Vasto, a former associate of Gandhi who lives only forty kilometers from the Larzac, unexpectedly became available to help mobilize the farmers and to publicize their plight. On one occasion, they took their sheep to graze under the Eiffel Tower. Another time, they drove their tractors hundreds of miles into Paris.

Over a seventy-year period, the people who lived in the area of the base had accepted it as a fact of life. Their imperial betters in Paris had put the base there as a camp for reservists, and it provided a number of jobs for local residents. Today, however, the institution and the careerism of the professional military are increasingly unpopular in Larzac and elsewhere in France. As a consequence, in August 1973, 80,000 Frenchmen descended on Larzac in an outpouring of national solidarity for the threatened peasants.

Predictably, the army, in turn, reacted—with

considerably more force than mere civilian "relocators" can muster. But in qualitative terms, the army's means were very similar to the mysterious middle-of-the-night fires and the other intimidating methods of U.S. hospitals, universities, seminaries, and speculators when their own expansionist plans are being thwarted by "recalcitrant" tenants, homeowners and shopkeepers. Under cover of darkness, tanks slipped out of the army camp, drove into the peasants' fields, and ruined crops. Daily explosions caused sheep to abort. On June 11, 1973, an 800 kilogram missile was fired over the area. If you live in the United States and have said "I won't move" to your institutional landlord, all this rings instant bells: the situation of everyone knowing exactly what's going on, who is behind the "small" but frightening fires, and who is responsible for the obscene telephone calls to lone women. In the stable of every expanding institution are a bevy of sophists and Pharisees, paid and unpaid, with the effrontery to demand: "Where is your proof?"

The tanks and the missile zooming over the Plaine du Larzac were to the peasants of that area what the unleashed, unmuzzled German police dog roaming through the halls of my apartment building was to me and my fellow tenants in our fight to head off Columbus Hospital's wrecking ball. Nominally, the expensive new dog belonged to the building's always-broke superintendent, who in turn was the hospital's on-the-premises representative. But Columbus denied all responsibility for the crude terrorization.

Transoceanic and transcontinental, the institutional objective is one and the same: to coerce people into moving against their will and their better judgment under the banner of less-than-honorable causes. Given this common denominator, one broadly conceived manual—

fittingly adapted to specific locales and circumstances—can serve a variety of institutional masters.

Plan A: "We'll ignore—or, at least in public, haughtily pretend to ignore—such inconsequential objections to our plans" (until long after even the most hawkish can see that something else has to be tried).

Plan B (borrowed intact, word for word, from bosses fighting unions and from oldtime Mississippi sheriffs vis-à-vis the NAACP in New York): "We'll blame everything on a disgruntled few or on outside agitators with vaguely sinister political motives." Hitherto, that was a tack that often worked. But it is increasingly ineffective amidst today's popular disaffection with authority.

Finally, after Plan B has been played out, there's the fallback Plan C position: "We'll scare 'em half to death. We'll bribe 'em one by one, with sleight-of-hand peanut settlements. And if they still dare to hold out, we'll ruin 'em" (with tanks, missiles, vicious dogs, enforcers in the night).

It is primarily that dehumanized mentality that knocks out early naïveté and illusions about reconciliation and "middle-of-the-road" solutions. If someone is out after the roof over your head or after your place of livelihood, there is no friendly and neutral middle ground. Would-be victims find themselves faced with the narrow choice of ignominious, individual surrender, or of collective victory after a protracted, painstaking, highly politicalized slugfest in which people get hurt.

The definition of victory can be a complete rout of the offending institution, when its position in a community has been made untenable by the pile-up of its own grossness, deceits and roughhouse stuff. In 1974, for example, in the face of a community stone wall, New

England Baptist Hospital withdrew a certificate-of-need application to expand that, just months earlier, had been portrayed as being essential to survive (a 500-car garage, a large doctors' office building, and a 250-bed replacement facility).

Or victory can mean simply the right of all concerned to remain in their ancestral homes and shops and fields, with a guaranteed end to bribes and violence and harassment. Victims who have learned the hard way can testify that, to mean anything, the guarantees need sufficient automatic penalties to be effectively self-enforcing. Fatal illusion Number 1 is to place the slightest trust in any word-of-mouth promises of those who head or speak for expansionist institutions. Unless bound by and fenced in by airtight legal stipulations that are prohibitively costly to violate, they will at first opportunity revert to their operational manual (Plans A, B, and C).

On-the-make institutions stoop low—very low— and play dirty pool. Only a marketplace hypothesis of money, of power, of pathological pressures for "keeping up" with competitors can adequately explain the motivations, even with a "nonprofit" figleaf to hide the truth.

Without such a marketplace hypothesis, how explain the private admissions by administrators of the Episcopalian New York Infirmary and of Beth Israel Medical Center—whose duplicating emergency rooms are a hundred feet apart—that they are indeed "competitors" in the five-block, four-hospital East Side area known as Bedpan Alley? In the lush arena of medical care, the 1960's brought the multibillion-dollar flowering of grantsmanship—the National Institutes of Health, the big and medium-sized foundations, the Cancer Society and the reconstituted March of Dimes, the Department of Health,

Education and Welfare—as well as the poorly audited slush of Medicare and Medicaid. Before those quickly corrupted programs became law with such high hopes a decade ago, hospital expenditures in 1964–65 were $13 billion. By 1971–72, prior to the period of double-digit inflation, they had jumped to $32 billion. While the Consumer Price Index for all items was going up 44 percent, hospital costs were increasing by 147 percent.

The spin-off from those billions becomes apparent with even a side glance at what has been called medical imperialism. Year after year, staff doctors have been earning more—much more. Contractors get more contracts to build and expand more hospitals. Pharmaceutical houses are able to peddle more of their stock items and to push more of the endless flood of hastily tested new pills with their multiple delayed side effects. Supply companies (boldly represented on the public-spirited boards of some hospitals) sell more supplies. For 1964, statistics of the American Hospital Association itself list a surplus of net revenues over expenses for all U.S. hospitals of $115 million. By 1969, as the billions poured in from Medicare and Medicaid, the "net surplus" (known in the business world as profits) had jumped to $400 million.

To spread these profits among the deserving few at the top—the medical boards and the chiefs of service, the well-paid administrators, and even the trustees and officers, as in the case of Miami's thoroughly looted Cedars of Lebanon Hospital during its expansion program—hospital boards need not declare anything so openly commercial as end-of-the-year dividends. Tax-exempt, nonprofit profits flow out along many ingenious channels; expansionism with all its sticky-fingers potentialities is high on the list of respectable outlets. Before the bubble of

36

corruption/expansion burst just weeks after President Nixon praised "private" medicine at the dedication of a new wing, Cedars of Lebanon Hospital, its hands deep into the federal treasury, was avowedly out to become "the Mayo Clinic of the South."

In unblinking grab-bag boldness in the face of admitted massive failures, the Veterans Administration is not far behind the medical establishment. In its late-1974 report to Congress, the VA acknowledged that veterans are "taking a chance" by seeking emergency treatment at the nation's 171 VA hospitals. The fiscal 1975 budget for these hospitals was $3.2 billion, up $329 million from the previous year. Nevertheless, in the same breath, the VA petitioned the House and Senate for an immediate $190 million increase in the 1975 budget and $236 million more for fiscal 1976 to "improve" (that is to say, to greatly expand) the "inadequate" physical facilities.

In making demands, under false colors, for all that money, the medical fraternity, despite its lobbying skills, can only be labeled pikers when measured against the despotic thirty-year New York reign on the grand scale of Robert Moses, at one time the holder of twelve simultaneous powerful city and state positions, and the man responsible in the quiet 1940's and the stagnant 1950's for the annual "relocation" of tens of thousands of dispensable New Yorkers.

The urban displacees had to make way for scores of Moses's bridges, for his parkways and tunnels, for two power dams (which he named after himself), for an absolutely essential Shea Stadium, for Lincoln Center, for the United Nations complex, for the Coliseum, for one "successful" and one (1964–65) unsuccessful World's Fairs—and, inevitably, for the series of scandals that finally helped bring Moses down in the middle of the last decade.

For, sooner or later, scandals prove to be the handmaiden of unresponsive, unaccountable, unregulated, multibillion-dollar power that Moses symbolized as chairman of the empire-pyramiding Triborough Bridge and Tunnel Authority. Triborough, and other similar bond-issuing authorities that he headed, continue and will long continue to fleece drivers, bus and subway riders, and the public in general—through eternal tolls decades after the bridges and tunnels were paid for, through increased transit fares from a nickel to fifty cents, and through billions just in interest payments to banks and other bondholders.

While adding up to impressive levels of scandal, the total of Moses-era slush and slop could not compare in scope with the wholly "legal" plunder of the bond market. In the wake of the national example set by Moses, today's expanding hospitals, schools and businesses turn primarily to this or that federal or state bond-issuing agency for the huge grants and low-interest loans they chase after.

None of this is new in our history. In the middle of the nineteenth century, when the Whigs were still electing governors in New York, the big argument in Albany, according to present State Comptroller Arthur Levitt

> was over what to do with the tolls flowing in from the "big ditch," the Erie Canal. Contractors were swarming into Albany with plans for bigger and better canals, with a feeder canal for every Assembly district. The whole state of New York would have become Venice. The argument was won by the State Comptroller, who became unpopular because he insisted the tolls be used for debt service.

As the man with overall responsibility for keeping the state's books, Levitt is worried about public agencies "which act above the people." That, he says, is "why I have gone to court to force public authorities to open their records for public inspection." He continues:

> Public authorities are big business. The outstanding debt of the statewide authorities is more than $12 billion. The debt of a single authority, the Housing Finance Agency [source of much of the money for hospital expansionism], is far greater than the full faith and credit debt of the State itself . . . which stood at $3.5 billion on December 31, 1974. . . . Why did this type of financing happen—not only in the State of New York, but throughout the nation? There are three quick answers, none very good: to get the job done, *to avoid public referenda* and to evade debt restrictions. [Italics mine.]

Today more than ever, the indispensable ingredient to implement antipeople, over-the-heads-of-the-people decisions is popular passivity and general ignorance. Like a house of cards, the whole game falters and eventually may crumble whenever even one intended victim bones up, says no, and begins to organize effective community resistance. From a "towering" Robert Moses down to the lowly administrators of a fifth-rate, expansionist Bedpan Alley hospital, contempt for passive public opinion is heavily laden with gnawing fear that at any moment the passivity can be converted into popular fury.

Indisputably, these angry times are no longer propitious for a bestriding and terrorizing Robert Moses. Today he would be an inviting target to be cut down in very short order. Because the many present targets in the expansionist fraternity are more dispersed and far less pyrotechnic, more organizational time is required to bring them down. But the tides of the 1970's and the slowly

39

coalescing community coalitions all point to a very inauspicious climate for the small fry—the Uriah Heeps of the expanding institutions.

Uriah Heeps, that is, when, hat in hand, they " 'umbly" appear before public bodies such as New York's community planning boards, asking approval for this "small" and "one-time" encroachment on a long-suffering neighborhood, or for that presumptuous out-of-tone zoning variance which would set a fatal precedent, or for some outrageous easement whose full implications for abutters they slickly glide over.

For me, the 1970–75 years of direct contact with Bedpan Alley expansionism have turned out to be the practical equivalent of a Ph.D. in urban affairs—or, more precisely, a doctorate in neighborhood manifestations of an acquisitive society. From that painful experience comes a rough rule of thumb for anticipating the reactions of those being squeezed in the impersonal vise of institutional imperialism. The higher the level of education, the greater the emotional stake in the overall status quo, the more enamored the individual is with the creature comforts that this society offers, then the more slowly, the more reluctantly, the more begrudgingly he or she hears, sees and *acknowledges* a "nonprofit" wolf huffing, puffing and hungrily panting at the back door. There are, of course, exceptions—and very honorable exceptions. But, in general, the correlation is direct, specific and unmistakable. The fewer our hard knocks in the past, then the less attuned we are to the schemes and machinations of those who deal professionally in hard knocks.

In a world as interrelated and as interdependent as ours has become, the luxury of remaining sidelined until one's own ox is gored by expansionist institutions

40

can no longer be afforded. In the late 1950's, in the aftermath of a "verboten" journalistic trip to China, I was preoccupied with lecture trips around the country and also with the defense of the right to travel in the passport case of *Worthy v. Dulles.* From yellowed and brittle newspaper clippings, I'm now belatedly aware of across-town developments then going on that I simply did not "see" from the perspective of my unperturbed and "unthreatened" East Side residence. Had I and my fellow tenants been alert to the citywide expansionist trends, we would have had a good head start for our own confrontation. We wouldn't have dwelled in a fool's paradise until the eviction notices of 1970.

Some half dozen blocks to the west of us and forty-five blocks to the north, small businessmen, the working-class population, and various ethnic groups in the area of 64th Street and Broadway were fighting a losing battle to preserve their homes and shops. It was People of the West Side v. the Wealth of Lincoln Center—and money won.

To the extent that I read the newspaper accounts at the time—and I don't at all remember—I conceivably permitted my love for *Don Giovanni,* for the Emperor Concerto, and for the beauty and radiance of *Giselle* to put me subconsciously on the wrong side. For one with a lifelong musical background, for a Bostonian who agrees that "life without music is a mistake," the glittering mental projection of a grand cultural complex must at the time have been very appealing.

It was not until 1970, when we on the East Side began researching Seymour Shapiro, his Urban Relocation Company and his court record, that we learned it was the same Shapiro who had been publicly attacked in

1958 by the association of businessmen in the Lincoln Center area for harassing them into moving out, in order to clear the large site for Culture.

In other words, Shapiro's malodorous "relocation" tactics of the 1970's, on behalf of Columbus Hospital and other clients, were equally acceptable earlier to the cream of the U.S. elite who pushed so hard and so effectively for Lincoln Center.

Given our conditioning, it jars our images and our sensibilities to have to acknowledge that it's not just second-rate parvenu institutions, but those with Ivy League credentials that knowingly ride roughshod over their neighbors. In turn, the Brahmin offenders become particularly unhinged when disruptive natives intrude into the serenity of tradition-steeped rites. After a half century in which not a single drop of rain marred her annual June commencement, Harvard University in 1970 would have gladly swapped a torrential downpour for the human embarrassment that abruptly broke her long lease on calm and decorum.

Mrs. Saundra Graham, who led an overnight camp-in and then broke up the commencement ceremonies with a demonstration that grabbed national headlines, is now a Cambridge city councilwoman. She still refuses to accept the label of "civil disobedience" for the protest.

"There's no law that says you can't break up the Harvard commencement," she pointed out in September 1974, when the *Boston Globe* asked her and others whether civil disobedience was a legitimate tool for Boston parents opposed to busing.

After a 5 P.M. march to the office of President Nathan Pusey, the night before commencement, Mrs. Graham and 150 of her Riverside–Cambridgeport community neighbors seized and occupied the caterer's tent in the Harvard Yard. They then demanded that the Harvard Corporation turn over 100,000 square feet of "largely vacant property known as Treeland" for construction of low-rent family housing.

These days, nearly every expanding institution finds money in its budget for a "community affairs officer" to head up its specific version of Operation Soothe. Edward Gruson, who bore that beguiling title at Harvard, told the 150 protesters that he could not "at the time" discuss the Treeland question. But he "pledged" that the corporation would build low- and middle-income housing "in the future."

Unhappy at not getting a nailed-down response and a commitment to which Harvard could be held, the protesters showed up the next day at the 319th commencement, to ask students to support their housing request for the site where the university was planning student dormitories. As 15,000 participants and spectators watched in total dismay, some twenty-five demonstrators from the Riverside Planning Team mounted the platform, which the *Boston Globe* reported was "filled with academic and political dignitaries in colorful gowns, striped pants and high silk hats." Using a bullhorn, after university officials had the microphones turned off, Mrs. Graham cited the futility of past efforts to meet with the Harvard Corporation.

"The students talk about fighting for the oppressed people," she shouted. "We are the oppressed people. We are tired of Harvard coming into our area and taking our homes."

After telling the audience "we refuse to live like animals," and after responding to shouts of "Go home" with "You go home; we've been here longer than

43

you'll ever be," Mrs. Graham's request for two minutes to air the community's grievances was granted by a pale and obviously frightened President Pusey. He had been busily conferring with the two corporation members on the stage who handled real estate and housing for the university.

She used the two minutes at the microphones to denounce Harvard for "two years of failure to carry out promises to provide low-cost housing for residents near the university."

"What Harvard isn't buying up in our neighborhood the speculators are," she charged. "Rents are going up, and we're being forced out."

Aside, perhaps, from being a bit more circumspect in "community relations," Harvard hasn't changed in the half decade since that ceremonial moment of supreme public embarrassment. Exactly five years later, at the 324th commencement, amidst a sea of umbrellas, senior-class orator Orrin Tilevitz alluded contextually to the same unresolved issue with the in-house irreverence traditional for the occasion:

He who blasphemes the name of Harvard in public shall be stoned. . . . Harvard is not a way-station on the road between high school and the world. Harvard *is* the world. . . . Harvard suffers from the same competitiveness and gigantism as does the rest of the world. We see the cutthroat world of politics and finance outside, but is this any different from the cutthroat world of premedism and prelawism and pretenurism at Harvard? . . . [O]ne could also say that ITT collects companies the way Harvard collects real estate. . . . Harvard owns an important part of Cambridge, the way the British used to own most of Africa. The reaction of the natives is reportedly the same.

Again it's necessary to confess a past blindness. During my 1956–57 Nieman Fellowship year at Harvard, I never found time—especially after my Christmas-to-early-February trip to China—to wander off the academic precincts and to make my way, very close by, to Mrs. Graham's Riverside–Cambridgeport neighborhood where, before I was born, my father for some years practiced medicine. Not once did it ever occur to me to inquire if housing had previously occupied the lot where I was routinely granted a reserved parking space. According to a 1974 conversation with Mrs. Graham, it was just about that time that Harvard's expansion spree was getting under way. (If research by the 1969 student strikers is accurate, Harvard in 1958 had no holdings in Cambridge apart from its own educational campus.)*

Mrs. Graham cites one old two-family frame dwelling that the university bought in the 1960's for the inflated price of $75,000. She says that 89 Putnam Avenue, to which her own mother was "relocated" around 1968, was purchased by Harvard for $60,000 when its market value was $12,000.

From a department chairman, I recently learned that another common Harvard practice is to buy particularly desirable houses from private owners—with the purchase price no object—and then to sell them at cut rates to much-sought-after "name" professors, in order to induce them to come to Cambridge. It's a neat device, worthy of a slick Yankee trader, for ever so quietly dishing out tax-free subsidies, at taxpayers' expense, of course. Whether it is clearly illegal (as an evasion of taxes) or is merely in the gray area of a grand academic hustle, the practice has

* "Harvard preceded Cambridge and is the most important thing going on her," President Nathan Pusey is reported to have said at Winthrop House in March 1969.

45

never been mentioned in any of the nickel-and-dime Harvard fund appeals that come my way annually as a Nieman alumnus.

Harvard is the oldest and the largest chartered corporation in Massachusetts, with a portfolio in excess of $1 billion. That the university is adept in using its wealth to further its power aims can be seen from an episode recently recalled by one of the student publications.

Ten years ago the State tried to take by eminent domain* one square block of houses for the use of the Massachusetts Mental Health Center. A march of 3,000 area residents on the State House blocked this action. Then Harvard's agents moved in and gradually bought up the disputed property. Harvard's money was used where the legal powers of the state had failed.†

Whether in defeat or in laurels, community resisters can usually look back and detect the factors that tipped the scales: either an indomitable fighting spirit or money. In Jersey City, over a period of some years, residents near the State Teachers College were pressured into selling their homes "at good prices." According to a faculty member, as late as the recession year of 1975, there is still "a constant encroachment. A high-rise college building was planned which would have cut the sun from a block of back yards. But fortunately monies ran out."

At Harvard and elsewhere, I happen to know—in some cases quite well—individuals involved at a high level in the expansion (or in public-relations justification of the expansion) of their institutions at community ex-

* The right of a governmental body to take private property for public purposes.

† From *The Present Illness,* a student-run tabloid "from the Harvard Medical area," September 1974.

46

pense. In their private lives, they are far from being monsters. But in the binding and the blinding institutional roles that they play, they insulate themselves from the visible human consequences of their actions. Psychologically, it is very difficult to train one's guns on culprits who are not personally diabolical, which is why journalists are enjoined to limit their friendships and dinner partners, especially among the powerful.

> He needs not to barter days in seeking friends,
> Nor to sell his freedom that he may keep them.

My own alma mater, Bates College, in the medium-sized industrial city of Lewiston, Maine, is casually buying up middle-class homes that fringe the campus. Because I was already attuned to watch for this kind of operation at any contemporary institution, I learned of this when there in 1972 for my class reunion. (Three years earlier, before mounting the barricades against Columbus Hospital, I wouldn't have "seen" what was going on.) Inasmuch as I heard neither of exorbitant purchase prices à la Harvard, nor of any improper pressures on homeowners to sell, the process seems more mindless than heartless, more provident than sinister. Provident, that is, in the sense of storing up treasure for possible use in the vague and distant future.

The lovely and always well-tended Bates College campus, with its student body of about 1,300, could almost be tucked away and lost in some corner of the sprawling and ever-expanding Charles River campus of Boston University, which in 1974 invited me to fill a visiting professorship in journalism and Afro-American Studies. In Boston, colleges and universities are a $1.3 billion business—the city's biggest, as a matter of fact, with close ties in some components to the military-industrial-medical complex. Between full-time and part-time undergraduates and graduate students, "private" Boston University lists a total enrollment of 23,000 and a full-time and part-time faculty of over 2,000. The university is, as one executive in the administration put it, a $90 million corporation, with several hundred buildings and, at the moment at least under the new president, a balanced budget.

Most of the campus growth has come over the last decade, although it was in the 1950's that dormitories (up to a total of 5,989 spaces) were built with federal monies then available. While the university officially says that no further large-scale building program is projected because of the flattening of the enrollment curve, *The News,* a student newspaper, reported on September 19, 1974, that expansionism nevertheless continues apace.

During that summer, unknown (as is typical) to the tenants, BU purchased an apartment building at 722–728 Commonwealth Avenue for $1,400,000. By the fall of 1975, after a complete renovation, 250–320 undergraduate students were scheduled to be living there in one-, two-, and three-bedroom apartments. Financial help for the purchase and renovation came from a bond issue of the Massachusetts Health and Educational Facilities Authority. (I doubt the average taxpayer in the state has ever heard of this Authority. By law and by sacred U.S. custom, however, interest and principal payments to holders of all official bonds must be given first priority in each and every annual budget.)

If the renovated building meets the standards of the U.S. Department of Housing and Urban Development—standards which apparently will mandate an all-student residence, at the expense of the present occupants

48

—then the federal government will help with $137,280 annually on debt service payments.

Item, item, item—the list and examples of the pattern could go on forever, here, there, and everywhere:

1. In 1972, in the *Boston Globe,* financial columnist David Deitch noted that an ever-declining proportion of the Gross National Product goes into *new* housing, which results in heavier speculative investment in *existing* residential real estate. This leads to steadily rising (and often prohibitive) rents, as in the areas around BU, Harvard, Columbia and other expanding institutions.

Deitch adds:

A tremendous edifice of mortgage debt rests on a stock of housing that is barely growing. This debt, held for the most part by big banks, would be jeopardized by any authentic move—private or public—to alleviate the housing shortage. . . .

If the banking–real estate complex wants to transform Lynn and Somerville into middle-class bedroom communities serving the central city, it wants to change Boston into a city of office skyscrapers, garages, and luxury apartment homes, assuming, of course, that the entire system doesn't go bankrupt in the process.

People in slum housing are living under a state of siege. Their misery stands between the banking–real estate complex and collapse.

2. *New York Times* correspondent John L. Hess noted in 1974 that Medicaid eventually pays the costs of new and old nursing homes—including some that are building expansionist geriatric empires, such as Florence Nightingale Nursing Home whose owner, Charles Sigety, has bought up nearly every building and apartment house in a two-square-block area of East Harlem. His

mortgage money has come from Chemical Bank, Aetna Insurance Company, and the U.S. Department of Housing and Urban Development, over the strongly focused objections of Spanish-speaking and other East Harlem residents who are being squeezed out of their homes.

3. On October 1, 1974, the *Boston Globe* headlined a speech by Mayor Kevin H. White before the National Association of Housing and Redevelopment Officials: "White Labels U.S. an Arrogant and Abusive Landlord."

The mayor criticized federal monetary policies for "destroying good housing, restricting family mobility, eroding neighborhood strength, impeding community development and ultimately strangling the cities themselves."

Washington's insistence that the latest apartment building purchased by Boston University be converted into an all-student residence—which dictates the eviction of the existing tenants—certainly "erodes neighborhood strength" in the vicinity of a "private" campus that each year receives $20 million of federal money, exclusive of government loans and grants to students.

Given Mayor White's own antipeople housing policies in various parts of the city, his speech, of course, falls clearly into the department of the pot calling the kettle black. The residents of those areas of Boston adjacent to White's pet Park Plaza urban-renewal project are appalled at his subservience to big real-estate developers, and at his insensitivity to the damage that Park Plaza would wreak on the abutting Public Garden, on historic Beacon Hill, and on parts of the downtown business area, such as the legitimate theater district.

But for good and sufficient political reasons, even an ambitious office seeker out to build national urban constituencies as a launching pad for a national bid in

1976 can sometimes indict with accuracy what is clearly indictable.

4. When it comes to erecting edifices that make no community sense, but which supposedly bring increments of glamour, prestige and power, large public institutions are not at all different, substantively, from those in the private sector. Whether operating in health care, in education, in culture, or in outright profit-making business, they are all birds of a feather. Spoken or implicit, the message comes through: Let the peasants in the community be damned.

"Could someone please answer a few questions regarding the lofty new addition to State College at Boston currently under construction on the narrowest neck of Huntington Avenue?" wrote *Boston Globe* suburban reader Catharine L. Motley in the autumn of 1974.

First, who authorized it? Did the city have no veto power? Or didn't it wish to exercise that veto power?

Second, who's paying for it? The taxpayer obviously will eventually foot the bill, but will the money be laundered in Washington first and come back to us in the form of a federal building grant for education?

Why an addition to State College at this time? University of Massachusetts at Boston has opened at less than full enrollment. The private universities are fighting to survive against competition of state and community colleges. Conventional classroom education is under fire, with the newest trend in education featuring community involvement, apprenticeships and on-the-job training. Why more classroom space at this time?

What of the density of this building, particularly when measured along with the existing State College building complex which it abuts? "Density" of a building, to quote the *Sunday Globe,* June 30, is "the ratio of floor space to land area." In the case of State College's new high rise, the land area is a minus figure. Since there was no remaining land on State College property the new building was simply plunked down in the middle of the street bounding the property, namely Evans Way, once a quiet avenue leading in from Huntington Avenue to the Gardner Museum.

What of the additional load on the MBTA [the local metropolitan mass transit system]? There is already, within one-quarter mile of State College, a heavy student population who must fight for space in the MBTA twice daily on their commute to school. There is Northeastern, Wentworth, Harvard School of Public Health, plus the Countway Medical Library and Peter Bent Brigham Hospital, not to mention Boston Latin and English High two blocks away.

If the new students commute by car there isn't parking space enough in the entire Fenway to accommodate this new influx. While Greater Boston businesses within Route 495 are being forced to cut the number of their commuter cars in half, the number of student cars in Boston Proper increases daily. Are the cars of the education community less polluting?

Private citizens living in the neighborhood of State College will have to battle with State students for simple sidewalk space, let alone for shopping, conveniences and municipal services. Have these citizens no rights? And what of the students themselves? Where will they stand when they come out of their building? On each others' shoulders?

Most of all, why has there been no publicity concerning the planning or groundbreaking of this building?

The only publicity for State in the local news has been generous coverage of State's programs, both the teaching and the training of teachers, to assist Boston's children with reading problems. State's activity in this area is, of course, most welcome to Boston educators and parents.

Students are just as susceptible to the woes of population densities as are slum dwellers or factory workers. Funneled into a cluttered area for their daily schooling, students will suffer the same frustrations and depressions as anyone else. It is sad enough when urban crowding closes in on a once spacious academic plant. To build a brand-new building in the center of such an area seems total madness.

5. At Pemberton Square Court House in Boston, the Massachusetts Supreme Judicial Court ruled in the autumn of 1974 that a $16 million Brookline apartment house that had recently been completed and partially occupied was built in violation of the town's zoning and environmental-protection laws.

The unanimous decision left the town building inspector trying to determine whether he was now required to revoke the certificate of occupancy for the eight-story 411-unit structure. Attorney Lawrence D. Shubow, who represented neighbors who had been battling the project for six years, called the court's ruling a "major victory for the public interest in local control of zoning."

6. Again in the same busy month of September 1974 and again in the Bay State, a twenty-seven-year-old commune farmer near Greenfield, Massachusetts, was found innocent—on a technicality, in a directed verdict— of toppling a 500-foot meteorological tower, which had become a symbol of community resistance to the coming of nuclear power.

Northeast Utilities had been planning to build twin nuclear power plants, and Samuel H. Lovejoy's trial was believed to be the first in the nation involving sabotage for ecological reasons. His friends and supporters filled the courtroom—always a vigilant "must" in political cases, since judges tend to be much rougher on unpopular defendants when they can dispatch them to jail unnoticed, invisible and unprotected. At the end of the trial, some jurors said that they had begun to lean in favor of Lovejoy's claim of civil disobedience as a defense.

Opponents of the nuclear plants feared the ruin of the ecology of Montague Plains where the sand and rock underneath are water-bearing formations that contribute to the Connecticut River. The plants would take twenty gallons of water per second from the river for cooling purposes. Arrayed on the other side, in a town with 11 percent unemployment, were Montague officials and construction unions, which looked forward to a boom in jobs from the $1.2 billion project.

Despite the bleakness of the local economy, Lovejoy's act of defiance did not spring from a political vacuum, any more than Daniel Ellsberg's "single-handed" disclosure of the carefully guarded Pentagon Papers fell from a detached, apolitical sky. Not long before, the Boston and Maine Railroad had wanted to excavate gravel from a huge and valuable bed of sand and gravel in the Montague Plains, right in the heart of the town, in order to fill the pit with the "sanitary landfill" from Boston, ninety miles to the east. The townspeople had vetoed this proposal that they meekly accept someone else's prestigious garbage so close to their homes. They were able to prove that the project would destroy the Connecticut River.

In his statement to the court, Lovejoy recalled how Vice President Charles Bragg of Northeast Utilities had boasted that local opposition "wouldn't affect us. We would have to go ahead with it even if there was a protest movement mounted by the citizens of the area." (Plan A.)

54

Bragg had also compared the development of nuclear power plants to the western expansion of the railroads. (The fallback Plan C position.) The Indians resisted the imperialistic corporate intrusion onto their tribal lands, and for this they were exterminated. The Braggs of our day, with their manuals for expansion, have deep historical roots. Today, after having long been pushed around, more and more people are beginning to do (with far better prospects of success) what the Indians did from 1607 in Virginia up until the massacre at Wounded Knee, South Dakota, in 1891: form their battalions and fight, in a variety of ingenious ways.

Lovejoy went on to tell the judge and jurors: "As a farmer concerned about the organic and the natural, I find irradiated fruit, vegetables and meat to be inorganic; and I can find no natural balance with a nuclear plant in this or any community."

Lovejoy and his colleagues in NOPE (Nuclear Objectors for a Pure Environment) expanded to create the NO party, and entered a slate of five candidates, including Lovejoy himself, for town elections—not in the hope of winning office, but in order to have a better and continuing platform for projecting the grave issues.

Radical politics was something new for that central Massachusetts community. Nevertheless, via the local press, the message got through. The NO candidates argued, with a clear and uncompromising political line, that "there can be no trade-off between money and public welfare" and that "the corporate giants not only extort us by preying on the weakness of the local citizenry, but they also degrade us with bribes." In cities such as New York, the expansionist forces dangle cash bribes in front of tenants, in order to get them to "relocate" and make way for parking lots and high-rises and excessive medical facilities. In a semirural community such as Montague, the bribes take the form of jobs in an antisocial nuclear installation.

For the NO party, the election results were both stunning and gratifying: instead of the generally expected landslide vote of 8–1 or 10–1 in favor, 770 of 3,000 voters came out in solid opposition to nuclear power in the referendum on the ballot—with the prospect that, later, a probable NOPE-sponsored countywide referendum might produce a majority against the twin plants with their two reactors.

With its thumb in nose, Northeast Utilities put the weather tower back up. But it didn't do the company any practical good. Community events and the state of the nation's economy had slowed, if not reversed, the all-important momentum for capitalizing the twin plants and for lining up favorable public opinion. Five months after Sam Lovejoy was acquitted, Northeast Utilities voted to delay until 1986 and 1988 the original construction target period of 1981 to 1983.

7. Man-bites-dog story, *The New York Times*, September 13, 1974:

HOSPITAL OFFERS HOTEL AS HOUSING

The French and Polyclinic Medical School and Health Center has proposed and the city's Department of Relocation has endorsed a plan to house Manhattan's temporarily homeless in the former New Yorker Hotel, which the center hopes someday to convert into a modern medical facility.

The proposal is being considered by the Mayor's office, and the medical center's officials plan to meet early next week with community leaders to seek support for the idea, which could put as many as 500 families in the 43-story 2,000-room hotel on Eighth Avenue at 34th Street.

The proposal would be dropped if it were op-

56

posed by the community, according to a spokesman for the medical center, who added, however, that the bankrupt medical institution would have to "seek new social-purpose programs that would generate enough money to allow us to keep the New Yorker."

The Hilton Hotel Corporation, from which the French–Polyclinic Medical Center purchased the New Yorker, has moved in Federal Bankruptcy Court here to regain the building on which the medical center has not made a payment since it filed on July 10, 1973, under Chapter XI of the Federal Bankruptcy Act.

Judge Roy Babitt, the referee in the case, said yesterday that he "would look favorably" on any plan that the hospital had to raise money to pay off the Hilton group. The medical center's monthly payments on the New Yorker are about $160,000 according to Judge Babitt.

Under Chapter XI, the medical center's debts of about $7 million are frozen, and it is allowed to continue operations so long as it is meeting current expenses and is working on a plan to pay creditors. It has been operating under a cost-control program instituted by John Battaglia, the executive vice president.

In the early 1970's, the hospital's ambitious purchase of the multimillion dollar New Yorker Hotel, which is one block from Pennsylvania Station, helped to grease a rapid decline into bankruptcy. Like Miami's Cedars of Lebanon Hospital so far—and, almost surely, like other expansionist hospitals in the foreseeable future as the financial pressures for lower patient censuses mount—French–Polyclinic's uncontrolled appetite for more real estate and grander facilities greatly exceeded its capacity to financially digest.

In itself, Watergate did not involve the corruption attendant on unaccountable institutional expansionism—aside, of course, from the White House's usurpation of unconstitutional powers. But in a country riven from Year One with nine-day scandals, the dimensions of that protracted and unforgettable landmark scandal have predisposed a hitherto trusting citizenry to scan the horizon for significant, even if less flamboyant, ripoffs.

It is in this new climate of national skepticism that New York State Senator Manfred Ohrenstein agreed with New York City Planning Commissioner Sylvia Deutch, at a September 1974 hearing, that there is "a backlash against construction." Locally, the senator attributed it to "years of almost criminal activity, block by block, against Clinton and other neighborhoods" in Manhattan.

Commenting editorially on the hearing, *The New York Times* on the following day remarked: "It was not until recently that the relationship between community health and the city's survival was perceived as anything more than a set of real estate transactions."

One is tempted to yell back: "Speak for yourself, Mr. *New York Times!*" There have long been those who shared among themselves a radically different perception. But individually, not to mention collectively, they had little access to the pages of the *Times.* As a great molder of public opinion, this newspaper does not accept its heavy share of responsibility for that earlier flawed perception. Now as always, it is the outraged victims of those "real estate transactions"—and not those with class and business ties to the victimizers—who are propelling the twisted social formulations up front and center for forced reexamination. "The worst and most corrupting lies," French writer George Bernanos was quoted as saying in a *Commonweal* article, "Atrocious Americans," "are problems badly stated."

The threat to the Clinton neighborhood of the proposed new Manhattan Convention Center—a triple threat of ferocious land speculation, traffic and air pollution—is, the *Times* correctly pointed out, to a stable community

that exists only by virtue of an irreplaceable makeup. This is an old-fashioned, mixed-use walk-to-work neighborhood of extraordinary health, value and resiliency. There are older, low-cost housing units affordable by blue-collar families, a support structure of jobs and industries, lively streets of shops and services, and a good part of the city's restaurant and entertainment business with related employment. All will be wiped out if the normal New York development takes place.

The backlash against construction is not at all limited to New York. "Humility Shines As Grandeur Fades" was a summer 1974 *Boston Sunday Globe* headline on its weekly architecture column. In analyzing a draft version of the long-discussed new Downtown Plan for Boston, columnist Robert Campbell noted

the complete absence of Flash Gordon visions of the future. A planner of a few years ago wouldn't even recognize this as a plan. . . .

Except for Park Plaza, a holdover from the grandiose past, there aren't even any neighborhoods proposed for (as they used to say) renewal, that is to say destruction.

The plan expresses what seems to be a widespread feeling that the days of heroic restructurings of the city are past and, in any case, maybe didn't work out so well, and that change from now on will be slow and incremental. . . .

Most poignant, as an example of the change in mood, is the case of the Central Artery. Proudly designed on the best Flash Gordon principles to carve its

59

dramatic, roller-coaster path through the city, it is today the subject of a study to determine if it can possibly be torn down or put underground, in the hope of knitting up the torn, humble, but as it turns out, precious fabric of Boston.

Globe reporter Ken Hartnett, a specialist in urban problems, revealed official doubts as to whether the "heartily detested and distrusted" Boston Redevelopment Authority (BRA)—"the agency with the bulldozer"—should remain the city's one and only planning and development agency under Congress' newly enacted Community Development Revenue Sharing (CDRS). Hartnett wrote:

> In Boston, grants under the CDRS program would almost certainly be used primarily for neighborhood stabilization programs—programs that [Mayor] White's aides say would be devised in collaboration with neighborhood groups.
>
> White aides are wondering out loud whether the BRA, so frequently in the past at loggerheads with the neighborhoods, can deal with sensitivity toward community groups in carrying out a CDRS program.

In part, the very fact that such a decentralist law, whatever its ambiguities and monetary limitations, went through Congress with support from the Nixon administration would seem to indicate that word of the popular backlash against renewal had filtered through to Washington. By having resisted here an expanding college or medical center, there an encroaching highway or nuclear plant, and elsewhere a noisy and unbearable airport, these groups by 1974 had vividly illustrated the slow, discouraging, cumulative principle that changes in quantity add up eventually to changes in quality. And by September 1975, the worm had turned so much that city, state and federal agencies were convening a three-day neighborhood conservation conference in New York to mark the new official line.

Popular, powerless frustration never turns out to be without limit, although the overreaching economic and political forces that ride high for a time try to assure that it will be. However unequal the forces for and against community stability, nothing as devastating as the extended decade of "urban renewal" goes on forever—even with the government, the bankers and the mass media dinning its glories into the public's ears.

Across the nation, the big-money urban policy of maximum demolition and new construction appears to have run its course. Said one of Mayor White's aides in 1974 about the Boston Redevelopment Authority: "They [in BRA] have been living from hand to mouth for two years now. There is no money, and money is power."

The unmistakable signs of the backlash do not mean that every tenant, every homeowner, every lowly Mom and Pop shopkeeper is home safe. For years to come, the charters and the pipelines of official agencies, whose names or even initials we've never heard of, will remain clogged with billions of dollars in "war" appropriations and with fearsome unrepealed "war powers" authorizations from the prebacklash period. The dollars, the powers and the will to spend and invoke them are still available for the asking to hospitals, to plazas, to universities, to museums, to convention centers that enjoy a patty-cake relationship with the officials of these agencies.

The "war appropriations" and the "war powers," of course, are for use against the people and against their expendable homes and shops. In *Store Front Organizing* by Sam Brown of the 1968 McCarthy-for-President movement, the author maintains that "Good organization of citizen groups can attack centers of irresponsible power and wealth in America."

But without organization, Brown warns, the best ideas in the world have no chance. More often than not, expansionist projects bear disarming names and labels, carefully selected—running from the presumptuous misuse in East Harlem of Florence Nightingale's image (to cover a profit-making scheme for a vastly expanded geriatric empire) to the trim and bland-sounding "Inner Belt" label (to suppress all thought of a city's added pollution and all memory of the dislocated families).

It takes active guard duty on a community's barricades before one begins to appreciate how much stratagem is invested in the planning and implementation of expansion projects. By and large, each local battle against one particular tentacle of the octopus has to be won locally. Nonetheless, for mutual support and reinforcement, all community preservation organizations ideally should be hooked into a nationwide federation. Those formal links would help every embattled citizen perceive that it's all one fight against the same octopus making use, in different settings, of the same Plans A, B, and C, and that political perception sustains morale and the will to go on fighting as long as the situation dictates.

In such a federation, members of Save Our Homes, Save Our Shores, Save the Old Man (of the Mountain), Save Our Playground and RAMA (Residents and Merchants Aware), etc. would quickly discover how much they have in common. Whether in the streets, in community newspapers, in court, in legislative halls, at the bar of public opinion, in Harvard Yard at commencement time, or in the loneliness of undercover acts of civil disobedience, all the groups are shaking their collective fists at entrenched institutional power, at great stolen wealth, at a vested insensitivity that rivals the historic attitude of Marie Antoinette.

Time has a way of taking care of villains, big and small. As the economy falters, those systemic fraternal ties to the rest of capitalist enterprise are beginning to create contradictions that politically savvy community groups can exploit. During the recently ended "good times," those who really run this country were quite content to look the other way as the hierarchies of "nonprofit" institutions milked the tills systematically—just as the politicians who serve the power elite are generally allowed to dabble in limited graft. Now, of course, many of the milked institutions—such as overexpanded urban hospitals —find themselves in financial straits, even to the point of bankruptcy.

In a replay of the Depression, the top financial decision-makers today know that the government must soon begin bailing out entire industries in order to keep the economy afloat. In the fall of 1974, "to meet its payroll," Pan American World Airways demanded a monthly subsidy in the tens of millions. Though denied for the moment, the airline will, of course, be heard from again. Under the terms of the 1973 Railroad Recovery Act, the Secretary of Transportation is empowered to "insure the continuation of essential rail services" through direct federal grants to ailing and bankrupt railroads, such as Penn Central. Washington calls this "grants" or "subsidies." To a family struggling to survive on Aid to Dependent Children, it looks suspiciously like another and more generous form of relief.

In defense of his administration's grants and subsidies as governor of New York in more affluent years, Nelson Rockefeller argued revealingly, after being nominated for vice-president, that "boosting the state's economic development called for 'capital improvements' such as building highways, hospitals [*sic*], schools and the octopuslike state university complex [also *sic*]." There, from one who should know, is the Establishment's perception of "nonprofit" health care and education as economic entities integral to the protection and the maintenance of the profit system. Even in the face of a depression, Arthur D. Little Inc., a Cambridge-based think tank headed by retired General James Gavin, projects that, by the end of the 1970's, the 1972 figure of $80 billion for health-care coverage, treatment *and materials* will double.

But henceforth hospitals and overexpanded schools will be passed over in favor of heavy industry. When any sector of our competitive system makes demands beyond the "acceptable" limits of acquisitiveness, other sectors step in to cut the offender down to scale.

This increasingly fierce elbowing at the public trough may give citizen groups opposing expansive institutional takeovers of their neighborhoods a chance to find some unexpected "allies" and draw increments of strength from them. Since about 1971, opposition by highly sophisticated elements of the ruling elite to any more hospital expansion and construction, for example, has been spread ever more loudly and insistently on the public record. Both in public print and most certainly behind the scenes, "Enough is enough, Doc" is what these elements are clearly saying. The Rockefeller-appointed Scott Commission, which called for a halt to all hospital construction, said it in 1973. In the same year, the top-drawer, business-dominated task force of the Committee for Economic Development said precisely the same thing. In 1972, the General Accounting Office, the Congressional watchdog over where the money goes, surveyed the hospital scene at the request of Senator Abraham Ribicoff, and found overexpanded hospitals all over the country. As former Secretary of HEW during the Kennedy-Johnson grantsmanship years, Ribicoff knew what to tell GAO to look for.

Richard Lyons of *The New York Times* has reported on the pressure now emanating from key conservatives in Congress—especially from members of the tax-writing Ways and Means Committee—to reduce the medical gravy train and to cut health-care costs before the medical entrepreneur system gets completely out of control and before it becomes completely discredited. For its own conservative budgetary reasons, the Nixon administration was more or less contributing to these pressures on hospitals to cut costs and to stop expanding.

After a healing or an educational institution is no longer popularly accepted on its own terms as quasi-divine and quasi-angelic, its naked vulnerabilities become obvious. With greed, power grabs and twisted notions of "prestige" behind virtually every effort at unwarranted institutional expansionism, it becomes possible to perceive that many such proposals are in flagrant or at least borderline violation of one or more laws. If you're still bewitched and blinded by an institution's contrived self-image, it never occurs to you to look for those illegalities.

In the most favorable situations, to call public attention, loudly and even raucously, to the violations is sufficient to block an entire project. More often, to assure such a defeat, a citizens' group has to organize early, to research all relevant aspects (leaving *nothing* to assumptions or guesswork and not taking at face value even sworn institutional testimony), and to mobilize a tight and determined and preferably disciplined people's counterforce at least equal in economic and political firepower to the institution. Without that counterforce and without the patent will to use it—in the face of sweet talk and fraudulent political efforts to "mediate" (defang)—the war can well be lost—in the courts (which are highly political centers of power and very responsive to angry citizens who are truly fed up), in the generally irresolute administrative agencies, and among top elected officials. Power is power, whether it's economic power, tenant power or minority group power, and it always has the last word.

In a community's tug-of-war with a self-serving institutional image, it is never enough merely to object to needless expansionism. Politically and practically, the wisest checkerboard move is for the community to present a plan or proposal of its own—even if it means just spelling out good and sufficient reasons for leaving a neighborhood intact and undisturbed. The paid spokesmen for hospitals, schools, churches and commercial enterprises that want to expand are smoothly expert at making objecting abutters appear monstrously unreasonable. These slicksters can throw an inexperienced save-our-homes group right off balance by demanding at a public hearing, "Well, what is your alternative?" The unspoken premise is that, *of course*, the neighborhood in question *has* to be "renewed."

In such instances, fortune favors the tough and imaginative mind. Take, for example, the case of Boston community activist and State Representative Elaine Noble. She discovered that the Boston School Committee had made a secretive, sweetheart deal to eliminate the one and only playground in a section of her Back Bay–Fenway district, and to hand it over to the Knights of Columbus for a parking lot.

She and others appealed the School Committee decision to another city agency. When a public hearing was called, Ms. Noble rented a bus to transport forty of the children who actually use the playground, and began to call all forty to the stand to testify, one by one. After only a handful of the kids had explained why they needed a place off the streets for safe play and games, the attorney for the School Committee—initially supercilious but by now shattered—approached her to seek a "compromise." Her position was adamant: Not one square foot of the playground could be infringed upon. Because she was uncompromising on this point of principle, the war was over at that instant.

Without exception, if an expansion project lacks merit, its sponsors try to ram it through before a community can get itself fully together. At a quick glance, their dressed-up arguments seem plausible. When closely examined over a period of time, however, the totality of the fraud emerges. Nearly always, neighborhood preservation groups need time to communicate this totality to a wider public, and to convince the frequently unsympathetic government officials who must pass on the proposal. Under these circumstances, delay and more delay becomes essential and morally valid. (Most attorneys for save-our-homes, save-our-shores and kindred organizations have to be coached and coaxed into these political pathways and out of their narrow, legalistic backgrounds. They need clear instructions to invoke every technicality that can serve to hold up official approval of the project.) When the offending institution or enterprise begins to squirm and to charge "stalling," the odds are that it sees its dream project going up in smoke under the hot glare of a thousand pair of eyes.

Those of us who have fought off parking lots and fancy new hospital wings for toenail research find nothing wrong in using the law's fine print to serve the public for a change. Most neighborhood groups that are battling against institutional disasters of one variety or another have to rely on volunteer labor, while the institutions are often using public funds to lobby for their favorite boondoggles. Community effectiveness and any meaningful assertion of community rights are often correlated with the healthy passage of time. Except in the depth of a depression, when so many are unemployed that full-time volunteers abound, organizational miracles can rarely be brought about overnight. The system is weighted against the kind of community participation that sociologist C. Wright Mills had in mind when he wrote in *The Sociological Imagination* that "Democracy implies that those vitally affected by any decision men make have an effective voice in that decision. This in turn means that all power to make such decisions be publicly legitimated and that the makers of such decisions be held publicly responsible."

If stalling is required to legitimate decision-making powers and to hold our public servants accountable, so be it. We are talking about war—cynical war on people's homes and jobs and safety and happiness—and in war everyone who's serious plays rough and plays for keeps.

Over and above battles imaginatively fought and tactical delays won is the decisive importance of correct political analysis. Veterans of community wars know that from a correct political line comes victory, and from an incorrect line come setbacks. A gut realization that no one up on the upper rungs of this society is going to solve our problems for us tills the soil out of which correct political analysis can come.

The playground v. parking lot illustrates the point. In Boston, Elaine Noble has come to symbolize the elected official emerging from the matrix of *com-*

munity activism and *community*-defined principles and needs—in contradistinction to the traditional on-the-make and unaccountable manipulators, who go whoring after elective office by being all things to all persons. Old-style politicians would have tried to pacify the parents of the playground children, while at the same time keeping open communications with the Knights of Columbus and the powerful politicians on the School Committee. That way lies a guaranteed sellout of parents and children. With the correct political line one has to conclude that here was a situation where equivocation would have equaled betrayal. When fighting off insatiable wolves who would steal a playground, there is no possible middle ground and no basis for "reconciliation." It's us or them. It's the people or the institutions, and one side has to lose. It's a psychology that consciously cultivates self-reliance—of handling one's own affairs, of relying on and trusting one's fellow tenants and comrades-in-arms, and of disciplining and keeping under strict group control one's attorneys and all others with expertise.

It's an awareness that everything must be questioned and reexamined in a post-Watergate light. That includes all our patriotic assumptions about who gets what rewards, *and how,* in an unplanned and irresponsible social order. From our ingrained frontier notions of individualism, it is not an easy switch to the stern concept of building a community to which all individuals and all institutions and all in government are held accountable, at all times and under all circumstances.

For those intent on institutional rape under cover of smoke screens, all this sounds dangerously radical. In actual fact, it's the rapists resorting indiscriminately to the wrecking ball who are partly to blame for the radical and the dangerous changes in the quality of urban life.

69

When the expansionist fraternity is finally vanquished and their policies are overturned, new neighborhood problems will meanwhile have surfaced that, for all we know, may indeed require truly revolutionary approaches. For now, it's almost embarrassing to acknowledge that the "save our . . ." cry has a deep conservative resonance to it.

Yet, saving from the scrap heap the adults and children who dwell in those homes and play in the threatened parks and playgrounds is what revolutions are supposed to be all about. The difference is that, in these neighborhood battles, the victories are virtually bloodless. Whenever there is an injection of violence, it almost always comes from those behind the bulldozers and not from the mowed-down victims.

Dramatis Personae

Columbus Hospital

Sister Cyprian Branco	(former) executive director of Columbus Hospital
Mother Josephine Migliore	President of Columbus Hospital Board of Trustees
Peter Schneider	Columbus Hospital Attorney
Nicholas Iannuzzi	Columbus Hospital Trustee
John Nicholas Iannuzzi	Columbus Hospital Attorney
Robert Valente	Public Relations Director for Columbus Hospital
Seymour Shapiro	Citadel Management Corporation/Urban Relocation Company

Tenants Committee

Lester Evens	Tenants Committee Attorney
Glenda Watson	Tenants Committee Secretary-Treasurer
Robert Ferrari	Tenants Committee Attorney
Harriet Putterman	Co-ordinator of the Neighborhood Save-Our-Homes Committee
Neal Hitzig	Chairman of the 201 East 19th Street Tenants Association
Assemblyman Andrew Stein	
Councilman Eldon Clingan	

The Master Plan (recapitulated)

Plan A: Ignore, or diligently pretend to ignore, all community opposition to expansionism.

Plan B: Blame a few "soreheads" or some (generally unnamed and mysterious) outside agitators.

Plan C: Scare 'em, bribe 'em, ruin 'em.

71

chapter 2
In Bedpan Alley:
Columbus Hospital

The wolf eats him who makes himself a lamb.
—BARTOLOMEO VANZETTI

At Christmas 1969, had a gypsy fortune teller informed me I would be taking five years out of my life —and possibly more—to resist the expansionist program of a small, backwater, Podunk hospital on Manhattan's East Side, I would have demanded either a second reading of my palm or, more likely, my money back.

Though twice a patient, briefly and long ago, at Columbus Hospital, I knew very little about the institution except that it was diagonally across the street from the building where I've long had an inexpensive, rent-controlled apartment. Like the hydrants and street lights, Columbus was just there, as part of the block. If I'd been queried by a public-opinion poll taker, my reflex reaction toward an expansion of medical facilities would have been favorable. Who would have wished to be labeled an obstructionist in the path of what nearly everyone would presume to be health-care progress?

As a small boy, I sometimes accompanied my father as he drove to Greater Boston hospitals to visit his patients. From this and from the general culture, I imbibed positive and even reverent attitudes toward these centers of healing. On lists of alternative domestic uses for the billions of dollars the United States wasted on the Indo-China war, even radical groups almost always put hospitals way at the top of the preferred priorities. During the early 1960's, when Local 1199 of the Hospital Workers Union began an intensive drive to organize the exceptionally low-paid workers in New York City's many "voluntary" ("nonprofit") hospitals, I even felt a measure of sympathy (which I don't for most bosses) when one administrator after another came forth with the plausible plea that they could not afford to meet the union's demands.

Sadder and wiser, I now realize that I hadn't done my homework. Since World War II, I hadn't kept abreast of the vast depersonalizing changes in the structure and functioning of hospitals. I hadn't come to realize that, except for declaring and paying dividends, businesses operating for profit differ little in operation and in purpose from today's deformed medical-care centers.

The pleasant East 19th Street residential block between Second and Third Avenues is halfway between famed Gramercy and Stuyvesant parks. We are part of a well-tended area that has traditionally been low in crime, remarkably free of racial and ethnic tensions, mixed and balanced in apartment buildings and in owner-occupied brownstones, heterogeneous in the income and age levels of its residents, and pleasant and attractive within the confines of contemporary urban living. If one stands at the Peter Stuyvesant statue in the park that bears his name, one can look three blocks down Second Avenue to the Eye and Ear Infirmary (where in 1970–71 working-class tenants, lacking indigenous leadership, were hounded out of their homes) and directly east past the park to New York Infirmary (with strong Episcopalian connections) and to its next-door acknowledged competitor, Beth Israel Medical Center.

Two blocks north, at a slight westward diagonal, lies Columbus Hospital on 19th Street. Founded in 1891 by Mother Frances Cabrini, the first-named saint of United States citizenship, and owned and operated by the Rome-based Missionary Sisters of the Sacred Heart, Columbus was long content with its undistinguished medical staff, its heavily Italian immigrant clientele, its Kuomintang patients from Chinatown, and until 1973 its 288 beds in a single unprepossessing building. Year after year, the *Directory of Internships and Residencies,* published by the American Medical Association, has shown Columbus to have a general death rate at least twice that of Bellevue, New York's largest and most famous municipal hospital. By law, overcrowded Bellevue cannot turn away any resident of the city, and a high proportion of its many poor patients are admitted in deteriorated states of health.

Over the years, if Columbus has made any serious effort to clean house and to upgrade its medical staff, it is a secret well kept from the community. Among knowledgeable people in the neighborhood, it is now generally understood that Columbus is not the place to go if ill. Each year, for all its sociological liabilities and its political neglect by City Hall, Bellevue has the pick of the crop of graduates from U.S. medical schools. Each year, the AMA Directory shows Columbus attracting virtually no U.S.-trained medical students.

By 1965, for those in the know in Albany, a trend was discernible that, by 1970, would make huge amounts of state funds available for hospital expansion. It didn't take long for Columbus to catch the bug. But character-

74

istically we in the community were not notified by either the nuns or the state authorities who dispense the low-interest, long-term mortgage loans. Even if we had been notified, few if any of us would have raised objections. Like most of our fellow citizens across the country, we had not then perceived the threat to stable neighborhoods inherent in wholesale, unplanned, uncoordinated, competitive institutional expansionism. Perhaps former patients who had been badly treated, medically or financially,* would have been skeptical (had they known) about adding to Columbus' size and power. But such individuals were scattered and disorganized. Certainly in the mid-1960's, they were not at all likely to come forward with any serious and sustained challenge. Thus, by community default, The Plan moved forward—quietly, stealthily, relentlessly. Like a silent plague, residential buildings on the site of the planned new wing were bought up, one by one; tenants were evicted over the signature of the superior, Mother Irene Connolly; the buildings were then torn down with no community consultation; the site was gradually cleared. Not even the faceless, voiceless dispossessed tenants protested. Our block slept on.

The Columbus neighborhood abounds with similar stark, money-grubbing stories. Invariably, they

* In 1955, a resident of 70 Irving Place (a professional writer) gave birth at Columbus to a baby daughter. Since the delivery was free of complications and since she needed to get back home to her other small children, she arranged to be discharged on the second day.

Her husband came to pick her up, and on the way out they stopped at the desk to pay the bill. To their surprise, it covered seven, not two days. When they pointed out the "error," they were told that patients were billed for a full week for childbirth, regardless of the length of stay.

Stunned, they declared they would not pay for services not rendered. Hospital guards then surrounded the mother, father and infant, and they were given to understand that they could not leave until they paid in full. They paid.

startle. On reflection, though, they don't really surprise us. For the end is in the beginning, and the beginning was acquisitive. In a May, 1973, *Reader's Digest* article on the canonization of saints, we learn that when Mother Cabrini, Columbus' founder, was up for canonization, the Devil's Advocate (Promotor General of the Faith) argued that "this simple immigrant had shown so keen a sense of money, and such cunning at dealing in real estate, that her charitable institutions eventually became a flourishing financial empire. Could this ability to amass wealth be reconciled with Christian virtues?" the *Reader's Digest* author asked. "It evidently could; Mother Cabrini was canonized in 1946."

Unknown to us across the street at 210–214 East 19th Street, the powers-that-be at Columbus Hospital had long had their eyes on our forty-eight apartments and four ground-floor storefronts. Ours is an old six-story walk-up, structurally sound, with a rather unusual mix of white-collar and professional tenants (including several actors and artists), blue-collar industrial workers, and elderly persons barely managing on pensions and Social Security. From the late 1950's through 1969, the building—all one structure with two entrances at 210 and 214—was owned and managed by one of New York's more reputable realty firms, Klein, Mayer and Korn. Heat and hot water were rarely a problem during those dozen benign years. Almost always, on request and without a hassle, these former owners painted our apartments according to the legal time-table. Repairs were promptly attended to when called to the firm's attention. Although rents were controlled and low, Bertram Klein himself told me after the building was sold that they had been making a "satisfactory" profit. Despite repeated offers by Columbus, they were "not interested" in selling. Klein, Mayer and Korn are not fast-buck speculators who buy today, sell tomorrow, and meanwhile let their properties deteriorate.

Then, in the autumn of 1969, Columbus raised its bid to $275,000 cash—twice the market value. At that point, the owner's reaction was that "we couldn't turn it down. It was an offer we couldn't refuse." Technically, Columbus' hand was still invisible. The offer and then the cash came from Marpaul Corporation. Despite vigorous and formal denials that Columbus was in any way involved in the purchase, all concerned knew that Marpaul was a front for the hospital. This was soon confirmed, in the nuns' usual unsubtle fashion. Sister Cyprian Branco, executive director of Columbus, turned up to sign the insurance papers as president of Marpaul when the time came to shift the policy on our building from the old owner to the new.

Needless to say, we tenants had no advance notification about the big deal going on over our heads. Coming as it did on December 15, 1969, the sale turned out to be our negative Christmas present. Long before we were formally told to pay our rents to the new management firm as of March 1, 1970, we received informal we-want-you-out signals from Columbus, in the form of intermittent heatless days and other curtailed services.

The new management came with two faces but with one unrelenting purpose: to get the tenants out by all necessary means. Citadel Management Company, headed by Seymour Shapiro, collected our rents, supervised the superintendent, and supposedly managed the building. Urban Relocation Company, headed by Seymour Shapiro and occupying the same offices at 205 East 42nd Street, was charged with the responsibility of placing us in whatever abodes elsewhere we would accept.

A decade earlier, Shapiro had first broken into

the news when prosecuted on kickback and conspiracy charges and, later, when accused of harassing West Side merchants and residents out of their shops and homes, in order to make way for Lincoln Center. Since early 1973, Shapiro individually and Urban corporately have been under a permanent citywide antiharassment injunction obtained by New York State Attorney General Louis Lefkowitz. In asking the State Supreme Court to issue the injunction, Lefkowitz submitted sworn tenant affidavits, including a dozen from our building, detailing Urban's tactics in behalf of Columbus Hospital.

From a conversation in the spring of 1970 with a woman aide to Shapiro, I perceived that they fully expected to be rid of us tenants by the end of that calendar year. That was their timetable—and, presumably, their pledge to Columbus. Urban sails into a situation such as ours with a well-practiced operational plan. The company faces x number of disorganized tenants, and plays one off against the others. ("We'll offer *you* this much to move out, but don't tell your neighbors.") Urban capitalizes on the U.S. individualism indoctrination of the devil-take-the-hindmost variety, and cultivates an atmosphere of "official" inevitability about a building's demolition. Little imagination is required to grasp what lies behind another permanent injunction, issued in 1971, that directed Urban to put, in large type, on all its stationery, building signs, business cards and notices to tenants: NOT A GOVERNMENT AGENCY.

Within weeks of Urban's arrival on the scene, a large sign appeared overnight on our front fire escape: THIS BUILDING SCHEDULED FOR DEMOLITION. In less than twenty-four hours, the Fire Department (the only city agency that has consistently enforced the law in our behalf) made the hospital remove the sign. But meanwhile, the intended panic had gripped many tenants. If at that time Urban had been legally obligated to add "NOT A GOVERNMENT AGENCY" in equally large letters, the sign's impact would have been considerably diluted.

Urban's overall plan usually works, right on schedule. Most of the company's clients are thumb-in-nose private speculators and insatiable developers, rather than sweetness-and-light institutions, whose very poses make them somewhat more vulnerable to negative publicity and to political pressures.

The superintendent, who had been with us for eleven years, occupied one of the forty-eight apartments. Except for a handful of us longtime residents who had gotten to know one another somewhat, nothing distinguished the forty-seven residential tenants from tenants in other sizable buildings all over New York. We hardly knew the tenants in adjacent apartments. We were faintly smiling bodies that passed in the halls. Not having been cursed with a neglectful landlord for almost fifteen years, we had no recent experience in struggling together for common aims. Psychologically and politically, we were disarmed and naked unto Urban and Columbus.

In retrospect, we can see that what saved us and our building from the wrecking ball was a combination of favorable items and circumstances: a clear decision to fight on the principle of preserving sound housing (as distinct from a mercenary haggling over "relocation" fees); the ability and willingness of several tenants to devote considerable time and energy to a fight that often became all-consuming and energy-depleting; the ability to mobilize community support and to generate citywide (eventually nationwide) publicity; the know-how in our ranks needed to raise funds; technical assistance from neighbors and others who are statisticians, architects, researchers, housing

79

experts and attorneys; political support from local elected officials; strategic advice from tenant organizers with a wealth of experience ranging as far back as the 1963 Harlem–Lower East Side rent strikes; and uninterrupted fumbling by Columbus, whose conceptions about us as pushovers and about their own absolute power were totally askew.

This is not to imply that only in that complex combination lies the formula for tenant success. It took us, for example, from March 1970 to August 1971 to rid ourselves of Urban Relocation Company. In five minutes, one group of Harlem tenants achieved precisely the same end. They beat up an Urban "enforcer," and warned that anyone from that company daring in the future to show his face in that block would be killed. To be successful, every fight has to be attuned to the climate and to the prevailing temperament of the surrounding community. Bedpan Alley is not a brawling neighborhood and, at least in prerecession days, would not support a rough-and-tumble confrontation. But if past periods of backs-to-wall upheavals are any guide, other communities not endowed with our wealth of intellectual and other genteel skills will fight back with whatever resources they do have.

We in our building also fell heir to the body of experience from tenants of other nearby hospitals—each with its own expansionist program involving "relocation." Months before our turn came, those tenants had begun to organize to defend their homes. In fact, it was Beth Israel tenants who were mostly responsible for calling the first (and well attended) we-won't-move meeting of us Columbus tenants in May or June 1970, immediately after word spread that the ax was about to fall on us. As we all now look back, we can discern the amateurish weaknesses of those early meetings held in the neighborhood storefronts of Congressman Edward Koch and Assemblyman Andrew Stein: the upward-and-onward tone; the unwarranted encouragement we derived from the unanimous we-won't-move votes when, in fact, some who so voted were already negotiating secretly with Urban Relocation Company for penny-ante bribes to move; the failure to see that a five-minute pep talk from Bella Abzug (who whirled by on a candidate's usual preprimary dozen meetings per evening) was no substitute for tedious, sustained, floor-by-floor organizing of timid and wavering tenants who above all needed authoritative, believable assurance—and then weekly reassurance—that they really would not have to move.

The May 15, 1970, letter from Urban inviting us to cut our own throats was as specific as it was misleading: "Your building is slated for demolition." At the time, none of us knew anything about municipal certificates of eviction, which Urban and Columbus would legally need if we refused to cooperate in our own "relocation." None of us knew that the John Lindsay administration had already imposed an informal stay on granting such certificates to institutions for company (staff) housing. We weren't yet aware that, since Columbus planned to substitute a twenty-seven-car parking lot for our forty-eight apartments, sufficiently loud agitation by us would make the issuance of eviction certificates politically infeasible for a mayor with Presidential ambitions. (As 1972 neared, the City Hall order went down through the ranks: "Make John look good in housing.") Five years later, we still know of no expanding New York City hospital that in the 1970's has taken the route of certificates of evictions. Lies, threats, bribes and con games are more fruitful ways to vacate buildings.

Partly because of inexperience, partly because

81

of language barriers (Polish, Spanish, Ukrainian, Chinese), those of us on whom leadership burdens devolved were too late, in many cases, in preventing Urban Relocation Company from convincing the more easily victimized tenants that $200, $500, $1,000 in "relocation" fees was "big money." In part to generate the feeling that "everyone" is moving out, Urban goes after non-English-speaking and more poorly educated tenants first. Usually within weeks it gets them to sign an agreement to move. In many cases, such persons have never held $200 in their hands at one time. When Urban benignly adds "We'll also forget about this month's rent if you move out by the first," the victim's cup runneth over. For Urban to dangle this kind of bait in front of easily bamboozled poor people was reprehensible. For a religious hospital to encourage Urban to utilize such cynical tactics was doubly damnable. Urban warns tenants who hesitate and who ask for time to think it over: "If you don't accept this offer now, you won't get *any* money later on, and you'll still have to move."

Leaders of the Tenants Committee that was slowly organized over the summer and fall of 1970 soon encountered a basic and serious obstacle: the matter of credibility when seeking to convince fellow tenants that, to win, we merely had to stay ensconced in our apartments and say no. No to all monetary enticements. No to intimidation. No to harassment. No to the tireless rumor-mongers.

I for one was astounded to discover how authority-minded so many of my neighbors were. The reasoning was "It's *their* property. *They* are powerful. If they say we've got to get out, then we'll have to move." Without exaggeration, it took at least one full year, with approaches from many different angles, to convince even tenants who desperately wished to keep their apartments that Columbus Hospital in fact did not have that absolute power of eviction, and that tenant rights could be effectively asserted over property rights. In the meantime, the Urban Relocation staffers were busily at work. By the time we forced Columbus to fire them, our numbers had dropped from forty-seven occupied apartments to twenty.

The requisite credibility built up slowly. In Psychology 201, one learns that people have to trust you as a person before they will trust your ideas. We in leadership roles recognized the necessity to be 100 percent accurate in the technical, legal and political information that we began collecting and disseminating. In a fight inevitably attended by crises in collective morale and by discouraging setbacks, there is always a temptation for organizers and leaders to withhold news of negative developments. It's a temptation that has to be resisted—if only because word will eventually get around anyway. Within the framework of a carefully planned struggle, people can absorb temporary defeats.

The sound political admonition to "serve the people" is also an indispensable ingredient in the long uphill efforts to win the trust of those being organized. In the context of a protracted tenant struggle, ministering unto others can mean everything from paying the utility bills of elderly tenants who don't have checking accounts, to replacing light bulbs for neighbors who can't climb ladders, to accepting parcels from mailmen and then climbing five flights of stairs to deliver them, to many other forms of mutual aid for which New York apartment dwellers are not particularly noted. While it is an open question how much a struggle such as ours changes the participants for the better—perceptibly, significantly, permanently— some of the tenants have caught the contagion of the underlying idea that "I am my brother's/sister's keeper."

83

Today we do think of group security and group comfort and group defense against a landlord that has yet to give up.

During the early 1960's, when the United States rushed from one self-defeating move to another in the desperate effort to reverse the Cuban revolution, the dean of Wisconsin State College at Whitewater asked me at a faculty lunch following a morning lecture: "Does Fidel have agents in the CIA helping to make policy?" From time to time on 19th Street, we've been asked if we planted a sympathizer on the Columbus board of trustees. *"Who* is advising them?" No other explanation seems to fit the endless series of hospital blunders. From August 2, 1970, when Columbus got the Tactical Police Force to dispatch 150 riot-trained cops (in two busses, half a dozen paddy wagons and twenty to thirty patrol cars) to evict and arrest half a dozen needy, harmless squatters in some of the empty apartments, until August 27, 1971, when both sides sat down to negotiate a contract, all tenant requests to meet with someone in authority at Columbus were rebuffed. No matter how polished the efforts to explain away this inaccessibility, it is impossible for an institution to maintain a good image in the community it professes to serve when it reveals itself so defensive about a twenty-seven-car parking lot that it dares not sit down and talk—even in bad faith—with a group of tenants.

On the day-to-day pragmatic level the blunders stood out. When Urban Relocation Company takes over a building to be vacated, sooner or later Mr. Shapiro puts in his own "trusted" superintendent. At that point the systematic, well-rehearsed, continuous harassment begins. The motor on the oil burner gets "stolen," and can't be replaced for days—*always* in the coldest weather. Radiators

84

in empty apartments start leaking down on occupied apartments below. In the halls and on the stairs puddles of urine appear. Garbage is not collected, and rats appear. Newly vacated apartments are sealed with tin—without first removing food and garbage. Usual security measures are scrapped, and well-timed burglaries increase. Obscene, middle-of-the-night phone calls to women tenants multiply. Day and night, tenants know they are being spied upon. An atmosphere of siege and war develops. There is no court and no official agency to which to turn for immediate remedy and relief.

Columbus made the serious mistake of allowing Urban Relocation Company to fire our seventy-year-old superintendent, who had been with us for eleven years. The letter dismissing him was crude and cruel, with a thirty-day get-out deadline, with no pretense that he was being fired for cause, and with no mention of severance pay or of the vacation pay due him. In routine fashion, Urban noted that a copy of the dismissal letter was being sent to the hospital administrator, thus inadvertently making it impossible for Columbus to feign ignorance.

We reproduced and distributed the letter, and took to the streets in the super's defense. Unfortunately, our efforts did not get him back his job. But through the press coverage of the demonstration, we began to transmit the information that a hospital, supposedly out to heal, was resorting to heartless tactics usually associated with company towns and ghetto slumlords.

The weight of the escalating publicity—99 percent of it adverse to Columbus—proved to be enormously helpful. Among other effects, it contributed to the steady demoralization of the hawks at the hospital and, at the time of our first lawsuit, helped make their hard-nosed policies untenable. But we never got caught up with the notion that publicity alone could organize a tight Tenants Committee and save our buildings.

At community meetings we often said that in the end we would lose, no matter how frequently we managed to get favorable stories in *The New York Times* (as indeed we did every couple of months), if tenants simultaneously continued to accept bribes and move out. A point is reached when a building becomes so empty that the few holdout tenants begin to tremble for their day-to-day safety. Their we-won't-move resolve caves in. If, for example, one lives on the fifth floor and if every night one must walk past several totally empty lower floors, where addicts and muggers might well be lurking, the temptation increases to accept "relocation" and to flee to *supposedly* safer turf. The irony is that tenants usually get "relocated" to remote, high-crime or highly inconvenient areas. One of our fellow tenants was driven to Far Rockaway by Urban Relocation Company to look at a new apartment, and then driven back to 19th Street—never thinking (as Urban surely knew he wouldn't) to check accessibility by public transportation. On his first night after "relocation," when he left his Manhattan job at 11 P.M., he discovered to his horror that it took until 2 A.M., via several subways and busses, to reach his new address.

Honesty requires us to admit to an early political naïveté that is embarrassing to look back on now. Because we shared the conventional positive attitudes toward hospitals, we for months could not believe that Columbus was aware of, let alone condoned, the overall treatment we were getting from Urban Relocation Company. Hence our repeated requests to meet with administrators or board

86

members, so that we could tell them, face to face, what we were being subjected to.

Happily for us, Columbus shattered that illusion before it had unduly undermined our fight and before our ranks had thinned beyond the point of no return. Christmas Day 1970 was a bitter cold day. On that day, Urban's imported superintendent—who was specially provided with three large electric heaters for his own apartment—cut off all heat and blamed it on oil burner "breakdown."

Directly across the street from us, Columbus has its own engineering and maintenance staff on duty twenty-four hours a day: plumbers, electricians, heating specialists, others. When the hospital refused us emergency service, our naïveté came to an abrupt end. In opening our eyes and in hardening tenant resolve, Columbus had again grossly miscalculated.

In the months before we got to know one another quite intimately, some of us worried about possible leaks to the hospital administration from tenants out to strike a better bargain on "relocation" fees. We watched for indications that the hospital had been tipped in advance to any of our surprise sorties—such as our disruption of the annual money-raising bazaar of the Women's Auxiliary, or our crashing Columbus' unpublicized community mental-health conference, to which psychiatrists from other hospitals and representatives of social and official agencies had been invited, and at which we distributed embarrassing fliers recounting the nerve-wracking harassment of us tenants. "Mental health, anyone?" was the ironic theme of the fliers, which the nuns scurried around to collect from the empty seats. During the question period, the minute I raised my hand, the chairman closed the conference. In that 1970–71 period, the nuns invariably called

87

the 13th Police Precinct a block away whenever two or more tenants assembled at or anywhere near the hospital. Eventually the cops, weary of being used, stopped responding to the "rabble at our door" summonses. Like everyone else, the police were openly unsympathetic to the proposed twenty-seven-car parking lot.

So far as we could ever tell, we were consistently lucky. There were no leaks of our plans and strategies. As our numbers dwindled and our ranks drew closer, our concerns about unauthorized disclosure of tenant secrets disappeared. By contrast, as time passed, our ability to know what the hospital was up to improved, especially after Local 1199 won a union representation election at Columbus in June 1972. Because we supported the union's organizing campaign and because union members in turn gained a better understanding of our struggle, our sources of information increased considerably. Among some of the white-collar and professional staff we also found sympathizers who were in a position to provide useful tips.

Partly because of all the volunteer talent available to us, partly because of genuine consultation and discussion on all important matters, our Tenants Committee has managed so far to avoid any serious errors of judgment. In reviewing the long progression of steps we have taken over a five-year period, we see that, consciously or unconsciously, the decisions we reached more or less reflected the ever-shifting power realities. Over the summer and fall of 1970 and into 1971, we devoted considerable energy to leafleting the neighborhood and to keeping block residents apprised of our moves. We are still very conscious of community relations. But our growing self-reliance and the 1971 birth of an excellent community newspaper (the *Gramercy Herald*) tipped the power scales, and enabled us to reduce emphasis on time-consuming, door-to-door circularizing.

While we were slowly organizing ourselves and building tenant self-confidence, citywide publicity was very important to us internally. Friends and fellow workers would tell tenants who had never before had a moment of glory and recognition: "I saw you on television" or "I read about your building in the *Daily News*." Tenants came to realize that the protective eyes of the city were on us and that, as a result, Columbus and Urban Relocation Company were inhibited from trying their ultimate tactics against "recalcitrants." Women in our building lost their justifiable fears of physical attacks. We all stopped worrying about nocturnal arson, for which nearly all New York's "relocation" outfits are notorious.

In January 1971, our first appeal to Community Planning Board 6 also reflected where we stood, in power terms, vis-à-vis Columbus. The community boards, a sign of the decentralist times, are appointed by New York's five borough presidents. Members serve without pay. What little authority they can exert is moral, not legal, and it depends upon the caliber and determination of the members and particularly the chairperson. Board 6 is known to be one of the more forceful of any in the city's five boroughs. Yet even it can do little more than take Columbus to a verbal woodshed and briefly embarrass it. We clearly could not tarry long at the level of mild moral chastisement. We had to build up for the big leap forward into the brass-knuckles realms of the courts and other centers of real power such as the regulatory and administrative agencies in the "fourth branch of government." In New York, it is the State Health Department that ultimately controls the expansion of all medical facilities, and it was the State Housing Finance Agency to which

89

Columbus was applying for a low-interest, long-term $39 million mortgage loan. *This,* we ultimately found, was the jugular vein.

Very early in our relationship with our first tenant attorney, Lester Evens, he advised us that "there is a long and honorable tradition in the United States of defending one's home" and that "if you tenants make up your minds that there will be no harassment, then there will be no harassment."

Parenthetically, one of the most difficult pieces of legal advice to get unsophisticated, partly scared tenants to accept is this: "First say, 'See my lawyer,' then close the door or hang up the phone." Fear, ego, a misguided wish to be polite to everyone—all operated to give Urban Relocation personnel a crucial foot in the door. We finally had to get everyone to sign a legal document, backed up politically by dire warnings from Congresswoman Bella Abzug, our councilman and our state assemblyman, telling Urban and Columbus to cease and desist from all solicitation. Forced to take one step backward under that concentrated pressure, Columbus instructed Urban to stop offering bribes to any and all tenants. A "relocation" fee was to be paid only if a tenant approached Urban. We quickly noticed that, with each involuntary step backward, the hospital was increasingly off balance and thus more susceptible to our next big onslaught.

Had the Columbus nuns ever switched from retaining an emotionally involved attorney, who told them what they wished to hear, to engaging a lawyer more attuned to sophisticated ways of defusing embattled tenants, and had the trustees simultaneously fired its entire incompetent public-relations department, the Tenants

Committee would have had a considerably tougher job of holding itself together. On January 30, 1971—the day on which our state assemblyman, Andrew Stein, and City Councilman Eldon Clingan held a news conference outside our building to denounce Urban Relocation Company and the hospital's "arrogance"—the chief of security at Columbus was ordered by his superiors to block the entrance to the hospital when the two elected officials, together with several tenants, sought to enter to discuss the issues.

No institution even slightly conscious of the sensitivities of politicians in front of their constituents and in the presence of reporters would subject them to the indignity of being physically barred by a private cop. Such crudity alone was sufficient to assure an eleven-paragraph story in *The New York Times* and to guarantee coverage on the evening television news shows. Hours later, when Channel 5, the Metromedia station, finally tracked down one of the always elusive spokespersons in the hospital's public-relations department, her statement on the twenty-seven-car parking lot was a classic of professional ineptness: "I know it sounds bad [to be throwing people out of their homes at the time of a critical housing shortage], but parking it is."

Juxtaposed to her on the Channel 5 news was an interview with one of the tenants, snowy-haired Mrs. Berta Norton (then age eighty-four), who graphically explained what it would mean for her and her two old cats to be evicted after having lived in her apartment for over a quarter of a century. Once elderly people reach a certain age and fragility, their legitimate worries about falls and broken bones make them leery about running around on the myriad errands that are essential to urban living. At that point in their declining years, they develop a support system: one neighbor's child buys the groceries; another neighbor (someone with better education) fills out all the complicated Medicare and Medicaid forms; another buys money orders at a bank to pay the rent and other monthly bills.

In our naïve period, we used to tell Columbus Hospital, in letter after letter, that elderly persons often die soon after being uprooted. We assumed that this would melt the hearts of those in policy positions. Eventually we were constrained to realize that they did not care, and once we forced them to emerge from behind their secretaries' skirts, they made little pretense of caring. On the contrary, they lied repeatedly in public by denying they had evicted anyone at all from the site of their new sixteen-story building (until we came up with a successful 1966 dispossess application signed by Mother Irene Connolly and by Peter Schneider, the hospital attorney). The hospital also adopted the public stance that one or two "professional agitators" among the tenants held a gun at the backs of the others, all of whom would otherwise be delighted to "relocate." (Plan B.)

In a very deep sense, the Missionary Sisters have never gotten over the deep shock of being called by the press on a Sunday morning in August 1970 and told that during the night squatters had moved into our building. In angry and embittered terms, these "daughters of Mother Cabrini" (patron-saint of the homeless and founder of Columbus Hospital) still refer to "the trespassers" who were "attracted to the building by these tenants through various devices, including the distribution of incendiary circulars," and who "battered down" the doors and windows of the vacant apartments.

For exactly one year, from the time of the squat-in until the signing of a contract between Columbus and

92

tenants, the hospital placed uniformed security guards outside our building on a twenty-four-hour three-shift basis. At a conservative estimate of three dollars an hour for such guards, this entailed a daily expense of $72, and a yearly expense of over $26,000. Even with the guards stationed directly outside, our apartments during those twelve months had a substantial jump in burglaries. In December 1970, at the end of an evening tenants' meeting, a dozen of us walked across the street to demand the stationing of an overnight guard outside the apartment of a tenant who had arrived home from work that day to find his door broken down and various bulky and highly visible items, such as stereo equipment, stolen. En route, we passed a guard, Salvatore, in civilian clothes, leaving to go home. When we demanded to know how the burglar could have gotten past him during his tour of duty, his answer was blunt: "I'm there to watch for squatters, not for burglars."

During the mid and late 1960's, before the rise of consumerism, there was absolutely no community involvement in the Columbus expansion project. Because then and now all the health and funding agencies are pathologically secretive about opening files to public inspection, the riddle of a fivefold cost escalation (even taking inflation into account) between 1966 and 1970 has yet to be unraveled. The original proposal, calling for a nine-story wing adjacent to its old building and raising the number of general (acute care) beds from 288 to 406, was to provide on-site staff housing, including a convent on one of the floors, and an on-site street-level garage at a cost of $8 million. By the time our Tenants Committee began researching the project in late 1970, The Plan had mushroomed into a sixteen-story wing, with no on-site staff housing and no on-site garage. With no increase in the number of the originally planned total of 406 beds,

93

the cost had jumped to $44-million—far beyond the annual inflationary 10 percent increase in construction costs and far beyond the prorated extra expense of the seven additional floors.

The to-us familiar readiness of Columbus to lie about its expansion program and to dissemble in public was dramatized at a January 1971 meeting of Community Board 6. As a result of tenant protests, the board asked Columbus administrator Joseph Toomey to appear before it. At the last minute, Toomey, a faceless careerist, ducked out of appearing himself and sent the community-relations director, who "explained" to the board that they needed our building for a twenty-seven-car parking lot because an "underground river" at the site for the not-yet-constructed new wing made an on-site garage impossible.

Even before we disproved the underground-river caper, architects informed us that such a body of water constitutes no serious obstacle to an underground, let alone a street-level, garage. Apparently the nuns, noted for doling out toilet paper as if it were made of gold, decided to save the expense of blasting underground where rock, not water, was the problem. A half-hour visit to the map department of the New York Public Library by tenant Glenda Watson clearly established that the nearest of Manhattan's numerous underground rivers turns northwest at the corner of 20th Street and Second Avenue and passes underneath the Police Academy across from Columbus. The academy has a large underground garage. The water comes nowhere close to any hospital property. Fortunately, we by then had learned to believe absolutely nothing the hospital said without independent verification.

When the Tenants Committee entered the picture in the fall of 1970, we discovered that, in behalf of

94

the $44 million proposal, the State Health Department and the State Housing Finance Agency (SHFA) had, by law, commissioned one of the "Big Eight" accounting firms, Ernst and Ernst, to conduct a financial feasibility study to determine the ability of Columbus Hospital to repay the proposed state mortgage loan.

The preliminary report of October 1970 was inconclusive. At the time of the City Hall hearing that our local elected officials called in May 1971, the final report was not yet available. Councilman Clingan's administrative assistant, Brian Murtaugh, was compelled to twist the arms of the two state agencies and of the Health and Hospital Planning Council before they reluctantly agreed to send representatives to the hearing.

Once there, they had no answers to probing questions put to them by a statistician neighbor of ours, Neal Hitzig, who presented a lengthy professional analysis of the preliminary report and of the unexplained restrictive instructions given to the accounting firm by the state agencies:

1. Conduct no investigation of the need for the sixteen-story Columbus Hospital addition in Bedpan Alley with its already existing 1,800 beds (five times the national average of hospital beds per capita).

2. Conduct no investigation of the financial position of "Mother House" (the Missionary Sisters of the Sacred Heart, owners and operators of Columbus Hospital and the guarantors of the loan).

3. Conduct no audit of the data provided by Columbus' management.

Thus, in effect, Columbus said to the accounting firm: "Yes, we can repay a $39 million loan." Under Albany's guidelines imposed on its staff accountants, Ernst and Ernst then told the state in its final report: "Yes, Columbus can repay."

Via sources in both the Health Department and SHFA, we ascertained that Columbus, which seems to have a chronic cash-flow problem except for cash purchases of nearby properties, had "a very hard time scraping up the 10 percent equity" ($4 million) to qualify for the loan.

Whatever the truth about its financial status, a real panic seized the Columbus administration on August 20, 1971, when Assemblyman Stein and two tenant representatives brought suit in State Supreme Court to enjoin construction of the new building and to block impending final approval of the state mortgage loan by the commissioner of health and by the SHFA. Within *hours* after being served with the legal papers, Columbus telephoned Mr. Stein to indicate readiness to sit down and talk with the tenants immediately—after having been totally inaccessible for a full year. The next week was taken up with preliminary sparring on the framework and the ground rules for the negotiating session as we tenants sought to assure the fruitfulness of such talks. At least three long evening tenant meetings were required for final decisions on our negotiable and nonnegotiable demands.

Fourteen months later, in answering our damage suit for breach of the August 27, 1971, contract, Columbus unintentionally revealed that the mere remembrance of the threat we posed to that $39 million state loan sent fresh shivers down the institution's back. Certainly our demands at the bargaining table would have been notably stiffer—and before signing we would have slept at least overnight on the negotiated terms of the contract—if we had known the extent of the trembling and the knee-knocking at the hospital. Here, from Sister Cyprian Branco's affidavit of September 26, 1972, is her

96

account of the impact of our August 20, 1971, lawsuit:

Page 5: [T]he [court] action was known to all the parties to be extortive, coercive, and in the nature of a "hold-up," in that by merely bringing the action, no matter how baseless, the plaintiffs had placed a stranglehold on the throat of Columbus Hospital.

Page 9: All these extra-legal [publicity and agitational] efforts of the plaintiffs to prevent Columbus Hospital from making lawful use of its own property [for the parking lot] were unsuccessful until August 20, 1971. On that date, they achieved instant success, however, by merely bringing their injunction suit, knowing as they did that the New York State Housing Finance Agency would not schedule the mortgage closing while the law suit was unresolved. To prevent the consequent *disaster* [emphasis mine] to Columbus Hospital we yielded to the plaintiffs and signed the contract that was their price for discontinuing their coercive law suit.

In a memorandum of law (pages 9 and 10) presented to the court during the same autumn of 1972, hospital attorney Peter Schneider argued that our 1971 lawsuit had "cast a cloud on the mortgage proceedings that required immediate action by the [State Housing] Finance Agency if Columbus Hospital was not to be irreparably damaged." On page 14, he continued:

In exchange for the discontinuance of the mortgage litigation, Columbus Hospital agreed to a lifetime tenancy for all tenants, agreed to make numerous and expensive repairs and changes, agreed to cancel 10-months back rent due from plaintiffs Wastock and Worthy, agreed to submit all future expansion plans to a community board, and agreed to establish a tenant-hospital committee for planning the future operation of the 210–214 property.

97

Attorney Schneider failed to mention that Urban Relocation Company, in behalf of Columbus, had for ten months rejected the rent of tenants Wastock and Worthy, and then took us to court on a nonpayment eviction proceeding.

Whatever the source of the scraped-up $4 million in equity funds needed to qualify for the loan, what is known is that, to repay the $39 million state loan, Columbus must add $17.80 per patient per day (or an extra $124.60 for a patient remaining one week) to its already steep basic room charge. The $17.80 figure comes from a formula for repayment of hospital debts, published by the Health, Education and Welfare Department in an April 16, 1973, memo: *Rapid Reference Guide for Estimating Impact of Borrowed Funds on Patient Charges.* (Under the gun of necessity, tenant and community groups quickly learn of the tremendous volume of available research documents that can be of inestimable legal, political and agitational value in a war with an institution. Many are free of charge and are readily obtainable through members of Congress and other officials. The only requirement is the imagination to inquire—of a librarian, of a public agency, of a Ralph Nader-type organization—if such-and-such a study or analysis or survey has by chance been made.)

Since a high percentage of hospital bills today are paid by third parties—Blue Cross, Medicare/Medicaid, Welfare Departments—we have here a merry-go-round of public loan funds being used to rip up a stable neighborhood in order to build surplus medical facilities. Then other public monies go to repay the loan that was unwarranted to begin with and that is helping to inflate the costs of medical care—and all in a fifth-rate hospital.

About the time of the May 1971 City Hall hearing on the pending loan application, our Tenants Committee began a conscious process of pacing our activities and our publicity efforts—partly to avoid burning ourselves out as we perceived a long struggle ahead. A year of very hectic agitation had by then convinced us that, no matter how intensively we might work, the fight to save our building from the wrecking ball would be protracted, with natural lulls in the confrontation alternating with busy periods, if only because inevitably our fight was part of a much bigger and slowly growing tenant movement. In that context, it is senseless to try to do today what can only be done tomorrow.

Pacing in publicity efforts necessitates a restrained and strategically trained appetite for breaking into the news. In March 1971, after it had become clear that Columbus Hospital had no intention of painting halls and apartments and of correcting numerous other violations, we staged a well-publicized Sunday afternoon paint-in. The *Daily News,* for example, carried a sizable picture story, showing Councilman Clingan busily at work in a painter's cap and Assemblyman Stein with paintbrush in hand, helping to brighten up our grimy first-floor hall.

On the cold morning of the paint-in, we awoke to an unheated house—a frequent occurrence in that see-saw period of the struggle. Urban Relocation Company's super informed us that he had "forgotten" to order oil. We telephoned Mr. Stein at home, and he in turn called the hospital. A few minutes later Salvatore, one of the hospital security guards, knocked on the super's apartment door. From down the hall, just inside my strategically located first-floor apartment, I could hear the conversation:

99

"I just came from the hospital, and Mother Innocent says you've *got* to give these people some heat."

The super was demonstrably unimpressed. So far as he was concerned, Urban Relocation, not Columbus Hospital, paid his salary (though the hospital was, of course, the source of the money). Urban, not Columbus, would be his employer elsewhere once they succeeded in hounding us out.

Salvatore, by temperament and by conditioning a true-blue company man who would remain loyal to Columbus if they were to burn him at the stake, was exasperated.

"I'm telling you that Mother Innocent says the hospital is catching hell. You've *got* to turn on the heat. She's one of the big cheeses."

Finally, the super saw that he had to comply. It just wouldn't do to have the New York press corps come, a few hours later, to a bitterly cold house owned by Columbus Hospital. The heat went on immediately.

On a number of similar occasions, by exerting pressure at just the right moment, we were able to obtain immediate results. Once, when Urban Relocation Company itself was on a hot griddle of unfavorable citywide publicity, we telephoned Owen Moritz, the very capable housing reporter for the *Daily News,* to say that the garbage pails in our courtyard were overflowing because Urban's super had neglected for a week to put them out on the street for the daily municipal collection.

Mr. Moritz telephoned Seymour Shapiro, the head of Urban, to say that a *Daily News* photographer was en route to our building to take pictures of the accumulated garbage. Within five or ten minutes the pails were out on the sidewalk, and other pails that were empty

100

and had been hidden away suddenly became available for use by the tenants.

At other times it was probably the edge in our voices that warned the hospital to ease up on the harassment. Around November 1970, a large howling German police dog suddenly appeared in the super's apartment. Soon it was running loose in the halls, unleashed and unmuzzled, lunging at tenants, visitors and mailmen, terrorizing everyone. Here again, in the classic fashion of oppressors, both Columbus and Urban seriously miscalculated. There was cold fury among the tenants, but no mass rush to move out ensued. Instead, by an initial phone call, by a visit to the hospital administrator's secretary, and by an acid letter (with copies to elected officials, to the press, to the ASPCA, and to Catholic Charities, from which Columbus derives some income), the tenant leaders let Columbus know that the vicious animal had to be restrained. Even the hawks caught the urgent or-else tone in what we were saying. Administrator Toomey gave immediate orders to the super to leash the dog at all times. Ever since, the hospital must have regretted its futile experimentation with dog terrorization. For we saw to it that, in the mind of the public, Columbus became forever identified with three easily remembered symbols: the German police dog, the negative connotations of the term "Bedpan Alley," and our cablegram in Latin to the Pope.

In terms of catching the public fancy, the cablegram turned out to be an imaginative stroke of genius, however unclassical the Latin translation may have been. NBC's Channel 4 blew up the Latin text in large letters and put it all on the television screen. *The New York Times* ran a humorous story, pointing out that everything

101

had been translated into Latin except the word "parking lot." And in the local *Gramercy Herald* the cablegram was headline news.

March 21, 1971

His Holiness Pope Paul
The Vatican
Rome
Sanctitas:

Tuum submisse deprecarimus. 210–214 East 19 Street, Manhattan, New York, U.S.A., habitamus. Dominus aedificatii, Columbus Hospital, aedificatium destruare intenderet.

"Parking lot" construere desiderant.

Tuum persuadere dominus aedificatii, Missionary Sisters of the Sacred Heart, rogamus. Domus amamus et stare desideramus.

Traditium magnum conditori, Mother Cabrini, eis succedere roge. Domus custodire succure.

(signed) Neighborhood Save Our Homes
Committee.

(translation)
Holiness:

We beg you to intercede for us. We live at 210–214 East 19th Street, Manhattan, New York, U.S.A.

The owner of these buildings, Columbus Hospital, intends to destroy these buildings. They wish to build a parking lot.

We ask you to prevail upon the owner of these buildings, the Missionary Sisters of the Sacred Heart. We love our home and we wish to remain there.

Ask them to follow the great tradition of their founder, Mother Cabrini. Help us to save our home.

Even today, we are still asked: "Did the Pope ever respond to that cable you sent him in Latin?" A top Madison Avenue advertising firm could not have dreamed up a commercial in our behalf that would remain so fixed in people's memories.

When we finally went after the hospital's jugular by threatening its public funds, we were able to perceive that one full year of battering publicity had had a softening-up effect. But publicity was not, in itself, decisive. A councilmanic aide fingered the reason when he told us: "You have half a million dollars of the Church's money tied up. And Sister Cyprian is not going to say 'I goofed when I bought that building.' "

Besides the $275,000 purchase price, Columbus spent tens of thousands of dollars in "management" fees to Urban Relocation Company, in "relocation" fees to thirty departing tenants (the last tenant to move prior to the August 1971 contract—an actor who needed a loft for teaching dancing—received $2,500), in salaries to our round-the-clock squatter-watching guards, and in maintenance costs and oil-burner repairs for a building only one third rented.

In addition to coming to see the value and the necessity of pacing—of easing up periodically on agitation and publicity, in order not to let the issue become boring to the public and in order not to go stale ourselves—we learned that each successful level of activity opens up new and ascending horizons. Early in the struggle we used to wonder what else, three to six months hence, we would be able to do to keep the issue alive and to remain on the offensive. Invariably, the question answered itself, as we advanced from all the conventional forms of protest to new and original ones of our own, and as we ran the gamut from prominent coverage in the local community

103

newspaper, to an unusually long "Talk of the Town" column in *The New Yorker* (November 1972), and from rejoicing over an early down-to-earth interview with retired tenant Charlie Mancini on small, listener-sponsored WBAI-FM, to network television coverage of demonstrations led by the Berrigan brothers.

In any kind of battle, a flow of intelligence on one's adversary's moves is essential. Diagonally across from us at the northeast corner of 19th Street and Third Avenue is 201 East 19th Street—a luxury building constructed in the late 1950's, with 187 apartments in the $250–$500 range. Through one talkative hospital trustee, we learned in late 1970 that Columbus was actively interested in buying 201; a bank loan was being sought. Then, in February 1971, a sympathetic source in the local post office informed us that hospital personnel living in Cabrini Tower—an even newer luxury building at 222 East 19th Street that Columbus bought in 1968 with an FHA loan—were being quietly infiltrated into 201, one apartment at a time, as vacancies occurred.

We promptly procured the precise 201 apartment numbers, prepared a flier with that information, and distributed it outside 201. Columbus has its nose under your tent, the leaflet warned. Unless you organize to resist a quiet take-over, you'll awaken one day to find yourselves living on feudal turf, surrounded by hospital "serfs" (many here from Asia on visas obtained by Columbus), who are completely beholden to Columbus for their jobs, their visas and their housing.

The impact was immediate. Within a couple of weeks, a core of the 201 tenants had gotten together and arranged for a building-wide meeting (minus the Columbus fifth column). Research soon uncovered an exclusive

104

and secret rental arrangement between the hospital and Greenthal Realty Company. People began reminiscing that in 1968, while our block was still slumbering, Columbus had evicted from Cabrini Tower (at 222), as their individual leases expired, nearly all nonhospital tenants. (At that time tenants in newer and non-rent-controlled buildings had no statutory protection against eviction.)

The enlistment to our side of the 201 East 19th Street Tenants Association was a valuable unearned increment. Without question, it helped to tip the power scales in our favor at a critical moment, and the wide assortment of professional skills in 201 has been of enormous help. Everybody—reporters, politicians, and other tenant groups—has remarked on the unusual mix in the two buildings: a united front that combines tenants on welfare and Social Security with the well-heeled who own boats and country homes and luxury cars.

It was in one of the spacious, gracious 201 apartments that we all met jointly on the evening prior to the negotiation of the August 27, 1971, contract with the hospital. Neal Hitzig, chairman of the 201 Tenants Association, had the week before joined Assemblyman Stein and me (as 210–214 Tenants Committee chairman) in the suit to block the $39 million state loan and to enjoin construction of Columbus' new wing. The almost instantaneous phone call to Mr. Stein after the legal papers were served on a surprised and then indignant Columbus administrator indicated that at last the hospital was to some degree coming to grips with reality. But aside from that obvious inference we had no way of gauging precisely their readiness to make meaningful and substantive concessions.

Hence, those long evening meetings, lasting

until after midnight, were an anguished effort to assess the balance of forces and to draft our negotiable and nonnegotiable demands accordingly. Our most difficult sticking point was on the proper position to take on the then twenty-seven empty, still rent-controlled apartments in 210–214. Did we have a moral obligation to desperately needy families to insist absolutely that they be rented? Did we have the power to make that insistence stick? Would such insistence blow everything with our highly emotional adversaries?

The greatest point of uncertainty about our arsenal of weapons was the disposition of our lawsuit in the courts if negotiations collapsed and if the case were to come to trial. No one can ever predict what a judge will do. If, in September 1971 (on the returnable date), the State Supreme Court justice were to have thrown our suit out, the State Housing Finance Agency would then have been free to meet and give immediate approval to the mortgage loan. And at that point our bargaining power with Columbus would have dropped to zero.

At the final joint tenants meeting, eighty-four-year-old Mrs. Norton finally left about midnight. As she passed my chair, she leaned over and said: "Don't ask for so much that we'll lose everything."

It was those words, ringing in my ears, that were for me decisive. Still morally perturbed at the thought of empty apartments being warehoused because of institutional stubbornness, I nevertheless voted—painfully but affirmatively—with the majority to make their rental a negotiable demand. The decision in no way precluded us, in the future, from pressing hospital officials to rent the apartments, once the passage of time extin-

106

guished all flickering hope of their "somehow" getting the twenty-seven-car parking lot.

To this day I believe it was the only practicable decision we could have taken. I base this on the emotional resolve of the hospital policy-makers—a resolve that was made manifest a few hours later. At 9 A.M. the following morning, Columbus Board member Nicholas Iannuzzi, the "dove" most influential in arranging for the negotiations with the tenants, opened the initially tense session by telling Neal Hitzig and me (the two largely sleepless tenant negotiators): "Let me make one point absolutely clear. We are *not* going to rent those empty apartments."

Unless Iannuzzi was a master of bluff, it seemed clear that that was one of the *hospital's* nonnegotiable positions—quite possibly a compromise reached between the sharply divided factions. Having vandalized the empty apartments after "relocating" the tenants—among other damage, sinks, toilet bowls, tubs and stoves were either smashed, disconnected or removed so that even desperate squatters would be deterred from moving in—the hospital was unwilling to invest the necessary money to put the apartments back into habitable condition, especially in view of the low rents they would bring under rent control.

It was a struggle to conceal how petrified I felt at the burden of responsibility for twenty fellow tenants in my building. But the proceedings went remarkably smoothly and swiftly. As Neal Hitzig and I, by prearrangement, alternated in reading from our list of demands, Nicholas Iannuzzi or his attorney son John would reply immediately: "We agree to that. Go on to the next point." Since the year-long policy of refusal to meet with the tenants had brought the hospital to the brink of "dis-

107

aster," Sister Cyprian, as chief hawk, and administrator Joseph Toomey, a close runner-up, had obviously been silenced for the day by the doves.

Aside from one ten-minute break for caucusing, no hitches developed. I'm sure that my expressive face registered surprise at the ease with which the hospital—that is to say, the Iannuzzis—yielded on some of the points. Our building was saved; the power realities being what they were, their $39 million state loan would now be approved by the State Housing Finance Agency.

Once the hospital agreed to negotiate with us, our 210–214 tenant attorney, Lester Evens, made one point very clear: "I will be there to advise you. But in this set of circumstances I will not negotiate for you. I am not a tenant in your building. I'm not suffering from the hospital's harassment. No matter how well you brief me, I can't possibly know all aspects of the situation you're living under, or all nuances of the tenants' grievances. It's your struggle, and you must do your own negotiating."

As a total novice at negotiating, I was stunned. My initial reaction was that the man was indifferent to our plight. Lester seemed to be condemning us to something less than an optimum settlement. However, after we had completed the negotiations, I came to realize he was absolutely right. Helpful though politicians can often be in community struggles, we had never relied on them to do our fighting for us. We had not relied on the mass media. We had not relied on the municipal housing bureaucracy. Nor did we bank on Rockefeller's state health and housing agencies.

Similarly, at the bargaining table, it would have been a serious political mistake to put our fate in the hands of a legal technician, however close his thinking was to ours. That was the moment of truth, the moment for Emersonian self-reliance, the moment for handling our own affairs, however shaky we felt. To the competent legal advice of Lester Evens, we always listened carefully and respectfully, and we kept in the forefront of our minds the legal realities that must constantly be confronted.

But as the victims on whom the guns of Columbus have been continuously trained, we've always reserved the right to make the ultimate decisions and to determine the contours of our very political hard-line struggle.

The hospital's chastened period lasted perhaps three months, during which the administration gave initial signs of more or less planning to abide by the *letter* of the binding contract. As Article 2 provided, Columbus within thirty days fired Urban Relocation Company/Citadel Management Company. Columbus also sounded out our building's previous owner, Klein, Mayer and Korn, about the possibility of their resuming the management duties they had responsibly handled for a dozen years. At the joint news conference on the contract signing, Columbus announced with a flourish its hiring of Taormina Contracting Corporation, which began immediately installing good-quality pick-resistant locks on all our apartment doors. As instructed by the hospital, a Taormina representative inspected the public areas and our apartments, listed housing-code violations and other needed repairs, and then submitted a budget to restore the building to a legal and more presentable condition. It took perhaps a week or more for the hospital's new we've-settled-our-differences line at the top to move down to the lower ranks. Then those of the hospital's security guards who had bristled at the mere sight of us ceased treating us as dangerous

109

enemies. They stopped demanding to know our mission before we could enter the premises.* With Urban gone, the year-long rash of burglaries abruptly stopped.

It was Taormina's reasonable budget estimate of $30,000 to $40,000 for mostly cosmetic repairs and painting (an average, including the public areas, of $1,000 or $2,000 per occupied apartment) that apparently ended what passed for Columbus' contrite, penitent, and public-relations-conscious mood. Robert L. Valente, the new public-relations director who felt insulted when the nuns put him in overall charge of our "tenement," called the figure horrendous. The administration, which is never short of funds whenever expensive real estate on the block can be snapped up (even if they have no foreseeable use for it for another fifty years), went into the same poor-mouth song and dance that the hospital's workers always encounter when pay raises are sought.

Before we came to realize that the hospital's good-faith compliance with the contract would be short-lived, our elation over the victory at the bargaining table †

---

* For those who doubt the efficacy of fighting long and hard for one's rights, it would be instructive to watch the change that, by 1975, has come over several of the originally unfriendly guards. It took our protracted agitation and the barrage of publicity for them to understand why we didn't simply fold our tents and steal meekly away into the mists of "relocation."

In 1970, one guard was ready to throw me bodily out of Cabrini Tower at the time we disrupted the bazaar, after I called him an Uncle Tom for being more royal than the king. Today he flashes us a pleasant smile and treats us with respect.

† At the joint tenants–hospital news conference on September 2, 1971, the WCBS-TV correspondent sat down to read the terms of the contract, and then bluntly said to Valente: "This contract reads more like a [directed] consent agreement"—that is to say, the type of settlement imposed on a party to a court action who, in effect, pleads: "I don't admit to any wrongdoing in the past. But I'll sign this agreement, Your Honor, consenting not to do it in the future, and promising to make amends for whatever bad things have occurred."

and our physical and emotional exhaustion led us into a trap of our own making from which the hospital, months later, unintentionally rescued us. At the *first* sign of Columbus' reneging on the contract terms, we should have proclaimed that fact to the world and launched a full-blown rent strike, whether or not the public at the moment understood.

Instead, out of excessive concern over not appearing peevish, petulant and unreasonably impatient in the eyes of the community, we stayed out of the news for months, while pressing quietly for the promised correction of "all violations in the public parts and in all occupied apartments." As a consequence, we lost precious momentum that was very hard to regain. Tenants will not stay on principle and fight indefinitely for apartments in disrepair. Our error was basically one of omission rather than of commission. In our haste to conclude negotiations, we neglected to insist that Columbus post a performance bond, and to include in the contract other self-enforcing provisions. It was a matter of naïvely failing to anticipate continued bad faith. A year later, we had to go to the trouble and expense of obtaining a court order to enforce the bans on relocation and solicitation.

Had we slept on the contract before signing it, almost surely we would have spotted these defects. But on the other hand we have no serious regrets over the quick signing. For after overnight contemplation by the other side, the frothing hawks at Columbus might well have blocked the signing—just as, in September 1973, at literally the last minute, they managed to block the signing of a carefully negotiated consent judgment. Since the autumn of 1971, several attorneys and realtors have told us that, if Columbus had been their client, they never would have let the hospital sign such stringent protenant terms that

111

gave twenty-one tenants (a couple of whom are in their early twenties) lifetime leases, and that pledged an end forever to all efforts to vacate an old building that stands on a very valuable plot of land.

Compared to these priceless, ironclad protections, the flaws in the contract have proved to be time-consuming nuisances, but not at all fatal to the preservation of our well-built, structurally sound building.

As we look back, we realize that we should have anticipated that Columbus would bail us out of the deadlock with some crude scheme that would antagonize us tenants, galvanize the crusading *Gramercy Herald,* and put the hospital back in the community doghouse. Through a sympathetic security guard, we learned (weeks after the fact) that on Friday afternoon, June 2, 1972, individually addressed letters from the hospital to each 210—214 tenant were left at the security office, with instructions not to hand-deliver them to us until late Sunday afternoon. The letters invited us to a meeting to be held in the hospital that Monday evening, at which time "a matter of great interest to [us]" would be discussed by Mother Josephine Migliore, president of the Board of Trustees and signer of the letters. From start to finish, the operation was designed to be a no-time-for-reflection, no-time-to-consult-counsel stampede.

Ideally, we should have told Mother Josephine to see our lawyer. Period. We should have unanimously spurned the Greeks-bearing-gifts invitation, coming deliberately as it did at the last minute. But a quick check of tenants' reactions showed that most were not politically prepared to take that clear, decisive, hard-line position. The letters triggered old working-class fears and insecurities. Several of the elderly tenants admitted that they didn't sleep that Sunday night. Because of the anxieties,

112

the majority sentiment favored attending the meeting. For half a year, during the drift, the tenant leadership had been more involved in neglected personal affairs than in keeping the Tenants Committee alive and in fighting shape. The trembling reaction to Mother Josephine's letter was the penalty for our neglect.

When we walked across 19th Street in a body and entered the conference room, Robert Valente, the hospital's new public-relations director, and Attorney John Iannuzzi both looked like purring cats who had already swallowed twenty-one canaries. Clearly it never occurred to any of those with the Columbus mentality that a group of (to them) raggedy-ass tenants would turn down a $168,000 bribe. Later, Lester Evens, our attorney, who could not attend on such short notice, remarked that unquestionably Mother Josephine was prepared, on the spot, to up the individual "relocation" offer from $8,000 apiece to at least $10,000, had we shown the slightest interest in haggling.

And had we done that, the site of 210–214 would have been transformed from what Joyce Kilmer called "a house that has sheltered life" into the world's most expensive miniparking lot: $275,000 purchase price; $210,000 final move-out bribe cost; plus the cost of having maintained a half-empty building for two years, plus all the fees shelled out to Urban Relocation Company and to twenty-six previously departed tenants. All tax-exempt. All ultimately at public expense.

Over a two-year period, as a result of our agitation, the public as well as the tenants had passed the point of even considering any parking-lot scheme. Therefore Mother Josephine's bribe offer was sweetened with a loose promise to erect luxury apartments on top of a garage. If we would agree to "relocate temporarily," our rents "upon return" would be vaguely pegged to a low-rent Housing Authority formula that our state senator assured us later was nonexistent.

During her presentation, Mother Josephine said she had available twenty-one copies of the proposed $8,000 agreement and would hand a sample copy "to your chairman" at the end of the meeting. When the session adjourned, Neal Hitzig at my elbow kept whispering: "Get that agreement. Get that agreement." In front of us all, Mother Josephine had several times said, "I know this relocation offer violates the contract we signed with you last year." Therefore, Neal was eager to have the physical evidence to supplement her oral confession. To our joyful surprise, Mother Josephine, confident of her ability to sell us the deal, had actually affixed her signature and the full date to the copy that she handed to me. The signed sheet became a prime exhibit that was submitted to the court in our subsequent breach-of-contract and injunction suit.

What more could we ask of our adversaries, blinded as they have been all along by the twenty-seven-car parking-lot obsession? Despite two solid years of their bad faith and worthless promises, they apparently did not anticipate the general tenant certainty that the so-called apartments above the garage would somehow never get built had we accepted the "temporary" relocation offer, scattered to the winds, and lost our cohesiveness and punch.

Sometimes the hospital's under-the-table and mendacious behavior needed no comment or interpretation; it was so clumsy as to be self-evident. Everyone at the meeting heard Mother Josephine threaten that our building would be sold at noon on Wednesday, June 7, 1972 ("and the new owner might not be as nice to you as we have been"), if we rejected her $8,000 offer. At 1:30 P.M.

114

on Thursday, June 8—some twenty-five and a half hours after the "sale"—a Columbus security guard hand-delivered to each apartment a forlorn letter (crudely dated Wednesday) from Robert L. Valente:

> During Mother Josephine's visit with you on Monday evening, she advised you that we had been negotiating to obtain suitable, modern housing for you. This was to accommodate you for the period the hospital would need in order to demolish 210–214 and build a combination garage-apartment house in their place.
>
> One building that had been under consideration is located at 207 E. 21st Street. This is a completely rebuilt 40 apartment building. Our last information indicated there were still 15 apartments available for rental.
>
> A second location involved a completely new building. This is the Crystal House, located at 24th Street and Third Avenue. Many apartments are apparently still available.
>
> Mother Josephine's financial offer would provide you with more than ample funds to cover moving expenses and the additional rental cost during the period of dislocation.

Before most tenants got home from work, Glenda Watson and Ted Kristian had visited both buildings and checked on the rents: $230 for a tiny studio apartment at 207 East 21st Street, $350 in Crystal House. Thus Valente was proposing a fourfold or a sevenfold leap into luxury housing from our average rent in a sound and livable building on a safe and pleasant street. We could only infer that he was catching hell from the nuns for having possibly sold them on the $8,000 "relocation" offer and that he wrote his predated letter in a moment of alarm about his year-old job. On the night that Mother Josephine tried to mesmerize us, the hospital was less than three weeks away from a union-representation election, at which Columbus hoped again to defeat the organizing efforts of Local 1199. Knowing that Columbus tenants and Columbus workers faced one and the same adversary and that our interests were intertwined, we arose early on Friday morning, June 9, to distribute hundreds of copies of the new issue of the weekly *Gramercy Herald* to workers arriving for the morning shift. The *Herald*'s supermarket edition had a banner headline on Peggy Berk's story of the Monday evening meeting with Mother Josephine: "Columbus Hospital LIED to This Community."

Previous distribution of *Herald* stories outside the hospital had always upset the sisters. Since they clearly regard the whole square block as theirs (either presently owned or to be owned in the future), it's as if we were circularizing on hospital grounds. Apparently the 13th Police Precinct had had to inform them that such distribution was constitutionally protected and that no grounds existed for placing us under arrest. But on the particular morning we were suddenly transported back into the Dark Ages of serfs, dungeons, ecclesiastical estates and unabashed thought control. With our own eyes we saw Sister Cyprian Branco, the executive director, and other nuns stand inside the main entrance and confiscate copies of the *Herald* as the workers walked in. Near the end of the hour Sister Cyprian looked me fiercely in the eye and snapped: "I guess you're satisfied with all you've done. Well, the building has been sold."

Of course, like book burning and other forms of censorship, the effort to ban embarrassing facts boomeranged. We saw to it that copies did get circulated throughout the hospital. Everyone was all the more eager to read what their bosses were desperately trying to keep from

116

them. Conceivably, the episode contributed to Local 1199's 197–103 victory on June 23, despite the nuns' last-minute display of a newfound interest in long-standing grievances. Editorially, the *Gramercy Herald* warned the union that, in view of the tenants' experience with Columbus, any contract they might sign with the hospital "may not be worth the paper it's printed on." We do know that workers on the union negotiating committee saw to it that nothing in their contract was left to the hospital's good faith.

In another editorial, the *Herald* recounted the confiscation of copies by the nuns and then thundered that the censorship

> is not too surprising in the light of other actions by Columbus Hospital. . . .
>
> The building has apparently not been sold. It would appear that perhaps the "out of town buyer" who so urgently wanted to buy the building never existed. . . . Columbus Hosiptal has shown a callous disregard for the meaning of "freedom of the press." To them, the media is to be used to announce decisions that make the hospital look good. The media is something to be shrugged off with "no comment" when the decision makes the hospital look bad. . . .
>
> [U]nlike the mass media, we are as responsive to small groups in the community as we are to organizations that have professional public relations staffs that know how to manipulate the media. For that reason, freedom of the press will not die, on East 19th Street or anywhere else.

With those words ringing in my ears, I left New York for my class reunion, confident that even diehard Columbus was now at the end of its rope and was stymied in any further effort to dislodge us. (Well before our next rent day on July 1, Columbus let each tenant know: Continue making your rent checks payable to the hospital. There was not a blush at having been caught red-handed in the lie about the "sale.")

Shortly thereafter, having failed to win us over via bribes, Columbus tried one of its few directly political ploys. Unknown to the tenants, the hospital retained former GOP national chairman Leonard Hall, of a Park Avenue–Garden City law firm, specifically to establish contact with our fast-rising state assemblyman, who, though a Democrat, is close to Nelson Rockefeller. Hall and two of his fellow attorneys met at lunch with Assemblyman Stein and Jed Kee, counsel to Mr. Stein. Vain purpose: to get Stein, a signatory to the tough 1971 contract, to sell us tenants on the high-in-the-sky apartments atop the "garage." At a reported $250 an hour for the time of senior partners in prestigious Park Avenue law firms, the nuns once again were throwing tax-exempt money down the drain in pursuit of their ever-elusive white whale.

(After the fact, when we learned of the luncheon, we politely let Mr. Stein know that henceforth tenant representatives must always be present at *any* meeting where tenant business is discussed.)

During the summer, Columbus was busily hatching more than just the futile luncheon with politicians. Our super was spreading the word that, contrary to Mother Josephine's original insistence on unanimity, individual tenants could now slip into Valente's office and collect the $8,000 to move. From a bustle of activity in her first-floor apartment, Beverly Wood and her small son were obviously on the verge of "relocating." Since 1970, just about every tenant who moved out was as close-mouthed as any billion-dollar oil company about his or her penny-ante deal with Urban or Columbus. So Beverly's reticence and that certain look on her face were the giveaway evidence

118

that the hospital was openly flaunting the contract by paying her to initiate a one-by-one move-out. In a court affidavit on October 13, 1972 (after we brought suit for breach of contract), Sister Cyprian stated: "During July 1972 Beverly Wood came to us and asked us whether we would pay her the agreed sum of $8,000 if she moved, even if the other tenants did not. We agreed to do so and on August 18, 1972, Beverly Wood did move and received from us the sum of $8,000." Sister Cyprian did not explain to the judge why Columbus was generously handing out thousand-dollar bills to help vacate a building that the hospital had "sold" on Wednesday, June 7!

So again came a midsummer moment of truth for the Tenants Committee. Either the 1971 contract meant something, or it didn't. The gauntlet had been flung at us. Were there to be no prompt retort, Columbus would logically conclude that at last it had us on the run. Enticement of individual tenants would assuredly be stepped up.

Three days after Beverly Wood moved to one of the high-priced buildings suggested by Robert Valente in June, tenant leaders met for a strategy session at the office of our new attorney, Robert Ferrari. The decision was not a tough one. We knew we had to file a breach-of-contract suit and to obtain a court order forbidding further solicitation and further payment of bribes. Outraged at the hospital, Neal Hitzig, chairman of the Tenants Association across at 201, on his own initiative put up the first thousand dollars for legal costs.

Little could we foresee the special urgent circumstances under which the suit would be filed a month later on September 26, 1972, or the emergency that prompted a State Supreme Court judge to sign a restraining order at his home that evening. T.K., hitherto one of the most active and reliable tenants, had sat in on the August 21 legal-strategy session. Two months earlier, he had been vehement, for all the right and principled reasons, in spurning the $8,000 offer, and had debated Robert Valente on this matter on a special Channel 5 housing program. If anyone in the building seemed solid, it was T.K., a bit actor with off-and-on luck in finding full-time office work.

The tip-off on his plans came as an overwhelming surprise. One morning, before dropping a letter in T.K.'s box, one of our mailmen asked me: "Is T.K. still here?" The startling word was "still." The details of T.K.'s rationale were personal, but bore a stunning resemblance to the self-seeking reasons that others had come up with. Nine months earlier, his roommate had been mugged in the fourth-floor hall by a drug addict—the one and only such occurrence I know of in all my years in the building. (Not long afterward, a woman tenant in Neal's luxury building, where there is twenty-four-hour doorman service, was raped. Nowhere is there a guarantee of absolute security.)

But T.K.'s main reason, specifically stated, was a sudden desire to live in an *elevator* building one block away where the rent is nearly $200 higher, plus a pile of debts. T.K. looked to the beckoning $8,000 bribe to bail him out, while ignoring the problem he'd have in meeting the higher rent when, within one or two years, the balance of the $8,000 would be exhausted.

Face to face and by phone, several of us pleaded with T.K. (a) not to cut his own throat and (b) not to hurt the rest of us at a pivotal moment in the struggle. We foresaw how Columbus would relish this defection of a tenant activist, and would gleefully interpret it as a major break in our dike.

I drew word pictures of the secret contempt that Robert Valente would have for him (a) when he'd go to announce his readiness to be bought off and (b) when he'd go back to pick up the bribe. I recalled to T.K. the memorable movie scene in *The Informer* when, cap in hand, Victor McLaglen goes to the Black and Tan (British police) station to collect his £20 reward for his tip on the whereabouts of an underground Irish revolutionary. With complete disdain, the police inspector tosses the money onto a long billiard-type table. Then, with a cane or long stick, he shoves it toward the already shaky man who has betrayed—and thereby helped kill—a friend and fellow countryman who is fighting British occupation.

And all just to use the money to emigrate with his girl friend to the United States. We reminded T.K. of two elderly tenants who, we all knew, would be very unlikely to survive "relocation" if ever general tenant resistance should crack.

It was like talking to a stone wall.

Our attorney Robert Ferrari was also shocked by news of a defector in our counsels. He saw what had to be done without delay. T.K. was scheduled to finish moving out on Wednesday morning, September 27, and then to turn in his keys in exchange for the blood money from Robert Valente. On Tuesday evening, when Mr. Ferrari and his loyal secretary, Harriet Melton, hastily completed drafting the necessary legal papers, he telephoned State Supreme Court Justice Arnold L. Fein and made an appointment to see him shortly at home. The restraining order was signed, and at 9 A.M. the next morning Mr. Ferrari served it on an astonished Valente in Saint Cabrini Tower.

"On pain of contempt of court, this order forbids you or the hospital to pay any more relocation fees," Valente was told, "and you'd better get a copy of it to the hospital attorney immediately."

121

Fifteen minutes later, from my first-floor box seat, I heard, then saw, the two roommates struggling out the front door with their last sizable piece of furniture. It is easy to imagine their amazement and disappointment upon being informed by Valente that the money they had counted on would not be forthcoming.

For weeks that we know of, and possibly for months, Columbus strung T.K. along, while privately their attorney was chortling that the hospital had gotten one tenant out for nothing.

By this time we were well along with tongue-in-cheek plans to co-opt a hospital anniversary of great importance to the Missionary Sisters. We got Father Daniel Berrigan to head "a processional to celebrate the feast day of Mother Cabrini, patron saint of the homeless, founder of Columbus Hospital."

In both English and Spanish, the carefully designed fliers for the demonstration read: "Mother Cabrini, Don't Make Us Homeless." "Come help liberate and save forty-eight rent-controlled apartments."

Predictably, the nuns rushed for the bait. We knew there would be no way for us and any squatters to hold onto the twenty-nine empty apartments once Sister Cyprian again called the cops to evict and arrest. Therefore we had no irresponsible plans to encourage the great unwashed to storm our building in search of decent shelter. But with their long-standing fears of another squat-in, that "mob scene" is exactly the image that our fliers conjured up in the minds of the nuns. Early on the morning of the demonstration, they had their uniformed security guards out in full force, in and around our building, in constant touch with a command post by walkie-talkies, indiscriminately stopping and questioning and antagonizing well-dressed reporters and every other stranger who attempted to enter 210–214.

As paced publicity for the processional was building up, the hospital came aboard and helped us build interest in the coming event. On October 24, 1972, a little more than a fortnight before the Derrigan-led demonstration, Columbus singled out three tenants and two elected officials (Councilman Clingan and Assemblyman Stein) and filed a million-dollar countersuit. The charge: the five of us had "conspired together with others to deprive Columbus Hospital of its property, to extort money and property from Columbus Hospital, and to interfere with the conduct, operation and management of Columbus Hospital."

The hospital went on to charge that on August 20, 1971, Mr. Stein and five others had brought our injunction suit against Columbus Hospital and the New York State Housing Finance Agency for the purpose of holding up construction of the new wing. Columbus asked the court to render judgment "rescinding as extortionate, fraudulent and illegal the agreement [with the tenants] of August 27, 1971."

When asked to comment on the charges, Councilman Clingan replied: "As for 'interfering' with the hospital, I would be derelict in my duties as a public official if I weren't concerned with the way in which public funds are spent." For the first time in the protracted struggle, Assemblyman Stein, a man with avowed presidential ambitions who had always been careful not to antagonize the Church, exploded at the hospital and called the officials "liars." "I'm still 100 percent behind the tenants," he added.

Certainly we expected no further help from Columbus on the processional publicity front. But again we underestimated Mr. Valente. Two days after Columbus became a laughingstock for having filed the countersuit, he sat down and initiated an exchange of letters with

Father Berrigan. To Valente's dismay, the *Gramercy Herald* published the letters as "The Valente Papers," and we distributed them widely to the New York media, to the Catholic press, and to the press in Italy, where the Missionary Sisters are based. After first contacting Father Berrigan's Provincial—in itself a bit of pressure—Mr. Valente urged the priest not to attend the planned processional. The full text of Daniel Berrigan's reply is worth reprinting.

WOODSTOCK COLLEGE

475 RIVERSIDE DRIVE
NEW YORK, N.Y. 10027

31 October, 1972

Robert Valente,
Columbus Hospital

Dear Robert,*

Your letter of Oct. 26 received. I find your letter frivolous and inaccurate. Let me say why.

1) Frivolous: to insist that Mother Cabrini is mother of the immigrant and not of the homeless is like insisting that Columbus hospital is interested in the sick, but not in the ill. Most immigrants, I believe, are also homeless. In the same regard, it boggles the mind to think that a hospital conducted by the daughters of such a mother, can think to heal some of the poor, while they

---

* Author's note: Inasmuch as Father Berrigan does not know Robert Valente, the "Dear Robert" salutation was a priestly put-down.

124

evict others from their (the hospital's) "tenement". (The latter is of course, your expression, rather than mine. For a hospital to own a tenement seems to me a little like a hospital experimenting in germ warfare. But the moral nicety is undoubtedly lodged in me, not you, and I beg pardon for bringing it up.)

2) Inaccurate. You mention an offer of Mother Josephine, who I believe is a spiritual daughter of Mother Cabrini. The offer, you state, is that tenants are to receive low-income rentals and first choice in a new building (not a tenement, rather a garage-apt.), to be built by the hospital. You are in contradiction of your earlier statement, or a statement of the hospital, that the rentals of the evicted tenants would be "all the market would bear."

Your offer to meet with me is tardy, if it is not mendacious. I understand that the hospital refused to meet with the tenants for over a year. Perhaps my interest in the scene is responsible for your quick offer of audience. Please join me, rather, in the streets on November 11, and extend the same invitation to Mother Josephine. Together, we can renounce our sins of injustice against the poor, which sins, Jesus tells us, "cry to heaven for vengeance."

The issue, I take it, is a simple one. When will the hospital start serving the poor, instead of victimizing them? Conditions in those famous "tenements" of yours are such as to ensure that you are indeed experimenting with germ warfare, and that by your fervent efforts, (to paraphrase Jesus), the sick we shall have always with us. It may be quite daring to assert that a hospital is for healing; but what is a tenement for? what are daughters of Mother Cabrini in business for? can it be for the encouragement of illness, and the creation of homeless people?   (Fr.) Daniel Berrigan, S.J.

Rev Daniel Berrigan

125

Although the weather on November 11, 1972, was foul, Columbus had so drawn attention to our processional that the attendance was good and the news coverage excellent (the *Times,* the *News,* radio, network television, and *The New Yorker* magazine). We adopted a suggestion from Raymond Rubinow, a neighbor on 20th Street, and arranged for a coffee klatch just before the demonstration, at which civic and community leaders met with Father Dan and with tenant spokespersons.

It was at this informal reception that Mr. Rubinow coined the phrase "medical imperialism," and it was there that Dan Berrigan from outside the community proclaimed as a hypothesis what we who live close to Columbus had long known as fact: namely, that any hospital that has treated its tenants so shabbily cannot possibly render tender loving care to its patients. Out on the street I saw Mr. Rubinow and other well-dressed neighbors who had never in their lives been on a picket line get caught up in the spirit of the day and join in the chanting demonstration.

Exactly four days after the processional, with publicity that we engendered, an already battered Columbus appeared in Criminal Court in an action we finally got the city to initiate because of flagrant and wholesale violations of the housing code. In the immediate aftermath of both the Dan Berrigan processional and the embarrassment from being in the dock as a slumlord, Columbus again publicly displayed a division in its ranks. The hospital's hawk attorney was pressing the million-dollar counter suit. Working at cross purposes, Attorney John Iannuzzi who had helped to negotiate the 1971 contract, approached our lawyer about a settlement of our breach-of-contract damage suit.

This time, it was clear that negotiations would

126

have to be slow, technical, and very carefully weighed. We wanted no more loopholes through which the hospital could blandly wiggle. In two and one-half years of eyeball-to-eyeball confrontations, so much blood had been spilled that negotiations between the lawyers, as suggested by our attorney, seemed the more prudent course.

Throughout nine months of negotiations Iannuzzi would try to use the alleged interference of Peter Schneider, his hawkish legal rival, as a pretext to wheedle unacceptable concessions from the tenants. While we never totally discounted his claims on that score, we surmised that he exaggerated the extent of Schneider's efforts and ability to abort a negotiated settlement. For until close to the nitty-gritty, sign-on-the-dotted-line stage in September 1973, Iannuzzi was constantly contradicting himself by boasting to our attorney that "I'm in charge."

For Columbus' first appearance in Criminal Court on charges brought by the city, we tenants didn't bother to show up. We knew their attorney would ask for an adjournment of a month or so and that the judge would routinely grant it. But for the second, third and fourth appearances we were there in force.

The procedure is not one designed to win paeans of praise from victims of slumlordism. Each time a different judge was sitting, and each time the tenants had to counterpose the facts of neglect and harassment to the sob story of the hospital's lawyer. On one occasion, sight unseen, the judge became convinced that, if the hospital "needed" our old building for expansion, we should gracefully exit. He cited the importance of the hospital "industry" as a provider of jobs in New York City, and offered his "impartial" services as a mediator to draw up an "airtight" agreement to protect our "relocation rights."

For the better part of an hour, we had to go on

127

repeating that relocation was not the issue, that Bedpan Alley was already saturated with hospital facilities, that preservation of sound housing is an essential ingredient in maintaining public health, and that the only issue before the court was the enforcement of the Housing Code. The judge, who was very conventional in his thinking but not really malicious, finally gave up when he saw he could not persuade us to be "reasonable."

Per count, the fines imposed on a total of seventy-two violations were, as is customary, nominal. They ranged, as I recall, from $15 to $50. But the significance of even these minimal amounts was that Columbus realized that if they didn't make the repairs, we'd have them back in court to face a new round of fines. Week after week, on the front page, the *Gramercy Herald,* which is widely read in municipal agencies (as are other crusading community newspapers), published horror photographs of several ceilings that could collapse at any time, with easily fatal results. The city bureaucracy would never have been able to profess ignorance of conditions in our building in case of any untoward event.

An enormous amount of tenant energy is poured into the protracted business of inspections, reinspections, follow-up on the computerized print-outs of the violations (a process that takes six weeks just to be officially entered into city records)—with not one but several agencies involved. There were the regular Department of Buildings inspectors. There were the inspectors from the Emergency Repair Program—a part of the Housing and Development Administration bureaucracy that was born as a direct result of the citywide 1963 rent strike. There were overlapping inspectors from the Office of Rent Control who came in response to our applications for rent reduction for deprivation of services. Why the Buildings

Department's reports could not have been used by the Rent Control Office—thus saving manpower for the city and time and bother for the tenants—is a secret of the bureaucratic HDA mentality.

Intermittently, we'd find ourselves admitting and escorting inspectors from the Boiler Division, come to check on the malfunctioning oil burner, still other inspectors from the (municipal) Environmental Protection Administration, who ordered an upgrading of the burner to reduce pollution. As late as 1973, I overheard the hospital's chief engineer "explain" to an EPA inspector that, since our building was "slated for demolition," the hospital really shouldn't be put to the expense of upgrading the oil burner. Since, in a sense, our day-to-day heat and hot water were more at the mercy of the engineering department than of anyone else, I had to weigh the wisdom of barging into the vestibule conversation, of advising the EPA inspector that demolition was long since *off* the agenda and of making a bitter personal enemy of an embarrassed chief engineer by showing him up as a liar. I chose to retreat unseen into my apartment and to correct the record at a later date.

The special attention that we and other organized tenants have gotten in cellar-to-roof inspections and finally in the city's Criminal Court action didn't just happen. Continuing publicity in newspapers, on radio, on television all helped. Every bureaucrat in HDA knew all about "the Columbus Hospital tenants." In addition, pressure on HDA from our elected officials—Bella Abzug and Edward Koch in Congress, Senator Manfred Ohrenstein and Assemblyman Andrew Stein in the state legislature, and especially Councilman Eldon Clingan at City Hall—more than counteracted any awe and fear of religious power and of hospital power. Every inspector who

129

entered our building made it clear that he was there on special instructions from the top. Given the widespread corruption and intermittent arrests in the ranks of different categories of city inspectors, it is entirely possible that some of the many whom we encountered were on the take elsewhere in their appointed rounds. But our building was too hot and too much in the spotlight for graft and payoffs to enter the picture. The inspectors' reports were models of thoroughness and accuracy.

We'd like to be able to claim great strategic foresight and brilliant long-range planning when, on January 1, 1973, we launched a rent strike that eventually stretched into 1976. But it didn't happen that way. At a Tenants' Committee meeting shortly before Christmas 1972, with correction of some pressing grievances in mind, we decided that, as usual, treasurer Glenda Watson would collect everyone's January rents (an act demonstrating tenant solidarity as far back as 1970). But this time the money would not be turned over to Columbus. It was all very informal. No special letter was dispatched to the hospital; they knew very well which violations were most troublesome and obnoxious, and they quickly guessed why the thousand-dollar rent roll was not forthcoming. In less than a month, our attorney was receiving whining complaints from the hospital's attorney that we were delinquent in our rent. It was always possible that Columbus could initiate dispossess proceedings at any moment in order to collect. In New York City, certain kinds of rent strikes are legal—usually when the courts hold the rents in escrow. Whatever the circumstances leading up to a landlord's dispossess petition, no one ever gets evicted in New York if he is able to come up with the rent when the case reaches a judge. The only penalty is four or five dollars in court costs.

In order not to taunt the hawks, we deliberately refrained from any publicity on the rent strike. We can only guess that the hospital was caught off balance and, not knowing quite what to do, did nothing. January became February. February became March. By early spring, as a result of the many-sided pressures on Columbus, the house was full of plumbers, carpenters, painters, and electricians from the hospital's maintenance department. Extensive and expensive repairs were made on the oil burner after a winter of unreliable heat. Columbus had little choice but to clear up those hazardous conditions that the inspectors had written up for the Emergency Repair Program. For the city gives a landlord about a week to correct emergency violations before contracting with a private firm to have the work done. The bill, which is often several times the going rate for such repairs, is then sent to the landlord and can become a lien on the property if not paid.

Throughout the first several months of the rent strike, our attorney, Bob Ferrari, believed strongly and legalistically that we should pay the rent. He also felt it would expedite his ongoing negotiations with John Iannuzzi. Politically, I didn't agree with Bob, but, given his unease, I was inclined on a personal level to go along with his repeated advice.

Fortunately, Glenda Watson, our conservative Republican secretary-treasurer, had firm counterfeelings, and her view prevailed. In the dynamics of any group, the person who actually sits on the group's money is ipso facto important and wields considerable weight, if only because of a sort of collective well-Glenda-handles-that attitude. Month after month, our withheld rent checks went into her office safe, and there they stayed for half a year.

By that time Bob had come to see the value of

thousands of withheld dollars as a bargaining chip. But he also worried that some of the half dozen tenants who pay by personal check might be tempted to spend the rent money on other personal needs, only to be left high and dry on the inevitable day when payment would have to be made. Therefore, on his advice, all checks and money orders were made payable to, and deposited in, his legal escrow account at Chase Manhattan Bank.

On all concerned, the impact of hard, tough experience in a struggle cannot be overemphasized. The rent strike certainly speeded up the ongoing process of demystifying and dethroning our institutional landlord and of reducing the common tenant sense of powerlessness. To be successful, a rent strike does not require unanimity. In our house, three tenants have not gone along with it. In other buildings, a bare majority or even a tightly knit minority have often been sufficient. If a landlord moves to collect the back rents and if a judge concurs, the tenants can pay up and then resume the strike on the very next day, thereby putting the landlord to renewed trouble and to the considerable expense of paying his own lawyer for court appearances.

Meanwhile, construction work on Columbus' sixteen-story new wing was running months behind because of a long strike of elevator workers in the building trades. Sympathetic workers who every noontime ate their lunches on our front steps kept us posted on target dates for completion of the wing. But the hospital was keeping the date for the grand dedication a deep dark secret. For one long decade, the nuns had been dreaming of a glorious Sunday afternoon when the cardinal would bless the new wing as part of a well-publicized opening ceremony, and when the Rome-based Missionary Sisters of the Sacred Heart would have their day in the U.S. sun at last.

132

A downpour had spoiled the cornerstone-laying around 1966, and Mayor Lindsay had not shown up.

And now, at virtually the last moment after all that patient waiting, the tenants of 210–214 East 19th Street had become the ants who were going to spoil the picnic. In the *Gramercy Herald,* in the spring of 1973, we wrote a letter to the editor announcing our intention to mount a counterdedication, to be led by Father Philip Berrigan, whenever Cardinal Cooke came to lead the dedication. The letter, of course, was directed more to the nuns and to John Iannuzzi than to the general readers. We had lines out all over the hospital, seeking word on the dedication date. Practically, it seemed like an impossible contradiction for the hospital to be planning a public celebration while withholding all information on its big day. Given our intelligence sources, there was no way for Columbus to extend invitations to politicians and to other public figures far enough in advance to get firm commitments of attendance without us tenants finding out. Ex officio, for example, and clearly by mistake, an invitation went to State Senator Manfred Ohrenstein, who represents our district and who had debated out in the street with hospital attorney Peter Schneider on the day of the Dan Berrigan–Mother Cabrini Processional. The senator immediately rejected the invitation and sent us a copy of his stern letter to Mother Josephine.

The secrecy on the precise dedication date was in fact maintained until three weeks before the dedication date, which turned out to be Sunday afternoon, September 16, 1973. But three weeks prior to the open disclosure, there was an unintended leak to us by a hospital volunteer, to whom the information had been entrusted. That gave us ample time to crank up all necessary preparation for the counterdedication and then to put everything on a

133

standby basis. For by then it seemed next to certain that a signed and sealed settlement of our damage suit would render our demonstration unnecessary.

In fact, in early May, as repairs proceeded apace, the two lawyers, after constant referral back to their respective principals, had reached agreement on a draft settlement in the form of a consent judgment and an accompanying stipulation. It included no cash damages—a point on which the hospital was adamant. But the consent judgment, if signed by both sides and a judge, would have enforced the key provisions of the 1971 contract through the State Supreme Court, with the power of contempt providing the necessary motivation for compliance. No solicitation to "relocate." No payment of "relocation" fees. No demolition.

The supplementary stipulation would have frozen our apartment rents for two years. In lieu of cash damages, this was to be a token of implicit recognition that we had been unmercifully harassed for three and a half years. Columbus was to hire a resident superintendent chosen by the Tenants Committee.

Two tenants, each with a compelling personal need to shift to other and better apartments, were to move shortly after the signing of the settlement, just as soon as the hospital rendered the two new apartments habitable. On the day after Labor Day, which was thirteen days before the September 16 dedication date, Columbus personnel actually began work on both apartments. By Friday morning, September 14, work in one apartment (for retired Charles Mancini) was at least half finished, and work was 90 percent completed in the other apartment for Juan and Janna Deligne.

On May 18, 1973, within ten days after we got the lawyers' draft, the Tenants Committee, in the longest and best attended meeting in three years, went over the consent judgment and the stipulation painstakingly, clause by clause. For advance study, everyone had had a copy for three or four days prior to the meeting. We all were looking for any conceivable escape hatch that might provide an out for the hospital at some future point. I found it very encouraging to hear tenants who, in 1970, could have been called timid and mousy now asking probing questions, in order to make certain that the settlement was for real.

When everyone's questions had been satisfactorily answered—some by legal information that Glenda Watson and I relayed from our lawyer, some by group analysis—we voted unanimously to ratify the settlement.

Joy and sighs of relief at 210–214 East 19th Street. "At last" summed up everyone's emotions. In return for the hospital's concessions we were only too glad to agree in the draft to turn over all rents due and owing, just as soon as both sides signed. Three years on the front lines were long enough for anyone's nerves.

June came. No word from the hospital on ratification. Knowing how difficult it is for Columbus to get itself together on anything, whether for halfway sensible or abysmally stupid decisions, we did not become unduly concerned. Then, before we knew it, July was upon us, and Iannuzzi was proposing in writing that both sides "get things rolling" by having a joint tenant-hospital subcommittee meeting for the first time in a year and a half. The nuns with the authority to sign, he claimed, were suddenly all in Nicaragua in the aftermath of the great earthquake there a half year earlier.

Looking back at events, we are nearly convinced —but cannot be absolutely certain because of some seemingly contradictory evidence and the wild irrationality of

135

our adversaries—that everything done by Iannuzzi, including the negotiating of the draft settlement over a five-month period, the convening of the joint tenant-hospital subcommittee, and the two weeks' work on the two apartments for Charlie Mancini and the Delignes, was part of a devious stalling design. If our surmise is correct, the nuns thought that, by their token action, they would be able to slip past the September 16 dedication without an embarrassing street demonstration, and without a signed settlement.

At the two midsummer subcommittee meetings —held at tenant insistence off Columbus turf for the first time—Bob Ferrari got the tenant representatives to strengthen Iannuzzi's hands vis-à-vis the hawks by agreeing to turn over six months' rent once our choice for the resident super was actually hired by Columbus, and once Charlie Mancini and the Delignes had moved into their new apartments. Sensing that Bob planned to propose something conciliatory such as this and knowing that politically Glenda Watson was the key tenant to convince, I persuaded her to leave her job early, in order to attend the late afternoon meeting.

Iannuzzi began raising with Bob our threat to picket the dedication. Our position throughout was "Sign now, and have a peaceful dedication." Nothing would have made us happier than to have no reason to demonstrate. On Friday morning, September 14, forty-eight hours before the dedication date when signing of the settlement by the hospital was scheduled for 11:30 A.M., Neal Hitzig, Harriet Putterman, and I hastily signed a formal pledge that there would be no demonstration on September 16. It was never handed over to the nuns because, at literally the last minute, they balked at signing the consent judgment and the stipulation.

136

Right after Labor Day, as Iannuzzi began to fudge on certain provisions in the draft settlement, he proposed an additional clause that would have waived forever our First Amendment rights to protest peacefully outside the hospital or to criticize Columbus publicly, no matter what their provocations might be.

It seems hard to believe that Iannuzzi, as a lawyer, really expected that any court would enforce such a broadly drawn waiver. And it is difficult to explain his seriousness in proposing anything so far out if his negotiations with Bob Ferrari were indeed anything other than playacting.

In retrospect, we apparently gave too much weight to the nuns' natural desire to have an untroubled dedication, and too little weight to their massive institutional longing to take over and eventually run our entire square block as they chose—even if the grand design should take another fifty to one hundred years, and even if they had no concrete plans for each and every building site. To have signed the settlement would have put the power of contempt of court behind our lifetime leases and behind our other protections in the 1971 contract (which, in itself, lacks self-enforcing provisions). The nuns would have been faced with the prospect that, at age seventy, young Bobby Lee, for example, might still be living in the same family apartment in the year 2023 as an untouchable tenant.

By midweek, we were all in a state of the highest tension. Essentially, our optimism held. But it was becoming more and more tinged with doubt in the absence of any designated time for the signing and in the face of Iannuzzi's constant efforts, by telephone, to trim this and that vital tenant protection in the draft settlement.

Our infrastructure for Sunday's counterdedication had been in place, on ice, since mid-August. In Baltimore, Father Philip Berrigan was standing by, ready to come to New York if we had to go through with the demonstration. Albert Blumenthal, New York State Assembly minority leader and one of the four major candidates for mayor, was also available to picket (and eventually did). For over a month, tenant activists around the city had had Sunday afternoon, September 16, marked on their calendars with a save-the-date red circle. Since 1970, all our demonstrations have been meticulously planned, and none has been a failure. In the pits of our stomachs, we were tense and agitated because of the delay in signing the settlement. But with another part of our consciousness, we were calm and confident about the success of our counterdedication if it had to be.

Columbus Hospital is free of direct control from the Catholic Archdiocese of New York. But "the cardinal is not without influence," as both laymen and sympathetic priests have advised us. Between Tuesday and Sunday of that crucial week, so much happened between us, our elected officials, the press and the Chancery Office that only tape recorders attached to everyone's telephones could have kept a complete record of the complex developments.

Tuesday: A tenant phone call to Father James Gilhooley, community ombudsman on the East Side, head of the Catholic Charities office in upper Manhattan, and chairman of the 1971 negotiating session that resulted in the contract. As requested, he promised to get word to the Chancery Office about the seeming deadlock over the actual signing.

Around Thursday, word came back that "the cardinal is deeply disturbed over the situation."

Wednesday: To the Chancery Office on Madi-

138

son Avenue and to Catholic Charities on First Avenue, I hand-delivered in midday a dummy of the flier that had been prepared for Sunday's counterdedication. An attached note informed the cardinal and his aides that we had no desire to embarrass His Eminence, but that we could not wait until the last minute to put the Sunday plans and arrangements into operation. If we did not have positive word by Thursday night that Columbus would sign, we would have to run off thousands of fliers, notify the press, and mobilize our forces.

Within an hour after the deliveries to the Chancery Office and Catholic Charities, Monsignor Eugene V. Clark, the cardinal's director of communication (public relations), telephoned us with an assurance of the Archdiocese's concern and with an implicit promise of intervention in our behalf. He volunteered his office night line and the phone number at his residence "where I may be reached up to eleven P.M."

To Ross Graham, an aide of our state senator, Manfred Ohrenstein, Monsignor Clark was explicit. "I want you to know, Mrs. Graham, that we are dispatching Father Cassidy of Catholic Charities down to Columbus Hospital to make sure that *those nuns* sign the settlement." But even with the power and prestige of the Chancery Office behind him, Father Cassidy did not in the end get "those nuns" to sign.

Further telephone conversations followed with Father Gilhooley, Monsignor Clark, and our elected officials. Bob Ferrari checked to see which judge would be sitting in Part 6 of the State Supreme Court on Friday— the last possible day for signing before the dedication. For, to be legally binding, after signing by both parties to the dispute, the consent judgment would require the judge's signature, which is usually routine, provided the judge sees nothing improper in the provisions. All along, we had made it clear to the hospital's lawyer that we would not call off the Sunday demonstration until the necessary papers were officially filed with the clerk of the court.

Finally came what proved to be the tip-off on the collapse of the settlement on Friday. For the past ten days, Columbus' carpenters, painters, plumbers, and electricians had been fixing up the new apartment for Charlie Mancini. By consensus of the workers and us tenants, the worst of the work was over and was at least half, if not two thirds, completed. Out of the blue, Iannuzzi said on the telephone that, earlier on that day (Thursday), it had "just" been discovered that a new ceiling would have to be hung in one of the rooms. Given the amount of work it entailed, would Mr. Mancini consider accepting, at approximately his same low rent of $36.09, an apartment halfway down the block in the luxury Saint Cabrini Tower?

I must say that John put the proposition smoothly and offhandedly. Although I instantly sensed that we'd be opening Pandora's box if even one tenant were "relocated" out of our building, neither Bob Ferrari nor I got the slightest inkling that the entire settlement would founder, allegedly, on this issue. My reply was that I couldn't speak for Charlie Mancini and could merely present the proposition to him when I arrived belatedly at the tenants meeting an hour or so later.

Bob let Iannuzzi know we'd type up the slightly revised draft; en route home I would leave a copy with the concierge at John's Gramercy Park co-op apartment building. Iannuzzi promised to take the draft to the nuns early the next morning before leaving for a federal court case

140

in Newark. Indeed, Neal Hitzig spotted him heading in the direction of the hospital about 8 A.M.

When the two lawyers spoke by phone around 9 A.M., Iannuzzi indicated surprise and disappointment that Charlie Mancini was not interested in his great offer of a luxury apartment in an elevator building. Nevertheless, Iannuzzi told Bob to be at the convent on 21st Street, where many of the nuns reside, at 11:30 A.M., and that Mother Innocent would be there to sign.

Bob felt, correctly, that to the nuns he was the least offensive person on the tenants' side. So it was decided that he should proceed alone to the convent. From Third Avenue and 21st Street, I saw an obviously unhappy Mother Innocent approaching from 19th Street. She turned and disappeared into the convent.

Later it turned out that several other top nuns were already inside, together with Father Cassidy of Catholic Charities and a lawyer whom Iannuzzi had dispatched in his absence. Not expecting much in the way of pleasantries or chitchat, I thought that a relieved Bob Ferrari would emerge, alone, in five or ten minutes and head downtown to the State Supreme Court.

An eternal half hour elapsed. From across the street I was discreetly watching from a distance of several hundred feet. Finally out came Bob, the nuns, a priest (Father Cassidy, whom I did not know by sight), and Iannuzzi's stand-in (also a stranger to me). Slowly and solemnly, intermittently talking, but for the most part silent, they walked east to Second Avenue, south to 19th Street, then next up our block. Bob caught my eye and nodded slightly, but I hadn't the faintest idea of what was going on. When the procession passed Cabrini Tower without stopping at the ground-floor administrative offices, I could only conclude they were heading for our building.

That, indeed, was the destination. Apartment 1, first floor, front, 214, to be exact. Mother Innocent had told Bob that it would cost the hospital $2,000 to $3,000 (a huge exaggeration) to complete the work for Charlie Mancini; they couldn't afford it (one month later they bought Neal Hitzig's building at 201 East 19th Street for $4.3 million); and now Mr. Mancini had rejected their kind offer of an apartment in luxury Cabrini Tower.

Where, she asked, was Mr. Iannuzzi? He had "promised" to be present, and in his absence she couldn't possibly sign the settlement with that clause guaranteeing the new habitable apartment for Mr. Mancini. Yet over drinks shortly afterward, the other attorney admitted to Bob that he had been with Iannuzzi earlier that morning when Iannuzzi clearly told Mother Innocent that he had to be in court in Newark. The whole refusal to sign, then, appeared to be a calculated and contrived affair on the part of the nuns.

One thin bit of hope remained. The Columbus board was to meet at 2 P.M. I was in immediate touch with Monsignor Clark, and he volunteered the remark that the matter of repairs for Charlie Mancini's new apartment was "not a substantive matter," and certainly was no valid basis for refusing to sign the settlement. Father Cassidy was to be at the board meeting, and the clear indication was that the cardinal wanted the board to reverse the nuns' stubborn refusal.

Except for an experience as a college freshman, when the college surgeon kept me waiting for hours on the great day I was to be released from the hospital after an appendectomy, I have never spent a longer afternoon than on that dreary Friday, September 14, 1973. Bob was

142

expecting a call from Iannuzzi, now hours delayed (though we didn't know it) in Newark by the criminal case he was trying. I was expecting calls from Bob and Monsignor Clark with the results of the board meeting. After 3 or 4 P.M., any approval of the settlement by the board that was contingent on our calling off the Sunday counter-dedication would have put us in an impossibly risky position. For, by then, Bob could hardly reach the judge and get his signature before Monday morning—at which time the hospital could try to renege and could come up with arguments against his signing. While to us tenants the signing was an emergency, it was unlikely that the judge would so view it were he to be approached at home after hours.

After 4:30 P.M. I could no longer get through to Monsignor Clark, who in the previous forty-eight hours had been readily accessible. Nor did he return my calls. Not until 6 P.M. did Bob hear from Iannuzzi, who professed ignorance of the day's events and promised to get back to Bob right after checking with the hospital. (The call-back came the following Wednesday.) In retrospect, we saw that, by keeping us in the dark on the board's final rejection of the settlement, Columbus hoped to leave us with so little time that we could not mount any demonstration at all by Sunday afternoon, let alone a meaningful one. On their end, plans were proceeding apace. The doorman at 201 told me that fifty nuns of the order had been bussed in from Chicago alone for the dedication. (In the Windy City, the Missionary Sisters operate Columbus, Cabrini and Cuneo hospitals.)

For us, Friday evening was the moment of credibility. Our trump card—the threat of spoiling their dedication—had not produced the settlement. To play that card now would mean that the nuns would never forgive

143

us, and that we'd have to look forward to an indefinite period of unresolved conflict. But *not* to play the card would signify to Columbus that we had gone soft. That would invite harassment and retaliation. The demonstration had to go forward.

Until late Friday night Harriet Putterman was on the phone alerting tenant activists to descend en masse on 19th Street for the counterdedication, rain or shine. Envelopes for hand delivery of a Tenants Committee press release all over town had to be addressed (with arrangements for follow-up reminder telephone calls Saturday night and Sunday morning). On Saturday morning, Marsha Friedman of Assemblyman Stein's staff especially opened their office in order for us to run off dozens of Xeroxed copies of the release, while tenant Bobby Lee with his bicycle stood by to make the rounds of city desks and television assignment editors. We asked both Mr. Stein and mayoralty candidate Blumenthal to issue their own reinforcing statements to the press, and they did.

Volunteers worked on the painting of slogans on large bedsheets, to be hung on our front fire escape facing the hospital and the street. Until late Friday night, elderly tenants in my building folded leaflets to be stuck into neighborhood mailboxes early the next morning. And a crew of neighbors experienced in the art of painting posters with waterproof colors went to work on the poster boards we had purchased just in case. Saturday was full but not panicky. Harriet Putterman firmly believes that the more persons who invest some time and energy in preparation for a demonstration—even if it's only the folding of leaflets—the more of a psychological stake they will have in its success.

It was not until early Saturday evening that I had a chance to begin calling the major news agencies

144

about the release (with leaflet attached) that had been delivered to them some hours before. I was not expecting the word that the Associated Press desk man came forth with. The thought had crossed my mind that, fed up with Columbus' intransigence, the cardinal might suffer a diplomatic illness on Sunday and simply not show up. I was happily dismayed when AP told me that, on Friday evening (just a few hours after the Columbus Board meeting), the Chancery Office—*not* the hospital—had telephoned AP to say that the Sunday dedication was cancelled.

By us, a quick decision was required. Do we go through with a counterdedication when the main event is called off? The consensus was that, with fine weather predicted for Sunday afternoon, we should proceed with the demonstration as a show of strength. Our only problem was to get the word of our decision around town so that scattered tenant supporters, hearing on the radio Sunday morning about the cancellation, would not assume that the demonstration was also off. By "beeper" telephone interviews on the two all-news radio stations (WINS and WCBS), we spread the accurate news.

It was from Pranay Gupte of *The New York Times*, who covered our demonstration and wrote a remarkably comprehensive account of the complex three-and-one-half-year dispute, and from Owen Moritz, housing reporter of the New York *Daily News*, that I learned that over the weekend Monsignor Clark was unavailable to them also when they sought details of the cardinal's unprecedented cancellation. For Old Guard church people, I understand, an unblessed hospital or other Catholic institution is almost as intolerable as an unbaptized child. Gupte began his story:

One of the oldest private hospitals in the city

145

assumed a new name and opened a new wing yesterday, but Cardinal Cooke, who was supposed to be the guest of honor, declined to attend the ceremony and neighborhood residents demonstrated, charging that the hospital was expanding at their expense.

So, with a ceremony that consisted of staff members greeting one another and listening to a piano recital, Columbus Hospital, at 227 East 19th Street, formally became the Cabrini Health Center, and the hospital's $39-million acute-care wing, which is 16 stories high and has 478 beds was officially declared open.

The *Daily News* account, with photos, began: "Dedication of the $39 million Mother Cabrini Tower at Columbus Hospital on Manhattan's East Side was cancelled yesterday after local tenant groups apparently persuaded Cardinal Cooke to bow out of the ceremonies."

The next issue of the hospital's house organ, *ColumbuScope*, had a paragraph buried on page 6: "The dedication of Columbus Hospital, planned for September 16th, was unexpectedly cancelled at the last moment, through circumstances beyond the hospital's control." Into this phraseology one could read a confirmation that it was indeed the cardinal who had cancelled the whole affair. Not trusting Columbus to tell it straight, His Eminence had used an aide to notify Associated Press.

The weather was so glorious, the turnout and good spirits of our chanting supporters was so heartening, and the press coverage was so extensive that all the depression of Friday afternoon dissolved in the warm Sunday sunshine. Philip Berrigan was just the right person to interpret the moral issues to reporters. The presence of Assemblyman Blumenthal, the mayoralty candidate, on the picket line proclaimed to the deaf, dumb and blind policymakers at Columbus that tenants resisting unwarranted hospital expansionism could count on significant political support. If the hospital failed to get the multiple messages, the sophisticated power brokers at the Chancery Office most certainly understood.

After Phil Berrigan headed back for Baltimore and after several million persons saw our spirited demonstration on network television shows, my own feeling was that the totally amoral institution we'd been fighting so long was well along the road to ultimate capitulation, however distant that might be.

Said Winston Churchill: "If we fail to come and face reality, reality will come and face us."

Whatever his personal motivations may be, hospital lawyer Iannuzzi is irrepressible in his salesmanship efforts. Quite soon after the dedication-that-wasn't, he brightly told our attorney that he had sold the nuns on a plan of his to gut-renovate our building. Implementation would require "temporary" shifting of the 210 tenants into 214 apartments while work proceeded on that half of the building, and then a shift of everyone into completed 210. While most of the renovated apartments would go to hospital personnel, the bait for present tenants was to offer us "luxury" apartments at approximately our present rents.

Two tenants were enthusiastic about being "upgraded." A couple more were interested if our lawyer could guarantee a number of safeguards. The great majority of us didn't aspire to "Cadillac" apartments, and we saw the proposal as the hospital's latest trick to get us out of the building. The greatest suspicion was that, during the renovation by some of the hospital's dubious contractors, the foundation or the structure would "somehow" be weakened, and that suddenly we'd all have to move out

147

of a building rendered unsafe. Once out and scattered, we'd never get back in. The parking lot would at last take our place.

Our attorney urged us to let him discuss and negotiate the proposal with Iannuzzi. If we didn't reach a settlement such as this with Columbus, he argued, he could foresee only endless acrimony. (Our basic position remained that nothing is ever settled until it is settled right, and that gutting in this case was not the right solution.) On a personal level, he repeatedly told us that, in adult life, he had moved from a very poor tenement childhood to his present duplex apartment in a luxury development four blocks from us. His goal was to elevate us into similar housing, whether or not that really met our wishes. (Hindsight wisdom: Be careful when your attorney, with the best of intentions, becomes a strong lobbyist for *his* position. That is not his proper role.)

The details of what went on from early 1974 to the spring of 1975 are complex. Partly because the majority wished to avoid antagonizing the two enthusiastic tenants by a summary veto—which, in retrospect, is probably what we should have done—and partly because we found ourselves before Housing Court Judge Stanley Nason on a rent-strike eviction proceeding—and the judge volunteered to help nail down what he called a renovation plan with ironclad protection for us tenants—we (against our better judgment) authorized Bob Ferrari to explore the matter with Iannuzzi. Bob gave us his absolute professional assurance that, under our lifetime leases in the 1971 contract with Columbus, ratification of any agreement would require unanimous tenant approval.

Before we knew what was going on, the judge was dominating all the proceedings—with a number of sessions in chambers between him and the two lawyers, with no tenants present.

In October 1974, the tenants at a meeting voted to reject what the three men had worked out in writing. Judge Nason was outraged. As required by court rules, he cleared a date with both lawyers, and then set down for trial the long-delayed eviction proceeding. The trial would mean not that anyone would actually be dispossessed (the rent money was safe in our attorney's bank account), but that we would demand, under New York law, that all code violations be corrected before our escrow rents since 1973 would be paid to the hospital.

In the intervening month before the trial date, someone at Columbus had a brilliant if belated long-shot idea: Why not argue that the tenants had earlier reached a binding oral agreement with the hospital, and that our vote to ratify or reject was superfluous? (For Columbus, the awkward angle to that was that, during the late summer and early fall, when tenants were on vacation, Iannuzzi was accusing us of stalling. Both he and the judge had kept asking our attorney: "When are the tenants going to hold their meeting on ratification and decide?" Bob Ferrari, in turn, responded to that double pressure by telephoning me long distance at least three times to ask: "When can we expect the tenants' decision?")

Even Bob, who was greatly disappointed at our rejection of the "Cadillac" scheme, said he could not see how any court could hold that a contract had been arrived at orally. Each of his five proposed drafts of the gut renovation scheme had provided individual lines for the *signature* of each and every tenant. But to everyone's surprise, the outraged judge did so hold. Bob was further dismayed when Iannuzzi then revealed that the hospital planned to chop up the forty-eight apartments into seventy postage-stamp-sized units, into which we and the hospital's transients, mostly foreign-born nurses, internes and residents, would be shoehorned. Recalling his assurances to us about "safeguards," a very subdued Bob said to me: "I *thought* the draft protected against that." His chastened tone of voice indicated that he, like us, felt he had been had by his two colleagues in the legal fraternity.

It goes without saying that Judge Nason's ruling was promptly appealed by our two new attorneys, Martin Hotvet and Nancy Le Blanc. *None* of the conditions, set in previous decisions on other cases by the state's highest court, for an oral agreement to be binding had been met in this case—such as a settlement reached in open court with a court stenographer present, and terms so brief and simple as not to lend themselves to vastly different interpretations. At the court conference sessions at which the oral agreement was supposedly reached, only a minority of the tenants was present—a fact acknowledged but glossed over by the judge in what the lawyers call his outrageous decision.

On appeal, Nason came a cropper. Having flouted *four* binding decisions of higher courts, including two by the state's highest court, and having switched dates and facts around in that ruling to suit the conclusion he wished to reach (as we documented in affidavits on appeal), it was only to be expected that the higher court would slap him down.

That is exactly what happened on June 13, 1975, when the Appellate Term of State Supreme Court unanimously reversed Hearing Officer Nason's verdict, in a brief but formidable opinion that fully upheld the claim of us tenants that there had never been anything even approaching an oral agreement in the informal court confer-

150

ences where Nason was the self-appointed mediator. The Appellate Term ruled:

> On this record, it is clear that it was the intention of all the parties not to be bound by the terms of any settlement agreement before it was reduced to writing and signed by all the parties. The understanding, if any, reached at the June 14th conference was "at best . . . an agreement to agree to the amplified terms of a future writing" [citation from one of the four binding higher court decisions]. . . .
>
> In any event, even assuming there was a definite and final agreement which the parties intended to be binding, the agreement was not enforceable since it was not made "in open court" or in a writing subscribed by the parties or in a writing reduced to the form of an order and entered [citations from two more of the binding higher decisions].
>
> Order, entered April 7, 1975 (Nason, H.O.), unanimously reversed. . . .

In 1970, that gypsy fortune teller would have had to be tops in her trade to have discerned in the clearest of crystal balls the twists and turns along the tortuous road to eventual victory.

chapter 3
The Way It Is,
The Way It's Supposed to Be

> Mayor Lindsay . . . suggested health services as one area of employment, saying this would be the fastest-growing single public industry in the United States in the next decade.
>
> —*The New York Times,* October 18, 1973

In campaigning for the vice-presidency in 1972, Spiro Agnew was harshly insensitive but not broadly inaccurate with his famous remark that if you've seen one slum or ghetto, you've seen them all.

Had he been differently oriented, he could have extended his observation to include both the systematized techniques for cheating the weak, and also the legal rules for sophisticated institutional ripoffs. I don't know if the professional associations of hospital and university administrators have workshops on the rape of neighborhoods at their annual conventions. But somehow the knowledge does get spread around and shared. In his essay on the corporate elite, "Power To Do What?" Andrew Hacker says, "It is clear that they know what is on one another's minds. . . . There is a community of interest and sentiment among the elite, and this renders any thought of a

152

'conspiracy' both invalid and irrelevant. . . . The lines of communication are built into the system." The same precepts hold true in the wondrous realm of "nonprofit" institutions.

By and large, if you've researched one expansionist institution (profit or nonprofit) anywhere in the United States, you soon learn on the second, third and subsequent investigations that you've researched them all. The local and individual variations are usually only in the size of the gravy train to latch onto, in the local laws on tenant-homeowner rights to violate, and in the hawkish or dovish (or sometimes mixed) approach to the nasty business of throwing defenseless people out into the street, of polluting people's shores, or driving a whole community insane with incessant and ever-louder airport noises.

With millions of dollars at stake for even a "modest" hospital expansion program, the medical-industrial complex moves into action against "recalcitrants" with the same covertness as the CIA before a coup, with the same arrogance, ruthlessness and steamrollers that the billion-dollar ITT employs against a "recalcitrant" foreign government. Of course, the guns and the assassination plots are absent from hospital and university battle plans because their brand of counterinsurgency is on a lower, "nonviolent" level. But otherwise the pattern and the modus operandi are uniform. The techniques are indistinguishable from the way in which the Green Berets forcibly "relocated" several million unwilling Vietnamese.

On the medical front, at the mother site, small or moderate-sized hospitals at first begin to add nonmedical structures: staff-housing towers, parking lots and garages, and private office suites for doctors.

The merger stage comes second, as in the business world. Larger medical centers and institutions begin to acquire smaller medical facilities. The latter are often in medically underserviced sections of a city.

Thirdly, the surrounding sites selected for hospital expansion almost always contain low- and moderate-rent housing. The wholly impersonal imperatives of empire-building call for eviction of tenants and for demolition of sound and much-needed housing.

Various cities and states impose more or less strict safeguards against the frivolous and unwarranted issuance of certificates of eviction. Since evictions often cannot be effected legally, health-care institutions finally resort to unconscionable harassment of tenants in order to induce move-outs.

Meanwhile, without any public guidelines or policy, the major business of expansion—funding, contracts, deals, payoffs—is being transacted, out of sight and over the heads of those whose lives are being disrupted. In most cases, getting the tenants out of hospital-owned buildings—ultimately by threats, by deceit, by bribes (or even by the setting of "small" warning fires in the middle of the night)—is cavalierly presumed at the start to present no insurmountable obstacle. Most men and women of money and power are not accustomed to being thwarted by their "inferiors." From the shocked reactions, it would appear that, until resistance hits *their* factory or *their* hospital or *their* university, they rarely anticipate it and thus are caught off guard.

Because the Establishment's own surveys show overbedding has become a nationwide problem, getting authorization for additional unneeded beds of necessity takes on aspects of a conspiracy and a cover-up within individual hospitals. And conspiracies are not hatched or implemented in free and open public discussion. A 1974 article in the *Bulletin* of the Health Policy Advisory Cen-

154

ter (Health-PAC) ("Oklahoma Crude—Everything's Gushing Up Hospitals," by health activists Bob Nichols, Eric Johnson and Deborah Roher) is a penetrating study of the secluded, antipeople politics of overbedding (i.e., unwarranted expansionism).

With a population of 700,000, Oklahoma City is richly endowed with eighteen nonfederal hospitals. One of the eighteen, University Hospital, is related to the University of Oklahoma. There are no county or municipal hospitals; the other seventeen are private and voluntary.

Medical professionals generally say that an 80–85 percent occupancy rate for hospital beds is an optimum figure that allows for day-to-day ups and downs in admissions and discharges. That rate range also allows a margin of safety in case of sudden demand following any disaster in the area. Four formulas, two of which derive from the 1947 Hill-Burton Hospital Construction Act, determine the number of short-term, acute-illness beds that a community needs and will need, by projection, in the future. Measured by those formulas, the three-county area around Oklahoma City needed 2,800 beds at 85 percent occupancy by 1975. In actuality, 4,746 beds were scheduled—or an excess of 1,946 beds.

An occupied bed costs $30,000 a year to maintain. Each unoccupied bed costs $50,000 initially and $20,000 annually to maintain. Over a period of thirty years—the usual life of mortgages for hospital expansion—the cost of these superfluous facilities will be over $650 million.

As elsewhere, the Oklahoma City hospitals plan to cover this loss by raising patient fees over the next three decades. For the period from 1968 to 1972, the figures for St. Anthony's, a Catholic hospital now finished with its current expansion program, show how the public pays:

155

Average daily census of patients up 1.6 percent.
Number of beds up 46 percent.
Operating expenses up 51 percent.
Total revenue up 62 percent.
Net income up 190 percent.

This net income or "surplus funds"—or profits —don't quite match the fabulous jump in profit rates of U.S. oil companies at the time of the 1973–74 energy crisis. But almost any businessman would envy so sharp an increase.

The neighbors of expansionist hospitals get taken in more ways than just evictions. Nearly everywhere, the "unprofitable" services (emergency rooms and outpatient departments) that are of most value to the nonaffluent are cut back in order that the hospitals may cope with their self-induced inflationary costs. In the same 1968–72 period, as the number of beds went up by 46 percent, St. Anthony's occupancy rate was down 31 percent, emergency-room visits were down 32 percent, and outpatient visits were down 54 percent.

Because St. Anthony's is not alone in Oklahoma City in building excess bed capacity—Presbyterian, Baptist, Mercy all busily compete with their own surplus beds —hospitals in the area by 1975 dropped to an average occupancy rate of only 55 percent. Several years ago, in warning against overbedding, a report commissioned by the Areawide Health Planning Organization (AHPO) predicted:*

* The federal Department of Health, Education and Welfare designated AHPO as the local Comprehensive Health Planning Agency for Central Oklahoma.

(a) unnecessary hospitalization, because of extreme pressure on hospitals to get some income out of the surplus beds;

(b) "a severe limitation in the hospitals' ability to explore new forms of health care" in the face of heavy debt burdens incurred for unused beds; and

(c) out of fear of losing medical staff, increased pressures on hospital administrators to meet doctor demands for glamorous and duplicative expensive equipment.

Just for repayment of principal and interest on the hospitals' mortgages, to patients in Oklahoma City hospitals the cost of current overexpansion soars to $180 million. Premiums for "nonprofit" Blue Cross "have to" be increased to help the hospitals meet their monthly payments to the bankers.

In a 1973 suit, the Oklahoma Consumer Protection Agency charged that the local hospitals have violated the state's tax-exemption law by refusing to admit indigent patients and by "refusing to discharge and threatening to refuse to discharge patients" until they have paid their hospital bills in full.

The contemporary use of the word "industry" to describe a precious healing art is no semantic accident. Nor is it without deep underlying marketplace significance that we now speak of the "delivery" of health-care services —like goods and merchandise being delivered off a merchant's truck. Typically, the boards of the Oklahoma City hospitals read like a corporate-banking-publishing-political Who's Who, many with a direct stake in the profits of overbedding. When Ralph Nader can say that we have a national excess of 300,000 hospital beds—at an annual waste cost of $20,000 a bed, or a total of $6 billion down

157

the drain—the problem has reached wild and pathological dimensions.

Two thirds of a continent to the east of Oklahoma City, in Boston, only the names of a dozen expansionist hospitals, of their doctors, of their administrators, of the lending banks, of the state agencies are different. The process itself is a carbon copy. Since 1969, for example, Boston University's 350-bed University Hospital has expanded rapidly—going from a no-debt status at that time to long-term indebtedness by 1972 of $14 million. Without exception, the new buildings are operating at a loss.

John Hancock Mutual Life Insurance Company lent $1.6 million to put up the acute-care Medicenters Building, with no space reserved for relatively less costly outpatient care. By the time the loan, at 8.5 percent, is repaid in twenty-two years, John Hancock will have raked in an additional $1.9 million in interest. We know that that lusty profit will not come out of the paychecks of the hospital brass.

Since 1950, the population of the South End, the section of Boston where University Hospital is located, has dipped from 51,000 to less than 25,000 today. Aside from the displacements of urban renewal, part of the loss in population is attributable to the demolition of housing that attended the expansion of several hospitals. A community group called the Ad Hoc Committee for a South End for South Enders has also pointed out in an occasional, self-published tabloid that, with the help of renovators, speculators and luxury developers, poor and low-income residents have been pushed out of apartments and out of hundreds of longtime lodging houses. A much smaller number of institution-affiliated professionals and students

158

have moved in. The South End, claims the Ad Hoc Committee, is being pushed into being an elitist-oriented Georgetown.

Across town, in Boston's Mission Hill and Fenway sections, community opposition to a massive hospital merger slowed up state approval until 1974. The resistance slightly trimmed the final construction plans for a $100 million Affiliated Hospitals Center (AHC), which had been in planning and in controversy for fifteen years. What the *Boston Globe* has called "Massachusetts's embattled certificate-of-need law" was the peg for neighborhood resistance. The law is intended to prevent construction of unnecessary health-care facilities. The dispute over the need for all 640 replacement beds that the Massachusetts Public Health Council finally approved gave community organizations, including the Mission Hill Health Movement and the Harvard Tenants of Roxbury, sufficient clout to extract concessions. The administrators of three of Boston's major teaching and research hospitals (the Peter Bent Brigham, the Boston Hospital for Women, and Robert Breck Brigham) were panting to get started on construction of the single new combined structure.

The concessions called for five "public" members on a seventeen-member trustee board, with nine members representing the three affiliated hospitals. The remaining three were to be chosen by the fourteen. The Center and the community groups also reached agreement on the nature of primary care to be provided, on future expansion, on the environmental impact of construction, and on the role of community representatives in long-range development planning.

Like other hospitals, AHC looked forward to

public financing of more than two thirds of the construction cost, by floating $73 million in tax-free bonds through a state of Massachusetts authority.

Six weeks before final state approval, *Boston Globe* reporter Nils Bruzelius pointed out that the Affiliated Hospital Center "has made only the roughest measures of how much its construction costs will drive up the cost of care at the new hospital, or how alternative plans might drive that final cost down—or up.

"As a major concern," Bruzelius wrote in a *Globe* column, "primary care—the routine, day-to-day care that most city dwellers find very hard to get—came rather late to the planning for Affiliated Hospitals."

The commentary went on to cite the fears of community groups and health planners that

> primary care at AHC will serve the teaching and research priorities of the hospital and its doctors more than the immediate needs of its patients. . . . [Across the country, the same complaint is echoed in many hospital communities.] Primary care must be of the community, not just for it. In the face of these questions, it is not enough for AHC to say, as it often tends to, trust us.

Globe reporter Bruzelius noted that some community leaders had been reluctant to participate in hospital planning because they did not wish to be co-opted, and because they had had no guarantee of a real voice—i.e., votes—on decision-making boards.

The fact that New England's largest daily newspaper kept a reportorial eye on the intricate tripartite negotiations among community residents, AHC and state health officials undoubtedly strengthened the hand of the organizations that were intent on preserving the area from institutional ravages. Powerful Harvard Medical School, with its octopuslike grasp on things medical in Greater Boston and far beyond, was also very much in the picture.

From the *Globe* stories it appears that the neighbors of Affiliated Hospitals forcefully threw onto the negotiating scales the basic issues of health care and neighborhood preservation. The rest was a matter of naked power. A decade ago, the three hospitals, with state acquiescence, would have openly thumbed their noses at the peasants who live beyond their feudal moats. Today they have been forced to recognize the ultimate untenability of being "hopelessly mired in hostility," in the words of reporter Bruzelius.

Just like their more mammoth sisters and brothers, financially weaker and politically less potent institutions also get bitten hard by the expansionist bug. They are just as prepared as is a powerful hospital or an influential university to trample on their neighbors. But when tens of millions of dollars are not at stake and when directors and administrators can't dangle the magic bait of jobs before mayors and policy-making agencies, a would-be putsch against a community can be more easily defeated.

Such was the case in early 1973 when, pushed by its small staff, the Massachusetts Historical Society prepared to raze a twenty-four-apartment, six-building complex it owned nearby, in order to create an MHS employee parking lot for a dozen cars.

I don't believe that anyone in the entire city of Boston came to the Society's defense. Even the Boston Redevelopment Authority, "the agency with the bulldozer," was on the people's side for a change. From the mayor down, the universal reaction was dismay that such a presumptuous proposition should even have been put forth in the first place, let alone clung to tenaciously.

161

Elected officials joined tenant groups and students from all over the city in mass picketing in front of the MHS building in the Back Bay. "Closed for the Day" read the sign on the door.

Nevertheless, even in the face of unanimous public opinion, the institution plunged ahead with demolition plans, to the point of cutting off the lights in the six buildings. At that point, a judge issued a restraining order against demolition.

Suggestions arose of possible tax problems for the bullheaded Society. That did it. From then on it was up to the Society to try to back down gracefully. MHS president Thomas Boylston Adams—of *the* Adams family —came to recognize that a convenience parking lot at the expense of desperately needed housing was not going to be tolerated. Provided funds could be raised for rehabilitation, the Society offered to lease the buildings to a community-based, nonprofit group. Under Housing Court and City Hall supervision, community residents led by the Boston Center for Older Americans opened negotiations with MHS, with the goal of seeking renovation loans from state agencies and restoring the six buildings to full occupancy.

To an outsider, it looks as if the determined MHS staff had sold an idea that was a lemon to a prestigious board. Most of the members apparently had no gut feeling for the severity of, or the social tensions generated by, the urban housing shortage. Not until the combined impact of public, political and judicial outrage hit them with full force did they awaken to their total isolation on the parking-lot scheme.

Although it has not been scientifically confirmed, I suspect that a carefully designed national survey would establish a high correlation between successful community resistance to institutional expansionism and the presence of a vigorous community newsletter or newspaper, no matter how modest its make-up or how journalistically amateurish. In the war of Fenway v. Massachusetts Historical Society, the community paper was the *Back Bay Ledger,* followed by the *Fenway News,* a no-charge monthly with a volunteer staff of a dozen, a circulation of only 5,000 copies (compared to the several million Bostonians and New Englanders reached daily by the *Boston Globe*), and a smattering of ads from merchants in the area.

In terms of the Fenway's ability to keep itself together, putting out the eight-page tabloid every four weeks is just as important as storming City Hall. The usual progression of news about a crucial block or neighborhood issue is from repetitive front-page coverage in a small community weekly or monthly, to occasional buried items in the metropolitan daily months or even years later, to a very belated "discovery" of the thorny story by the local television stations. If the community paper doesn't manage to survive and pound away month after month, the sudden bright-eyed discovery may never come.

In June 1974, the *Fenway News* published a two-page special report, "The Community Saves Some Apartments." The story begins:

> Before you read any further, go get a copy of your apartment lease. You say you don't want to, that it gives you a queasy stomach every time you read it? That the only right you have is the right to give the landlord your rent?
>
> How would you feel if you were required to form a tenant organization and elect a tenant representative? If your landlord had to give you a financial statement every year? If you could repair housing-code

163

violations if the landlord refused, and be reimbursed for your expenses? If any disputes between you and the landlord had to be settled by binding third-party arbitration? If you could fire the managing agent if he or she wasn't doing the job? A dream would you say?

If you lived at 15–25 Hemenway Street, though, these are some of the clauses you would find in your lease. The lease was negotiated with the building's owner, the Massachusetts Historical Society, by members of the Fenway community with the legal advice of Dan Sullivan from Boston Legal Assistance Project. . . .

Rents are calculated according to a set formula and cannot be raised, even if rent control is ended, without a meeting with the tenants and without arbitration. . . . All the rent money goes into a special account that is used to pay building expenses, and all surplus stays in that account.

What had happened, after the society was enjoined from going through with the demolition, was that the community successfully negotiated with MHS for the lowest-cost rehabilitation of the six-building complex; the contractor agreed to hire local residents; John Sharratt, a local architect, agreed to monitor the work for the community. At 5 percent interest, the society borrowed $50,000 from the nearby Christian Science Church and $211,000 elsewhere. After the work was completed, a community committee with a list of criteria selected the tenants—with the first priority to former residents. The task of picking new tenants in the future will be the responsibility of the present tenants.

The unprecedented scope of the victory could not have been foreseen in December 1972 when only one barricaded holdout tenant remained. The mayor himself turned up for the big ribbon-cutting ceremony. Nevertheless, said David Scondras of the Boston Center for Older Americans:

We didn't get low enough rents; that was our biggest fail ure. [Rents range from $140 for a one-bedroom apartment to $190 for a three-bedroom—higher than anticipated, as is usual in inflationary times, because of construction cost increases and tax increases.] We stretched the system to its limit, but that limit is not good enough. We must now develop alternatives—cooperative action like the Mission Hill Food Co-op and the Health Clinic—that will be strong enough to survive on their own and provide us with the services we need at the prices even the poorest of us can afford.

Even in the short run, when community activists reach that level of candor in self-criticism—instead of just crowing over a tremendous achievement—expansionist institutions don't stand a chance.

For the most part, the country's assignment editors have not yet awakened to multibillion-dollar institutional expansionism as a jazzy issue deserving prominent display and follow-up coverage. Early in 1974 in Miami, Cedars of Lebanon Hospital became an exception. A month after President Nixon dedicated a federally subsidized new wing and praised Cedars as a model for "privately" financed health care, it "collapsed figuratively," in the words of the *AMA News,* "under a mass of defaulted loan payments and assorted debts, including a total of $814,000 sought by Internal Revenue Service for unpaid withholding taxes."

In rapid-fire order in the spring of 1974 came these developments:

1. An international manhunt for Sanford K. Bronstein, the "nonprofit" hospital's president and operating head, who was out to create "the Mayo Clinic

165

of the South," following his sixty-four-count indictment for forging twenty-one checks totaling $525,000. Bronstein was located in the Bahamas and was brought back to Miami to face trial.

2. Federal Bankruptcy Court put Cedars of Lebanon in receivership after the institution could not pay $13 million in accumulated debts.

3. The office of the Dade County state's attorney "suggested that [part of] the missing cash (totaling well over a million dollars) may have been used to bribe government officials to clear the way for Cedars' ambitious $62 million expansion plan" (*AMA News*, June 3, 1974).

4. In early April, the *Chicago Daily News* reported that Senate investigators from Washington were "particularly interested" in ascertaining "whether Nixon's old friend, Charles G. (Bebe) Rebozo, and his Key Biscayne Bank were in any way involved in the financial maneuvering that led to Cedars' expansion."

As the pieces of the scandal began to fall into place, it became known that it was William Pelski, the former local FHA director, who in 1970 had approved a federal guarantee of the $62.1 million Cedars expansion loan over powerful professional opposition in both Miami and Washington. Pelski was serving eighteen months in a federal prison camp, following conviction on charges of taking $70,000 in bribes from a Miami homebuilder. In 1975, Pelski was a key prosecution witness in the federal bribery case against former Florida Senator Edward J. Gurney, who was indicted while serving on the Senate Watergate Committee. Gurney, Nixon's staunchest defender on that committee, was charged with selling FHA mortgage insurance guarantees in exchange for contractors' cash kickbacks to his $233,000 political slush fund.

The scandal's origins extended back to 1969

when the Comprehensive Health Planning Council of South Florida warned against the financial feasibility of an expanded Cedars of Lebanon Hospital. It was then a small eight-year-old viable institution with 252 beds. The Planning Council noted that, within five hundred yards of Cedars, there already was an eight-hundred-bed Veterans Administration hospital, and that the 1,191-bed Jackson Memorial Hospital was directly across the street. In other words, still another Bedpan Alley. Both Cedars and Jackson are teaching affiliates of the University of Miami School of Medicine. It is impossible to understand how medical-school faculty could go in and out of Cedars over a five-year period and not pick up even occasional vibrations of something being rotten in Denmark—on a multimillion dollar scale.

Although the Health Planning Council projected a 4,548 bed surplus in Miami by 1975, Cedars, under President Sanford Bronstein, insisted on leapfrogging from 252 to 700 beds. The council firmly rejected his country-club plans for a health-testing laboratory, hotel space for patients' families, apartments for physicians, a swimming pool, restaurants, and other luxurious facilities.

Neither Florida's certificate-of-need law nor Section 1122 of the 1972 Social Security Amendments (both designed to prevent overbuilding) fazed the Cedars empire builders. Mr. Bronstein and William Bayer, a hospital trustee and also its paid lobbyist, took their plans directly to the White House, where Bronstein already had ready entrée. *The New York Times* reported (April 15, 1974) that he "is a member of a group of conservative Miamians regarded as friends of the administration who are challenging the Federal license of Miami Television Channel 10, owned by the Washington Post Company."

As Nixon was denouncing socialized medicine

167

during the February 14 dedication ceremony, Cedars, the model hospital, was already two weeks late in its mortgage payments totaling $98,000. By mid-April, with a lack of cash and a lack of patients, the hospital was in default on the $13.8 million mortgages covering the north wing (one of three new unneeded buildings). Said the New York *Daily News:* "There is little hope that the $62 million mortgage will ever be repaid." Which means that, through the FHA loan guarantee, we taxpayers must make good on the principal and interest to the banks holding the mortgage. It won't be the last such default by shaky institutions that never could have expanded without access to the public till. But Cedars may be unique in that the corruption was so flagrant that its highest official (instead of some underling) wound up with a twenty-five-year prison sentence after conviction on all sixty-four counts. During his five-week trial, President Sanford Bronstein's defense was that the $862,750 he stole from hospital accounts was used to bribe state and federal officials who approved the expansion program. The sentencing judge called Bronstein's crimes "a diabolical scheme to defraud a semi-public facility."

Since 1969, health planners in Miami had charged that Cedars' daily room charge ($92) was too high and was already $16 above the average hospital room rate in Dade County. Until everything collapsed in disgrace, those same critics had calculated that interest payments by the hospital on the FHA-guaranteed loan would have necessitated an increase of at least another $10 a day.

In May 1974, Wood C. McCue, executive director of the South Florida Health Planning Council, told *Modern Healthcare* magazine that there was "every sign of overbedding as early as July 1969" and that his agency had set out to study the problem.

Of twenty building or expansion projects the council turned down after that, McCue said "probably thirteen have survived" in some form. "We lost at Cedars and at a hospital the AFL-CIO wanted to build. We were overturned at another level." Given the bribes and pay-offs, it's easy to understand why professional opinion was so frequently overruled at the top level.

Knowing how word and rumblings invariably get around in concerned circles when institutional hanky-panky anywhere reaches wholesale levels, one wonders how many private and publicly paid professionals in Miami's health-care industry knew what was brewing at Cedars of Lebanon and failed to blow the whistle.

One of the best informed of a new breed of medical journalists is Richard D. Lyons of *The New York Times*. In 1972, it was he who, nationally, broke the story of a documented hustle at the expanding, 430-bed Altoona (Pennsylvania) Hospital. Locally, a crusading newspaper, the *Blair* [County] *Press,* through two sixteen-page supplements ("The Altoona Hospital Papers"), opened up all the cans of worms for public inspection.

The case could be docketed as Altoona Hospital Trustees and Administrators v. Angry Townspeople, the State Insurance Commissioner and (strangely) Blue Cross. And it all boiled down to money. Money for a $20 million expansion program; a hospital demand for more Blue Cross reimbursement money (part of the increase to finance expansionism); hospital money for liquor bills; hospital money for cocktails and dinner for 120 persons at a local country club; $22,228.67 to one doctor for one month's services; $200,000 to one radiologist in one year; $3,800 for the purchase of a hundred ashtrays; $300,000 a year to a computer company for admittedly poor service; a hospital charge of a dollar for a popsicle for a young patient; and hospital money to pay for doctors and their wives to vacation in Las Vegas and Miami.

Fifty embarrassing photostats of these and other hospital expense accounts and vouchers turned up in the two special supplements. In such a brew, it doesn't take a trained journalistic nostril to sniff kickbacks, split fees and other forms of larceny at public expense.

Since economically depressed Altoona—"a fading railroad town" of 63,000, in Richard Lyons' words—has lost 20,000 people in forty years, the rationale for the most expensive hospital in the area to expand had been widely challenged in the community. The town also got up in arms when, for a six-month period, the hospital cancelled its Blue Cross affiliation. It was at that point that Pennsylvania's well-known State Insurance Commissioner, Herbert S. Denenberg, joined the fray and launched an investigation.

Denenberg denounced the trustees and the administrator, Bernard F. Carr, who at that time doubled as president of the State Hospital Association. Among other charges, the insurance commissioner accused ten of the twenty trustees of conflicts of interest because of their links to local banks. Eight of the board members were associated with the Mid-State Bank of Altoona, from which the expanding hospital had borrowed over $1 million.

Denenberg also brought to light the report of the hospital's own auditors, which stated that, far from losing money (as claimed in its rejected appeal to Blue Cross for a higher reimbursement rate), Altoona Hospital had been making money in recent years. $2,250,000 had come out of operating revenues in the 1960's to finance an initial expansion program.

In 1971, the state of Maryland created a powerful new State Health Services Cost Review Commission that finally began work three years later in the summer of 1974. The commission immediately took on Suburban Hospital in Bethesda and three Baltimore-area hospitals. The commission cited studies that showed Suburban "may have compromised patient care for profitability." Profits as of 1974 were running to more than a million dollars a year on patient revenues, in addition to another million on more than $17 million in investments.

Suburban protested that $12 of the $17 million would go to build a 115-bed addition to the existing 350 beds if state and county officials would permit the expansion. Just as elsewhere, the building plans were embroiled in community complaints about the already existing quality of care. The *Washington Post* cited "assertions by neighborhood associations and others that new beds are needed more elsewhere, and that hospital officials have been unresponsive to neighborhood and community needs."

Three days after the commission publicly took off after Suburban, the *Washington Post* (July 4, 1974) published excerpts from a letter to Suburban from Neil Solomon, Maryland's Health Secretary, giving the hospital until September to correct "several significant weaknesses in the quality of care and services" as a precondition to any granting of approval to expand.

Solomon ordered the hiring of more nurses, more laboratory and X-ray employees, and a control officer to curb infections.

A unique feature in this case was that, in 1973, the *Washington Post* reported that the hospital's own doctors were openly raising serious questions about the services provided to patients. The Nader Health Research Group was also involved on the side of local health-care and neighborhood associations. One medical staff officer, Dr. William H. Killay, publicly denounced Suburban's "obsession with economy" and the "generation of profit" that have "consistently led to undermining of vital services."

Health Secretary Solomon also directed the hospital to "make strenuous efforts to encourage meaningful community participation" in its planning for any expansion and in its future general policy decisions.

Next to money, community participation in policy-making is invariably the sorest point with hospitals that have been run for so long as nonaccountable fiefdoms. They take to a partnership relationship with the community in the same way that the Devil takes to ablutions with Holy Water.

Besides fighting expansion on professional health-care grounds, the community groups in Bethesda also raised strong zoning objections before Montgomery County zoners. Since hospital officials and their architects often pay little heed to zoning restrictions, that is one battlefront where their expansion plans can sometimes be effectively blocked on the smallest technical violation of the code. Institutions by their actions tell themselves and tell the public, "We are the law." Because arrogance sooner or later leads to gross carelessness, they are vulnerable up and down the line. If the regulatory agencies are weak, then the courts may enforce the law, or vice versa.

So worried was Suburban Hospital by the arrows coming from all directions that, on the same day the *Washington Post* published Secretary Solomon's letter, the trustees cancelled their plan to let the School for Practical Nursing die on December 31, 1974, when federal funds were scheduled to terminate. Instead, the trustees promised to keep the school open with an annual $65,000 commitment from the hospital's own funds (profits).

Solely because health officials everywhere feel

172

constrained today to pay more respectful attention to community wishes than was the case as recently as five years ago, Suburban Hospital's new wing was at least delayed. Probably only the American Hospital Association knows precisely—and they aren't telling—how many "Suburbans" dot the nation's landscape.

Some time soon, someone with the requisite prestige is sure to call a national action conference of hospital neighbors, community groups and displaced residents who have specific local grievances against health-care quality, expansion plans and patient costs. In a way, such a conference will resemble the initial regional and national comings together of new militant industrial unions in the period leading up to the founding of the CIO in the mid-1930's. Intentionally or not, lines of communication among kindred souls always prove to be the first step toward united action. The launching in 1975 of *Shelterforce,* "a national housing newspaper" published in New York for tenants and housing activists around the country, is a clear harbinger of a nationwide get-together.

I'm not sure that the biggest indoor hall in any of our large cities would be big enough to hold the delegates. As public consciousness grows of a likely scandal in most hospital filing cabinets—financial scandals, scandals of medical care—there will be more and more staff and patient tips to investigative reporters and to district attorneys, with more and more criminal prosecutions, as at Cedars of Lebanon Hospital in Miami. Ambitious district attorneys will come to realize that there may be more long-range mileage in dealing with substantive public grievances than in exploiting the cry of "crime in the streets."

For there is already under way a nationwide movement toward greater state regulation of health-care facilities. That movement has originated not among state legislators or among state commissions, but rather in countless communities where sometimes as few as a half dozen dissatisfied health-care consumers have rebelled against lousy treatment, extortionate fees, and totally unwarranted hospital block-busting. In every situation that I have become familiar with since my own tenant battle with Columbus Hospital began in 1970, it has taken only a handful of determined residents, shopkeepers or patients to put an offending hospital wholly on the defensive, to stall official approval of expansionist plans indefinitely (or at least sufficiently long to force concessions to the community), and even to jeopardize bank loans or public funds that the institution had been taking for granted. It always comes as a pleasant surprise to newly recruited activists to discover that powerful bank officials get terribly upset and fearful when community groups come barking at their doors.

So long as community activists know politically what they are doing and learn where to turn for information, for research, for publicity, and for political support, and so long as they refuse to be bribed, cajoled, threatened, co-opted or exhausted into surrender, large numbers of troops are not really needed in an active sense on a day-to-day basis. The main body of troops can be held in reserve for special and necessary occasions, and individual soldiers can divide up assignments that are not burdensome in terms of time and energy, on a steady week-by-week basis. At root, what *is* important is to put politics in command and people first.

In Manhattan, early in the 1970's, the upgrade-your-health-services-or-else demand constituted an important part of the community's resistance, ultimately unsuccessful, to New York City's sale, for one dollar, of

174

eight blocks of highly valuable air rights over the East River Drive to three medical institutions. The one-dollar deal called for five major medical buildings to be erected over the famous thoroughfare.

In the end, after a four-year fight, the combined Establishment power of ritzy New York Hospital, of heavily endowed Rockefeller (medical research) University, and of the Hospital for Special Surgery proved to be too great for the wide range of community groups in opposition. Lacking in the power equation was hard-line political leadership tough enough to keep challenging the very premises of medical imperialism. Absolutist positions often become untenable in the real world, and sometimes a fallback to haggling over concessions is unavoidable for groups fighting expansionist institutions. But a clear, loudly articulated, antiexpansionist position should at least be put forward at the beginning wherever the proposed expansion is unwarranted.

It would take robber-baron "nonprofit" institutions to propose so open a steal of a city's prized resources. These days, a private, for-profit enterprise would hardly dare. Yet the directly affected community never managed to stir up a citywide stink, to induce some of New York's crack reporters to take a long hard look at the three audacious institutions, and over a period of time to turn public opinion solidly against the raid. Clearly this could have been done—most certainly over the four-year stretch.

With a large number of residential York Avenue buildings threatened by the expansionism and with so many tenants involved, a full-time organizer was quite possibly a prerequisite to effective resistance—first and foremost to handle regular communication among the scattered tenants and to keep everyone organized, house

175

by house, and constantly alerted; and secondly, to mount a steadily paced barrage of publicity stemming from a solid base of tenant activity and community cohesiveness. Residents eager to defend their homes and neighborhood could have assessed themselves one or two dollars a month to cover an organizer's salary and expenses. A neighborhood or a cause or an organization can go only so far on news releases that have no substance, no base of unremitting activism behind them. One doesn't win against anything with Rockefeller in its name on a loose, hit-and-miss, random publicity effort.

In *The New York Times* letter column, one important piece of information did come out. Properly exploited in continuing publicity and pursued to the limits of legal sanctions, it could have turned the tide. In a letter, William Johnston, vice-chairman of Tenants Against Demolition, wrote that these eminently elitist medical institutions had ousted 238 families from East 70th Street by using certificates of eviction that the city issued on fraudulent grounds. If the York Avenue–70th Street community had forced a naturally reluctant district attorney to criminally prosecute those responsible, the air-rights expansionist program could have been smothered in a backlash atmosphere generated by the unique trials of the guilty doctors and administrators.

Johnston's letter concluded: "Entities which operate under the aura of medical, educational or religious purity, in particular, cannot stand above and beyond their neighbors."

Or as Pennsylvania Insurance Commissioner Herbert S. Denenberg put it in a Latin slogan that adorned his office: *Populus iamdudum defutatus est.* "The public has been screwed long enough."

176

chapter 4
Enough Is Enough: Expansionist Juggernaut over Graceful Boston

> The whole point of autocracy, Crispus observed, is that accounts will not come right unless the ruler is their only auditor.
> —TACITUS, *The Annals of Imperial Rome*

Section I   An Impacted Neighborhood: The People of the Fenway v. the Christian Science International Center

If an incorrigible rapist is out in the community stalking ingenuous victims, it sure helps to be nonprofit and to exude ultrarespectability.

Though a native Bostonian, I and many slumbering others belatedly awoke only in the late 1960's to the staggering dimensions of what the Christian Science Mother Church was up to. The Church has the patience appropriate to solid, nonspeculative wealth, and it is low profile to the point of facelessness. Who could name a single leader of that religious body, or a prominent Christian Scientist known for his/her active church role—dead or alive—other than Mary Baker Eddy?

177

In a general and loose way, Bostonians in the Back Bay–Fenway section long knew that the Mother Church was buying up private houses, theaters, apartment buildings with ground-floor storefronts, and whatever else owners were willing to sell. The target area ranged from and along Huntington Avenue up to Boylston Street via Massachusetts Avenue, and included all the narrow and well-kept-up side streets. By 1973, purchases covered thirty-two acres of choice midcity real estate. Money for the multiple acquisitions was never an object. Parcel by parcel, building by building, assembled block by assembled block, just about every lot and site except Horticultural Hall and historic Symphony Hall were snapped up.

Everything operated on the layaway plan: homeowners who sold out were "graciously" permitted to remain and pay rent to the Church, until . . . (No date was ever assigned to "until." Since hope springs eternal, no doubt some who sold their homes dreamed of living out their days undisturbed.) To a nonarchitecturally trained eye, the area in toto seems at least equal to the broad expanse of Times Square from 42nd Street to 50th Street. Under section 112 of the National Housing Act, the city of Boston was eligible for $2 in federal renewal grants for every $1 spent by the Church and other expanding tax-exempt institutions for the procurement *and clearing* of land within one mile of the Fenway Urban Renewal Project. One need not be cynical to stop looking for any further explanation of why city officials, regardless of who was mayor, went along with all the highfalutin and pompous schemes for wholesale community rape.

Because the process was so stealthy, and because the Church's leadership was so tightlipped, thirty-five years went by before the grand design for an International

178

Center surfaced. (Architectural drawings dated 1930 have been uncovered by community activists.) In the area, tenants and small shopkeepers on ever shorter leases had known that "something" was going on that was utterly beyond their control. They were chronically uneasy. But what does one do when hard information is deliberately withheld? To whom on the outside does one turn for help and experienced guidance—especially in the early decades when nothing even resembling a tough tenant movement existed?

It's hard enough to tackle and sink one's teeth into a well-heeled, fast-buck commercial developer with good political connections, who is modestly and more or less openly trying to assemble one's street, or at most a square block. Unless one is a veteran of block-busting wars, how does one even conceive of locking horns with a closed, unhurried religious institution?

Because everything was so vague and formless, my guess is that nearly everyone who felt threatened sat back and trusted in magic, with each individual praying that he or she would somehow be spared on the day of churchly judgment.

It never works out that way. In their institutional incarnation, religious groups are no less ruthless than any other builders of empires.

Until I myself had had prolonged personal contact with a deaf and unresponsive institution, I never could understand the dozens of parents in the small Welsh mining village a decade ago who continued to send their children to a schoolhouse directly threatened by a huge accumulated slag heap. For years, under both Labor and Conservative governments, the parents had protested to the Coal Board in London. The careerists who staffed the

179

board took absolutely no action. And one fine day, as frequently predicted, the unstable balance was tipped. The slag came pouring down a hillside, killing all in its path.

Between 1970 and 1973, fellow tenants and I fought (successfully in the end) to get the New York housing bureaucracy to crack down on our hospital landlord for life-threatening code violations. While awaiting the invocation of criminal sanctions (mild fines), I suddenly realized a transformation that had come over us. Even with our strong determination to exact justice, a certain fatalism had seeped into the equation. Violations or no violations, life has to go on. Working people have to report to jobs every day. Yes, those terribly unsafe ceilings might collapse at any moment, inflicting instant death on anyone underneath. But given the unavailability of a choice in housing and given the anarchy in corrupt don't-care big-city housing bureaucracies, what more besides steady protest can one do except start a revolution? And given the reality that, for both educational and parental reasons, children must be packed off to school, what else could those Welsh parents have done?

So, too, in Boston's fashionable Back Bay, where the prospect of a bulldozed home or small business was the nagging equivalent of the long-standing slag heap and the counterpart of the long-dangerous ceilings.

From Christian Science sources—specifically, from the 1974 annual convention—about all we knew about the organization is that it "is not in debt" and is "financially solvent." Which is what everyone had surmised all along. DeWitt John, the new Church board chairman and, until 1970, the editor of the *Christian*

Science Monitor, told his 6,500 coreligionists at the convention that the new $75 million international headquarters had been paid for upon completion in 1973.

What the surrounding neighborhood knew directly by then was that 137 merchants were ultimately slated to be driven out, with an initial seventy already out by mid-1973. Figures on the total number of residents evicted or eased out are hard to come by. Who kept tally over a forty-five-year period? But in view of the wide thirty-two-acre area and the number of demolished buildings, the total human casualties in dislocation could easily and conservatively reach high into the four-figures range. In 1972, the Church's own development consultant acknowledged that "construction of the Center, including perimeter parcels, calls for removal of a total of 553 housing units." That was a good decade after demolition was well along, to make way (as is typical of expanding urban institutions) for large, lucrative, temporary parking facilities.

By the early 1960's the Church had acquired, on Huntington Avenue, the Uptown Theatre and, on Massachusetts Avenue, Loew's State Theatre. After rechristening as the Back Bay Theatre, Loew's had become the home of the Boston Opera Company and of the Boston Ballet. From childhood, I remember both buildings as two of Boston's most graceful movie houses. Well before the end of the 1960's, the Fine Arts Theatre, which specialized in showing foreign films, had been knocked down after the building housing it had become part of the Church's portfolio in real estate. In 1967, the Church rejected out of hand the idea of building over and around the Back Bay Theatre in order to save from demolition the

181

cultural activities that were centered there. In a statement that qualifies as the quintessential creed of institutional imperialists, Carl B. Rechner, the same development consultant for the Mother Church, is quoted in the *Christian Science Monitor* (March 14, 1967) as saying:

> The building itself is quite obsolete. It is today an economic misfit. It has no parking, no air-conditioning. The seats are small and uncomfortable. The building's income doesn't even meet its operating expenses, and there is an annual deficit. This building is too large for opera. I'm told that the ideal size for opera is about 2000 seats. The Back Bay Theatre has more than 3400 seats.

Under the Church's rigid box-office means test, virtually every opera house, concert hall and museum around the world would become an immediate candidate for the wrecking ball.

It strains the imagination to conceive of upright and decorous Church officials greasing the itchy palms of Boston's urban-renewal Establishment. Unless appearances are totally deceptive, that really doesn't seem to be their modus operandi. Yet, in geometry, we're taught that things equal to the same thing are equal to each other. By whatever devices, the Christian Science Center has managed to circumvent 1965 promises to the community that were made by the Boston Redevelopment Authority (BRA) when urban renewal for that area was first being broached.

To the City Council, BRA promised to spare buildings that could be rehabilitated. BRA also pledged 3,500 new low-to-moderate-rent apartments. By 1973, it had scaled this figure down to 2,654, with only 1,552 scheduled to fall within the promised rental range. After eight years, only 324 had been made ready for occupancy.

For a money maker, the Christian Science Center had developer Max Wasserman erect an eleven-story, 508-unit, two-block-long luxury structure called Church Park that stretches 782 feet along the west side of Massachusetts Avenue—the largest apartment building in New England, with 60,000 square feet of commercial space on the mall level (half of it still unoccupied after having been two years on the rental market). So far as BRA's commitment to relocate merchants is concerned, Church Park has meant nothing to the shopkeepers who were displaced. For the monthly storefront rents per square foot would have jumped from the merchants' previous $2.50–$3.50 range at their old sites to the $8.50–$10.50 range. In each business week, how many more pounds of cod, scrod, mackerel, hake and flounder would Folsom's Seafood Market—a fixture on Massachusetts Avenue for as far back as I can remember—have had to sell as a Church Park commercial tenant in order to meet a tripled or quadrupled rent? And for its customers, how high would Folsom's have had to jack up retail prices if increased sales volume proved insufficient to cover the new rent?

It almost goes without saying that it was a $19 million public loan from the Massachusetts Housing Finance Agency that set the Church Park project in motion. MHFA financing, as distinct from conventional financing, reduces interest rates and extends amortization payments over forty years. It amounts, of course, to a public subsidy for a public screwing.

Small "relocated" merchants like Folsom's, who do little more than earn a week's pay, feel lucky to be among the few to have obtained five-year leases farther up the avenue—at exorbitant rents. (In one eating place now under that half-decade sword of Damocles, the rent jumped from $400 to $1,400, and the cost of an egg-salad sandwich, for example, jumped from fifty-five cents to $1.05.) And after 1978 when the leases run out? Finished. Because by then their present locations will also have been swallowed up in the divine design.

In the *Christian Science Monitor* of March 26, 1973, a straight-faced Church board of directors assured the public that "the Mother Church does not seek the ownership of land or buildings as a means of investing its funds or for profit. Where the Church has owned rental property that was acquired for needed improvement or redevelopment, it has consistently kept rentals below market, in effect subsidizing the tenant and operating at a loss. This is why it will not develop or build, and does not wish to be a landlord or own real estate as an investment."

Like the small merchants, the residential evictees were also out of luck. Few of them could meet the apartment rents in Church Park, which range from $217 to $290 for one bedroom, and from $310 to $410 for two bedrooms. To add esthetic insult to the monetary injury, the tasteless, uptight and constipated architecture of Church Park flagrantly violates the 1965 BRA vow that both rehabilitation and new construction would be "compatible with the original layout and structural character of the buildings."

Sharon Basco, writing in the weekly *Boston Phoenix* in 1973, cites a conversation with a BRA official that shows the willful intent to renege on commitments

184

to the community. A neighborhood leader, Karla Johnson of the Fenway Interagency Group (FIG), asked David Baker, assistant director for the local urban-renewal project, why certain buildings were being torn down instead of being rehabilitated in tune with the neighborhood.

"Those are solid old buildings. Why can't we save them?" she asked.

"Because it wouldn't look right to have a three-story brick building next to an eleven-story cement building."

Since the 1950's, the BRA has an unbroken record of joining with private developers in promising anything and everything to an about-to-be-raped community in order to induce easy and unprotested moveouts. In 1965, BRA promised the Fenway–Back Bay community sufficient "park and recreational areas and facilities . . . with special consideration for the health, safety and welfare of children residing in the project area." Those pledges too were broken, as fully intended from the start. Which was why, in June 1973, during a community protest at the Christian Science International Center, children in the area swam in the Church's two-acre reflecting pool, which is only to look at and ogle, and by no means to swim in and cool off in.

The occasion for the demonstration was the Church's three-day annual meeting, which drew 12,000 Christian Scientists from around the world. The meeting was closed to the press and the public. Alton Davis, consultant to the Church's board of directors, told reporters that the protest "has had no effect on the annual meeting." Davis added, with the noblesse oblige of those who forget that the First Amendment does cover demonstrations: "We have exercised patience, allowing community

185

people to carry out their activities." Inside the meeting, the faithful flock was "assured" that Church officials "had been in touch with" the Fenway group.

It is all the more ironic that this king-sized development should have been slipped over on Boston's Back Bay, traditionally the city's most liberal, most libertarian, most artistic, most musical, most education-oriented section. If any part of Boston should have been able to organize itself, to stall this ecclesiastical coup d'état for at least a half decade,* to bargain with brass knuckles if unable to stop the takeover permanently, and to settle for a much scaled-down empire, it should have been this unblighted area next door to Symphony Hall, Horticultural Hall, the old Repertory Theatre, the New England Conservatory of Music, and Jordan Hall (the Sunday evening meeting hall of famed Ford Hall Forum). The then Boston renewal chief Edward J. Logue was correct when he called the Fenway and the Back Bay "one of the most exciting areas in the city," containing much of the charm and flavor that distinguish Boston from other U.S. cities.

But by keeping tight secrets and by cultivating its low profile for forty-five years, the Church slickly forestalled any uprising by the unruly and the great unwashed. With the acquiescence of the federal courts, it even got away with dispossessing seventeen stores and fifty-four

---

* Before the State Department of Commerce and Development in 1967, one attorney for a local businessman argued that the Constitution prohibits a church from taking property by eminent domain for private commercial use. In 1965, to no avail, the separation-of-church-and-state issue had been raised by a city councilman, because of the Church's heavy involvement, through its proposed new center, in the governmental Fenway urban-renewal project.

186

families from a row of structurally sound buildings in the 200 block of Massachusetts Avenue, just to create an expansive front lawn (a landscaped, open-plaza area that, especially amidst a socially dangerous housing shortage, can only be labeled superfluous). Let 'em eat grass and sleep in it. A together community might have been able to provide the solidarity and the collective moral fiber to persuade at least one owner in each targeted block to refuse to sell out—whatever the tempting price—to irresponsible rapists. That kind of checkerboard recalcitrance alone could have stymied the empire-builders indefinitely.

To "balance" the new architecture, Church Park II, an eleven-story twin, is planned for the future. After a May 1972 demonstration by the elderly in the community, the Church consented to include 177 subsidized apartments in Church Park I. Rents would be limited to one fourth of the tenant's income. It was a tiny enough concession in view of the official 1965 BRA promise that low- and moderate-rent housing would be built on that very site.

Where small family-type businessmen have been forced out—in some cases, after several generations on the same spot—high-priced, chain-type enterprises have moved in, and the whole tone of the area has changed. In 1973, as the displaced children swam in the reflecting pool outside the Church's annual meeting, their parents were performing a community-written play about Christian Science Urban Renewal. They also mounted a mock funeral procession and a funeral service, with two women of the area hauling a large black coffin.

In a litany that greatly embarrassed those running the convention, the mourners chanted:

"O God, who can't read or write, who is on

187

welfare and who is treated like garbage: Help us to know you.

"O God, whose job at Hutchinson's Market is gone because the market closed and left the neighborhood . . .

"O God, whose church down the street has helped to close our shops and move away our neighbors,

"O God, who is old and lives on forty dollars a month in one crummy room and can't get outside,

"O God, who lives in the projects of federal, state and city institutional indifference,

"O God, whose toys are broken bottles, tin cans, whose play yard is garbage and debris, and whose play house is the floors of condemned buildings . . .

"O God, who is unorganized and without strength to change her world, her metropolis, her city, her neighborhood, Help us to join you.

"O God, who is overwhelmed by the indifference, and apathy and status quo of so many who are good Christians, and in church on Sunday,

"O God, who carries a sign, sits on the ground, dumps debris at City Hall, strikes his rent, pickets oppressors. . . . Help us to join you."

The mourners deposited the coffin on the steps of the Mother Church and threw dead flowers and dirt on top before departing. Among the demonstrators were community people who originally came from other "renewed" areas of the city, only to have BRA and the Church Center overtake them at their new residences (a not unusual bit of double and even triple jeopardy that the defenseless face in today's urban areas). Among such two-time displacees is an increasing number who now say, in almost exactly the same words: "There's no place left to go and hide. Problems must be faced where they first arise." The ancient U.S. tradition, originally launched by many of the seventeenth-century emigrants to the New World, of "moving on" to a problem-free Eden no longer works, if indeed it ever did.

Ten months after the mock funeral, in April 1974, a federal court class suit, originally brought in 1972 to regulate future urban renewal around the Church Center, ended in a consent agreement that has the force and effect of a court order. The agreement gives community residents a formal planning role. In the absence of any environmental impact statement, the U.S. Court of Appeals a year earlier had enjoined new construction in the Symphony Hall area. The chief judge, Frank M. Coffin, who wrote the majority opinion granting the injunction, also filed a concurring opinion. In it, he indicated he would have gone further and immediately ordered an environmental review for the 60 percent uncompleted Fenway project.

The agreement, which was signed by attorneys for the defaulting BRA, for the Church and for the eleven plaintiffs, set up the Fenway Project Area Committee (FEN PAC). BRA pledged $103,000 for a three-year budget, a small staff and office space, in order to assure that FEN PAC "actively participates in all stages of planning." (With the six-figure budget as leverage, BRA later managed to take into camp the FEN PAC members—another indication that final victories are an illusion for any community that doesn't remain eternally vigilant and battle-ready.)

The agreement covered eight parcels of land, mostly vacant lots. At least 25 percent of the new housing units on most of the parcels was to be for low-income

189

rentals. One of the church's parcels was to be limited to a height of twelve stories. The other church parcels could rise to no more than twenty stories, and would have to contain a mixture of low- and moderate-rent apartments.

Because of the community's late start, it took years to bring the Church even partly to bay. Given today's emphasis on neighborhood participation in planning, one can say that the Church barely squeaked through in time with its empire-building. Had its unilateral forty-five-year plan been scheduled to unfold from, say, 1965 to the year 2010, the alerted people of the Back Bay, riding the crest of the times, would have easily been able to strangle the idea in its cradle. Temperamentally as well as politically, an ultrarespectable institution with an un-ruffled and trouble-free image is highly vulnerable to community wrath when it is unleashed, through street action, in early, timely stages.

Whenever I walk toward Cambridge, through Christian Science turf where the once-busy sidewalks now seem silent and almost deserted, I feel morally certain that, if a decade ago even a handful of "unruly" Fenway–Back Bay residents had occupied the Mother Church and its administrative buildings for a week at the most—thereby focusing world attention on the top-secret plans for community rape—the Grand Design would have begun to wither on the vine. For the planners of the Christian Scientist International Church Center are a nervous lot not psychologically equipped to handle confrontations. Even better than some municipal office where two-bit corruption is rampant, they exemplify what an activist neighbor Bernie Goodman told me early in the Columbus Hospital fight about government officials, about private developers, about institutional expansionists, and about others who are not out to serve the people:

190

For good and sufficient reason, what they really fear is the people. "Us," said Bernie, "and people like us."

Section II   *Unhousing the Poor: University of Massachusetts at Boston v. People of Columbia Point*

There's nothing like a commuter college you can't commute to . . . but there will be in September [1973] when UMASS opens for business at inaccessible Columbia Point.

—the *Boston Phoenix,* January 7, 1973

It's not often that a seaside marsh filled with twenty-five years of garbage wins a political popularity contest and becomes the new urban campus of a state university.

Past service as a garbage dump wasn't Columbia Point's only liability in the site-selection process. At added cost and trouble, deep piles were needed to support campus buildings. Gas pumps were required to dispose of the methane gas produced by decomposing garbage. Because Boston's Logan International Airport is very close by, builders had to provide extra soundproofing in an effort to reduce the noise from jet planes taking off and landing.

In the blunt calculations of a task force, Columbia Point's glaring disadvantages were outweighed by one paramount transcendent political consideration: the opportunity to isolate and sidetrack a feared student body onto what one white Dorchester legislator called "the largest underdeveloped tract in the city." The task force's language was even more pointed:

"[W]hat better place could be found for unruly and possibly fractious students than on a peninsula jutting

191

into the harbor with only one access road and 6,000 housing project residents for their only neighbors?"

To almost every Bostonian, Columbia Point over the last few years has conjured up strongly negative racial connotations of end-of-the-line blight, mainly because of the violence associated with the large, twenty-two-year-old, 1,499-unit housing project there. Nationally, Columbia Point came into focus in the autumn of 1973 when a retired white resident was stoned to death while fishing near his home. (Both Columbia Point and the larger Dorchester community are parts of the city of Boston.)

In 1968, Robert Quinn, the Dorchester legislator who later became the Massachusetts Attorney General, saw the racial composition and the poverty component of the housing project as a threat to the city's stability. He suggested "dispersing the residents, because so many people concentrated is not good. They become alienated and isolated." Quinn's "solution" as well as his "underdeveloped" remark were in the context of the then-frequent ghetto and campus rebellions across the country, including what is known as "Boston's police riot" in Roxbury the previous summer.

Given the student body composition at other new inner-city colleges cropping up in that period across the country, it seemed reasonable to assume that U Mass Boston would attract a majority of lower-income students, with heavy representation of minority groups. And at first, at its temporary downtown Boston location, it did. On this disadvantaged-student theme, a majority of the legislature was sold on the justification of setting up still another university in the Greater Boston area, where there already were over seventy institutions of higher learning.

The legislature authorized the creation of the

Boston campus, but did not choose the permanent site. Enrollment opened in the fall of 1965 at the temporary headquarters, and "temporary" lasted eight years, until September 1973. Meanwhile, largely out of public view, a war over site selection raged. Originally, the university itself suggested a readily accessible fourteen-acre campus in fashionable Copley Square, in the Back Bay, right in the heart of the city and practically next door to the excellent Boston Public Library. With their eyes on the coast-to-coast campus turmoil, the business and civic voices of Back Bay were vociferously against it. Leading the howling pack was John Hancock Mutual Life Insurance, which had designs on the Copley Square area for a high-rise office building of its own—the ultimately famous one where strong gusty winds in the early 1970's kept blowing out millions of dollars worth of window panes. Later, it turned out that, as of 1966, John Hancock owned 1.2 million square feet (forty acres) of land at Columbia Point where eventually the new campus went up.

In the top-level power struggle over the choice of site, the Boston Redevelopment Authority (BRA), which since the 1950's has specialized in urban dislocation, was another powerhouse. The BRA staff published a brochure entitled *Campus by the Sea,* with flagrantly inaccurate data on Columbia Point's accessibility by car and by mass transit. On the face of it, one would hardly expect some 120–130 acres of isolated, vacant dump land to be well served by roads, busses and rapid transit facilities. In the end, it was BRA director Edward Logue, whose power at times seemed as great as, or greater than, that of both the mayor and the governor, who selected the Point for the $355 million public investment. Given BRA's history and Logue's connections, he could hardly have been unaware of the lush opportunities for quick profits that any such major development brings in its train.

Before urban planner Robert Wood became president of the University of Massachusetts (at its main campus in the lovely, midstate town of Amherst), he openly regarded as "atrocious" the bitterly resented proposal to invade the troubled and remote Columbia Point ghetto with a huge new campus—especially when alternative and much more accessible sites were available. Once Wood assumed the presidency, however, he abruptly switched his position and endorsed the Point campus enthusiastically. Wood's about-face is not at all unique in the pressure chamber atmosphere of institutions. As Andrew Hacker wrote in *The New Sociology:*

> These institutions have lives and purposes of their own. If the man at the top sits at the controls, the car rides on rails he cannot move. . . . The time has come when the institution in fact directs the man who in theory presides over it.

The general expectation was that the Point's inaccessibility would inevitably produce tremendous student-faculty pressure for at-hand housing. From the beginning, provision for student housing at the Point was never in the university's construction plans. Understandably, in this light, the housing-project residents have all along felt threatened. By any number of episodes and straws in the wind, they have been convinced that the school is really out to push them out of their homes, which would then be appropriately renovated for faculty and for an increasingly middle-class student body—the Commonwealth magically laying its hands on the requisite

194

monies which are not now available to correct the abysmal slum conditions there.

Like all public-housing authorities, the Boston Housing Authority chronically teeters on the brink of bankruptcy. Despite an overall policy of encouraging attrition by not renting apartments once vacated, the BHA chairman ruled that U Mass students who fell within the Authority's income guidelines would be eligible to rent apartments in the twenty-year-old decrepit Columbia Point project. As of 1974, one out of every four apartments at the Point was vacant, partly because of the Authority's long-time neglect of repairs, and very much because of the lack of adequate security. (The Point's crime rate in 1969 was 179.71 per 1,000 population—the highest of any housing project in the city—compared to 65.77 for Boston as a whole.)

To the old-time residents, newly conferred student eligibility for apartments could only be interpreted as the camel's nose under the tent. The ultimate fear is that the project will be purchased outright by the university for university use, leaving the present tenants—50.8 percent of whom are below the poverty line; 55.5 percent of whose households are headed by women—with no place to go. In light of the steady racial trend in the university's admissions as more white, more suburban and more higher-income students apply, the much maligned housing project, if placed under campus ownership, would change its present nonwhite coloration, and would become as white as the university itself. Boston's officialdom paid no attention when an elected committee of the project's tenants came up with an imaginative design plan to renovate and socialize the dehumanized project in order to save it for its present non-student, low-income residents.

Columbia Point is so far off the beaten path, anti-pollution considerations on the hemmed-in peninsula would so limit the number of on-campus *commuter* parking spaces, it would take so many years to extend the city's rapid-transit system to the campus (even if the $9 million were readily available to build a proposed new nearby station) and to extend the subway lines from several different directions, that a prudent person attuned to social dynamics would bet on eventual university encroachment on the entire Point, and most especially on the housing project. By the early 1970's, the poorer minority-group students constituted only one third of the student body—the rest being white kids whose grades didn't qualify them for Ivy League schools, or whose parents couldn't quite afford the cost of private tuition.

Two radical community groups, Dorchester Tenants Action Council and The People First (TPF), had foreseen and projected all this as the new campus plunked itself down in the area. But once $355 million is placed on the scales in any community, the balance of power becomes so tipped—even without the barrel of a gun—that events flow "logically" and inexorably. This is quite aside from the difficulty of organizing large numbers of beaten-down, demoralized housing-project tenants, who exist from one inadequate pay or welfare check to the next.

So instead of U Mass Boston being a "war college" for Kennedy-type managerial liberals—that is to say, a base for training working-class and minority-group cadres who will catch and co-opt potentially disruptive "elements"—the curriculum is under some pressure to swing to the liberal artsy orientation that one group of academic planners originally advocated.

If the university sooner or later takes over Columbia Point in its entirety, then poor people will be out of their housing project, scattered to who-knows-where. Restless low-income students will be out of the classrooms. A "dying" and embarrassing ghetto, with its drug and crime problems, will have been eliminated (in one of those final solutions). And all will be well in the town of Boston—until the explosions come.

Will that course of events have been determined by purely impersonal forces, without deliberate human intervention? Under faculty adviser Hubie Jones, a group of seven U Mass Action Program students took a closer and a skeptical look at what was going on. They reported their findings with considerable indignation.

In 1971, for example, the sprawling project lost the shopping center that a West German company had established years earlier. One by one, the stores in a 280,000-square-foot mall closed down. When the supermarket went out of business, the project's tenants had to be satisfied—in the cradle of liberty—with mobile trucks hawking overpriced, insanitary food, flea-market style.

Without basic life-support systems for the residents, frustration and desperation inevitably continue to mount. Efforts at self-help, including collective actions to set up community-security programs, were unable to attract public funds. Municipal police protection, the students found, was minimal. Only three officers patrolled the high-crime project from 8 A.M. to midnight—until, like magic, the city assigned additional cops to the Point once the University of Massachusetts set up shop there. With the new Point patrols came an eight-foot-high fence, sealing off the campus compound from the project.

"The 'containment' strategy hasn't worked, and

it won't work," says Hubie Jones, the faculty adviser who supervised the student survey. He points to a spillover of vandalism from the project to the campus, including severe damage to the gymnasium floor.

Mr. Jones, a social worker by training who formerly headed the Roxbury Multi-Service Center, anticipates the scenario:

"The stabbing of a white coed will provide the rationale to close the project down."

If indeed that happens, it won't be some random, unforeseeable circumstance. Equally predictable and devastating, in the context of Boston's present racial atmosphere, is the likely citywide political impact.

In this setting of conscious social neglect and of waiting for the inevitable to occur, is it relevant to wonder about the long-range designs of the U Mass planners? And is it appropriate again to recall the legal adage that, like individuals, institutions are presumed to intend the natural consequences of their acts?

Section III   Logan Airport

Letter to Editor of *Boston Globe* by two East Bostonians December 29, 1973.

Please allow us to explain to your readers . . . who do not understand East Bostonians in our opposition to Logan Airport expansion. . . .

We've yielded hundreds of homes and thousands of citizens for the C-1 North, elevated highway. Congestion on streets and pollution . . . our reward. . . .

We've yielded waterfront properties to construct highrise apartment buildings. Our gift . . . deprivation of access to waterfront usage.

To the airline industry—we've sacrificed 75 acres of recreational area (Wood Island and Amerina parks). . . .

Our gifts in return . . . noise to destroy our hearing and disruption of education . . . plus enough air pollution to put it far above that which the government determines a tolerable level. . . .

More waterfront property is being sought for airport related industries. . . .

How much more are we expected to yield?

With Massport's intentions of extending two runways, construction of STOL runway and implementation of Category II system on Runway 15R-33L not only will it subject more people to air and noise pollution but a multitude of dangers. . . .

July 1973 brought the worst disaster ever at Logan when a DC 9 crashed. That plane could have been forced to use Runway 15R-33L if the Category II ILS System had been implemented as proposed, at the residential end. . . .

Any plane tragedy could not only wipe out the Neptune Road residential area, but also cause serious damage to our Eagle Hill section. . . . Of course, this does not exclude possibilities of damage to East Boston and Chelsea should a crash occur into the oil stored under the flight path of Runway 15R-33L.

Must such a holocaust happen before it is realized that the citizens of East Boston were right? Pray God that all that are responsible will see the light before it is too late.

John Porzio
Rev. E. Marshall Bevins,
Cochairmen, Legislative Council, East Boston

In the long history of empire preservation, it is not at all unusual for individuals to get so deeply committed that saving the empire becomes more important than life itself.

At the end of the film *State of Siege,* this phenomenon emerged when the kidnapped CIA agent in Uruguay defied the Tupamaros guerrillas. He opted to go on upholding the interests of the United States empire, instead of striving to save his own life. After his execution, the movie's final scene shows his successor from Washington arriving, with family, at the Montevideo airport waving, smiling, almost as if his predecessor had just gone home for a routine reassignment, instead of in a flag-draped coffin.

At first glance, it may appear to be melodramatic to draw a political parallel between a tough, hard-lining, police-trained, gun-toting CIA agent and Edward J. King, long the all-powerful executive director of the Massachusetts Port Authority (Massport), which among other responsibilities regulates airports.

King lives in Winthrop, Massachusetts, on the edge of Logan Airport's expanding runways. King maintained that the intolerable health-destroying twenty-four-hour din never bothered him, but that the state's peace-torn economy did.

Around 1920, appalled by the first-time military use of air power during World War I, poet John Drinkwater wrote a famous letter to the *Times* of London, in which he proposed a total global ban on the building and flying of planes. A half century later, at least in this country which was untouched by the aerial bombardments of two world wars, the plane has not yet suffered the loss of glamour and prestige that polluting cars have—except among the neighbors of big, overwhelming airports.

As the letter to the editor of the *Boston Globe* made clear, the problems besetting the Logan Airport community are not limited to eighty decibels of around-the-clock noise. East Bostonians never know when dozens or hundreds of them may be wiped out without a moment's warning. Massport for years has been pushing for a third tunnel under Boston Harbor, connecting the mainland directly with the airport—a further disruption of East Boston which the residents fear would, in turn, encourage more expansion of the existing airport sprawl.

In addition, Massport has stood foursquare behind a proposal to build on the East Boston waterfront a $37 million container terminal for ships, on the grounds it is needed to handle expected growth in harbor traffic. Residents have been against it because of the anticipated additional truck traffic. The C. E. Maguire consulting firm did a feasibility study for Massport. Originally, it maintained that, of a half dozen possible sites, East Boston was the "least acceptable." Later, Maguire shifted and termed the area the "most suitable."

In the decades before institutional expansionism became a serious national problem touching millions of us, East Bostonians who were fighting airport expansionism didn't enjoy many pockets of support or even a great amount of empathy outside the boundaries of their own island. As long as the airlines and auto industry were riding high, with "progress" accepted by most as a basic premise, the rest of Boston, let alone the rest of the state and nation, really wasn't listening to all those Italian malcontents over near Logan.

Thus while largely unsuccessful to date, the long list of official scalps won and citizen scalps lost has made East Bostonians perhaps the most cohesive and the most sophisticated of all communities seeking to defend and preserve their homes and their sanity. Even if the tide of battle begins to shift in their favor, they have learned enough over the past forty years to know that their struggle must go on indefinitely. Expansionist forces never give up. In other words, in any root sense in this complex social structure, nothing will really change fundamentally until everything changes. If one theme underlies the fight that has preoccupied East Bostonians for so long, it probably is the demand for transportation for the people who can't afford cars or planes. In 1932, an Italian grocer named Vitagliano lost his grocery store—and thus his livelihood—to Sumner Tunnel, the first of the two existing underwater tunnels providing passage for cars from downtown Boston to East Boston.

Today, that grocer's son, John Vitagliano, heads up East Boston's Little City Hall (one of a number of Little City Halls designed to bring Boston's municipal services to the city's multiple communities). In that capacity, he helps head the interminable war against Logan's expansion, and he once asked publicly: "Who is the most powerful administrator in the state, Francis Sargent [the governor at that time] or Edward King [the executive director of Massport]?"

It was not an idle question. Once the governor appoints the seven-member Massport board, he loses all control over the agency. By law, it is answerable to no one. It collects the quarter tolls on the busy Mystic River Bridge, and it can and does put those millions of dollars —and the accompanying political muscle—to any use that it sees fit. Currently, it wishes to spend over $47 million to extend Runway 9 by 1,855 feet and Runway 4-Left by 2,000 feet, and to build a new 3,820 foot runway on East Boston's Bird Island Flats. In May 1974, by a 6–1 vote, the Massport board awarded a $7.66 million contract for

202

the job to a Framingham contractor—over what the *Christian Science Monitor* called "stiff opposition from residents."

Over a five-year period, Massport director King and his registered lobbyists killed two hundred bills introduced by state legislators to bring Logan Airport under control. In 1973, the lobbyists turned up to defeat, 179–52, in the House of Representatives, a bill that would have given the governor veto power over any Massport project costing over $1 million—such as the airport runway plans.

The proposed sacrifice of the Bird Island Flats to "progress" reminds East Bostonians that, in 1965, Logan expansion obliterated seventy acres of Wood Island Park —leaving one solitary tree standing. For easily discernible psychological reasons and because of upward social aspirations, some U.S. ethnic groups are not particularly known for militancy—like elements of the black bourgeoisie who fantasize that they have it made. But there have been times in the past when Italian and Irish residents have resorted to civil disobedience by blocking Massport construction crews bound for the airport. If pushed beyond endurance at a time of hopeless economic hardship, that spirit of resistance could begin to hark back to the frontier days of defending one's home against marauders.

Indispensable, as always, for information and morale purposes, has been a local paper, the *East Boston Community News*. Boston's metropolitan dailies certainly carry the Logan news highlights from time to time. But, as has been pointed out before, any community under siege needs its own "community bulletin board"—which is what a good, *engagé* community newspaper usually evolves into.

To East Bostonians there is nothing "unbalanced" about yelling to the outside world, day after day, that one of Logan's flight paths takes incoming and departing planes directly over the Samuel Adams Elementary School, and that some homes would find themselves within a thousand feet of the proposed new runway.

It was with this in mind that East Bostonians, joined by the City of Boston, went into both state and federal courts in June 1974, to seek orders against extension of two runways and the building of a short-takeoff-and-landing (STOL) strip. Superior Court Judge Harry Zarrow immediately granted a temporary injunction against Massport and Perini Construction Company after being told that increased air traffic would cause "serious disruption" to schools in the area, and that Massport had ignored the requirement of the Environmental Protection Act for a study of the impact the construction would have. Another party to the suit was a coalition of environmentally concerned neighbors of the airport, the Massachusetts Air Pollution and Noise Abatement Committee (MAPNAC).

MAPNAC rejected out of hand a "memorandum of understanding" between Massport and the State Secretary of Transportation to "restrict" use of the new runways. No community with four decades of experience under its belt falls for *any* provisions of a pact that go contrary to the expansionist nature of institutions. If Logan or any other airport gets new runways, planes will be around "necessitating" their use at all times. The bureaucrats know this as well as the people. But they never tire of efforts to con and soothe. Said MAPNAC about the "memorandum of understanding": "[There is] nothing [in it] to prevent a future Massport board and a future state administration from scrapping the so-called restrictions." Poor people, Manhattan poverty lawyer Lester Evens once said, are so trusting. But not poor people with

204

forty years of scars, scratches, fractures and concussions in their collective memories.

In the lawsuit, MAPNAC and the City of Boston also charged that Massport reached the crucial decision to proceed with construction in a closed executive session, in violation of the Massachusetts open-meeting law.

Like Job's, East Boston's afflictions never seem to abate. At exactly the same time as the airport's neighbors were embroiled in a showdown on the new-runways issue, Massport announced its invitation for an Anglo-French supersonic Concorde (SST) to fly to Boston from Paris in three and one half hours for dedication of a new $32 million International Terminal at Logan on June 13, 1974.

Aside from objecting, on even a one-visit basis, to the Concorde's well-known excessive noise and its questionable safety, the Citizens League Against the Sonic Boom feared that the flight would be a precedent and an excuse for easing the way to eventual regular SST landings at Logan. Sweetly, in all innocence, as if it had a reputation for honor and honesty, Massport of course denied any such ulterior motive. But its denials carry no weight among East Bostonians, who know that efforts to sell the Concorde to United States airlines are continuing, despite the plane's noise, despite its cost, and despite its limited range.

From Washington, Massachusetts Senator Edward M. Kennedy denounced Massport for its "lack of compassion for the communities neighboring Logan Airport." Kennedy continued:

Massport has ignored the concerns of local residents and moved forward with runway extension projects prior to the completion of an approved master plan. . . .

Next week, the landing of the supersonic transport will be the latest affront in a decade of decisions by the Massachusetts Port Authority which is incompatible with the goals of the communities bordering Logan.

In what the *Boston Globe* called Kennedy's "strongly worded statement," the Senator encouraged residents to continue their fight to make Massport members "responsive to the environmental and social costs of their decisions."

Largely on technicalities, both the U.S. District Court in Boston and the usually open, sensitive and receptive U.S. Court of Appeals for the First Circuit refused to enjoin the Concorde landing. With the appropriate fanfare, the plane indeed came. In the courts, the supersonic issue, like companion airport issues, was primarily political. But except among Logan's harassed neighbors, city and state voting patterns so far do not turn on public reaction to Massport's highhanded policies. There are only 16,368 voters in East Boston—less than 7 percent of the city's total. Which means that dependable and permanent legislative and injunctive relief remains something for the indefinite future—unless, of course, dozens of children burn up in the Adams School as a result of a statistically foreshadowed plane crash, or unless hundreds of passengers and residents are incinerated in an inferno around the oil tanks stored near Runway 15R-33L. At that point it would be hard to find a frightened judge not eager and ready to sign all necessary permanent injunctions, even if he should have to make up law on the spot.

When the Massachusetts House was debating the bill to return Massport to something resembling accountability, an opponent argued that the legislation would make Massport a political football.

Retorted Representative Barney Frank, whose district encompasses Beacon Hill and parts of the Back Bay: "Anybody who doesn't think Massport is political must have been out of town for the last ten years." On criticism, Massport is as supersensitive and as highhanded as some egomaniacal ward politician from the Daley or Rizzo machines. In mid-1974 the agency placed against the *East Boston Community News* an "embargo on the expeditious flow of information."

In the summer of 1974, the tides of battle surged back and forth. On August 1, a federal judge in Boston said he had "no present power to enjoin" the Logan Airport expansion because, as of that date, the Federal Aviation Administration had not yet approved a $2.29 million matching grant that Massport applied for under the Airport Development Aid program (ADAP)—one of those socialism-for-business federal subsidies. Such an approval, the judge ruled, would then become a "major federal action" (under the National Environmental Policy Act) substantially affecting the environment. The City of Boston filed a prompt appeal, arguing that FAA and the U.S. Department of Transportation were already partners in the expensive project, and that federal law mandated a prior environmental impact study.

At 2:30 A.M. on Saturday morning, August 3, Governor Sargent, "his voice husky and his pace slow" as the *Boston Globe* reported it, sat in his office and told reporters he felt "disappointed, cheated and resigned" about the just-ended legislative session. Among the defeated pieces of Sargent's "must" legislation was permission for a third vehicle tunnel under Boston Harbor—a tunnel bitterly fought by East Boston residents because of the congestion impact it would have on their already disrupted neighborhoods, and because of the symbolic encouragement it would have given to Massport and other advocates of Logan Airport expansion. The $300 million Sargent tunnel would have emerged inside the airport upon completion in 1981.

On August 23, 1974, in a 5–1 vote, the Massport Board decided to continue gung-ho construction of its runways extension and to hold in mid-September a final hearing on the airport's master plan, which includes the runway projects.

East Boston Little City Hall manager John Vitagliano called the hearing a farce because the construction work had been under way since May (the old familiar stake-in-the-ground procedure).

At the same Port Authority meeting, the board heard their communities-affairs director report on the agency's most recent depredation: fourteen three-family homes on Neptune Road purchased by Massport, eleven of those houses razed, and thirty-three families "relocated." Forty-four houses on the road, which is two hundred feet from Runway 15-33, were, as of August, still privately owned.

Five days later came a setback for the expansionist forces. A state judge temporarily halted all work on the three runways in dispute, pending state approval of an environmental-impact report. Judge Arthur M. Mason rejected Massport's two main contentions: that the project was not covered by the state Environmental Policy Act and that the project would not cause significant damage to the environment.

The health of the public was at stake, the judge ruled, since noise, air and water pollution were all involved. But the arrogance of the Port Authority and the debilitating slowness of the legal process were highlighted by the Massport executive director's boast that by the time he pulled 150 workers off the runways in response to the judge's injunction, 30 percent of the expansion work was already completed. It's hardly a telling argument for "working within the system" if a war can be 30 percent lost before the system of equity and justice even becomes operative.

And on August 12, *The New York Times* reported from the tiny community of Lennox, California, that the residents there pray for fog, because on the rare days when Los Angeles International Airport is fogged in, there is a respite from the one thousand incoming daily flights. Lennox lies directly under the landing approach, where every two or three minutes the high-pitched whine of a jet drowns out all conversation, interrupts all teaching in Fulton Avenue Junior High School, makes students more tense, and contributes to fights and discipline problems.

In 1971, California led the nation in enacting legislation requiring jetports to reduce noise "significantly." Under the new law, airports were supposed to face a $1,000 fine for each unduly noisy flight. But the costly and complex noise-monitoring equipment at Los Angeles Airport has registered no reduction in noise, and not a single airline has paid a penny in fines. Typically, the state's Department of Aeronautics has caved in under the pressures of the marketplace. The airports now have until 1985 to reduce their "cumulative noise" level.

California had Reagan, an avowed right-winger. Massachusetts had Sargent, a liberal Republican. Their appointees sit on the relevant commissions and the regulatory agencies. In Lennox, California, and in East Boston, Massachusetts, the din goes on. The people are mocked. Over and over again the system plays games and fails them.

However limited the occasional successes of the East Bostonians, they can pride themselves for inspiring an *early*, well-coordinated and sophisticated movement in Boston's scattered suburbs to block any expansion of suburban airports.

The villains here are the same Massachusetts Port Authority and the Massachusetts Aeronautics Commission. Both of their 1973 annual reports projected great increases in traffic at Logan. To meet the problem, they recommended diverting the extra load into one of four suburban airports—with "appropriate" expansion, it goes without saying. Although this was a matter of public record not to be denied or erased, Massport's executive director, Edward King, continued to make speeches saying there were no plans for suburban airport expansion. Were Mr. King to transfer his talents from transportation to any secretly expanding hospital, he would have no difficulty—and show no embarrassment—in reconciling similar firm denials with easily ascertainable truth. About forty or fifty years ago, Berthold Brecht wrote that the people know, when statesmen weep for peace and publicly abhor war, the mobilization order has already been signed.

On the suburban resistance front, one heartening factor is the participation of a commercial airline pilot, Robert Rioux of Weymouth, Massachusetts, whose technical expertise has been invaluable in ripping apart official lies and half truths.

Though his airline disapproves of his involvement, Rioux says:

210

My airline didn't want me to get involved in this, but I had to set priorities too, and I decided that my home and family come first. I'm not going to let them put a major airport in Weymouth.

We don't want to have a jetport here [Weymouth]. It's time they got their priorities straight. People are more important than airports. Our lives are more important than some businessman's trip to New York.

The protesting group in each of the suburbs coalesced into the Suburban Coalition to Resist the Airport Plan (SCRAP). A Weymouth woman who is active in the coalition says bluntly:

We don't believe them when they tell us they're only going to send a few general aviation planes over here. We've seen the politicians in action, and we know that once they get started it will grow and grow.

But we're learning how to handle them. We're sticking together so they can't single out one community to send their extra airplanes to.

We're ready to fight. Weymouth is made up mainly of people who have run from the core city because of the problems they had there. But you can run only so far, and then you decide to stay and fight.

At Massport, the official line is that Weymouth, site of an underutilized Naval Air Station, "is too close to Logan," and that it would interfere with flight patterns at the Boston airport.

When Mary Thornston of the *Boston Globe* asked Massport's public-relations assistant where he got that information (since military jets use Weymouth regularly all the time), he replied: "I just heard it around somewhere."

The same public-relations assistant tried to lull

211

Weymouth community opposition by falsely maintaining that the Navy is not willing to share its facilities—when, in fact, the Navy, until the end of 1973, had a joint-use agreement, with the town of Weymouth, covering civilian use of the field. It was the town that let the agreement expire because no civilian aircraft took advantage of it. The naval commander indicated the agreement could readily be revived and renewed.

So strong is public sentiment in the suburbs that, in suburban Norwood, the local municipal airport commissioner hesitates to let the Federal Aviation Administration install a bad-weather Instrument Landing System (ILS). Although aviation officials claim that the runways are much too short for jets, skeptical residents worry that the ILS would pave the way for jet landings.

The *Boston Globe* in May 1974 quoted the Norwood airport manager as saying his townspeople "don't even want us to keep the runway in good repair, because they're afraid it will encourage more airplanes."

Pilot Rioux and his colleagues in SCRAP charge that none of the expansionist-minded state or federal agencies has given careful attention to alternatives to airport enlargement, such as the long-discussed proposal for high-speed rail transportation in the Boston–New York–Washington corridor. Nor are the agencies at all innovative in scheduling. Says Rioux:

> Instead of having three DC-9's per hour to New York, they can schedule one L 1011. And they can spread flights more evenly throughout the day rather than schedule so many flights at rush hours. It's all a question of priorities—trading off convenience against maintaining a quality of life.

Weymouth's representative in the state legislature says bluntly: "This [proposed airport expansion] would be the most awful thing that could possibly happen to the town, and I wouldn't be reelected if I allowed it to happen."

"There is no way they're going to be allowed to do it," pilot Rioux swears. "One way or another we're going to stop it. And if they succeed, there'll be a row of graves leading to that airport."

Section IV   Kennedy Library–Museum

Anywhere in Massachusetts, and especially within the family's Boston bailiwick, to challenge a project bearing the Kennedy name is not at all easy, psychologically, politically, or practically. Kennedys do not like to be crossed.

In full knowledge of this fact of life, the Kennedy Library Corporation confidently went forth with its unilateral multimillion dollar plans from its inception in the mid-1960's—right up to the spring of 1974 when community opposition to the memorial complex finally began to sink in.

At that point, Stephen Smith, the Kennedy brother-in-law who is corporation president, journeyed quietly to the Boston area to consider for the first time alternative sites for the museum.

Also for the first time, on June 7, 1974—a full eight years after the Commonwealth of Massachusetts donated 12.2 acres of publicly owned land—Smith and his chief architect, I. M. Pei, deigned to appear in person to explain their proposals in an open news conference in Cambridge. It goes without saying that tax exemption has been bestowed on the project.

Before being forced in June 1974 by community resistance to redesign and scale down its plans drastically, the corporation in June 1973 had unveiled plans for a $27 million library-museum complex close to heavily trafficked Harvard Square. The new plans, billed at $15 million, eliminated an eighty-five-foot-high glass pavilion and a large crescent-shaped building. (Invariably, expansionists weep and wail, and initially argue that absolutely nothing can be altered or reduced in scale.) Substituted for the latter were a building for the library (archives) and museum, and another for Harvard University's Institute of Politics and the Kennedy School of Government.

Other changes called for three acres of landscaped green space, reduction of the total floor area by one third, reduction of the library building length from eighty-five to forty-nine feet, elimination of two four-hundred-seat movie theaters in the exhibit areas, and substitution of brick for concrete as the primary building-facade material.

Even after all the changes attributed by Stephen Smith to "community concerns and the press of inflation," the plans remained subject to revision after completion of a $184,000 environmental-impact statement. Possible court challenges by Cambridge community groups held out the prospect of further reluctant concessions by the Kennedy Library Corporation.

By law, the General Services Administration (GSA) had to arrange for the environmental study. The contract carrying a 120-day deadline went on February 14, 1974, to C. E. Maguire, Inc. It took the Kennedy Corporation 108 days—up to the day of the Smith–Pei news conference—to tell Maguire the basic facts about what would be built. As a consequence, the deadline had to be extended three months. Meanwhile, GSA had launched

214

an investigation into Maguire's credentials as a result of charges of unprofessionalism by both East Boston and Cambridge citizens' groups.

On top of the accusation that the firm had knuckled under to political pressures in an East Boston waterfront study for the highly political Massachusetts Port Authority, Cambridge City Councillor Barbara Ackermann pointed out that Maguire had hired two leading proponents of the long-debated Inner Belt Highway, which Cambridge homeowners and many others successfully fought during the 1960's. The two had held important official posts: Massachusetts public-works commissioner and Cambridge traffic commissioner. Again and again the incestuous lines and connections—and the multi-million dollar signs—intersect and double back, regardless of whether the issue of expansionism happens to involve culture, mass education, public transportation, high-priced medical care, organized religion, or straight commercial development.

When it comes to systematically shaking down the public under the guise of high moral purpose, everything meshes in the backrooms. The personalities at the top interlock, as in the corporate world. If from the standpoint of community resisters it's all one struggle, to the proponents of institutional expansionism the lush proceeds all flow from one source: the frayed pocket of the taxpayers—with enough goodies *to date* to spread amongst the "in" institutions. As the economy slides downhill at geometric rates, among erstwhile friends the competition for the loot and for the accompanying prestige will become fiercer and fiercer. There will be fallings out, with quite possibly the losers squealing on the winners.

Because the Kennedy museum would generate the most traffic with the greatest number of tourists, Cambridge critics of the complex long suggested that the museum be built elsewhere, apart from the library. The Kennedy Corporation took the rigid position that federal legislation covering presidential libraries mandated a single site. But an attorney for the Cambridge Civic Association challenged Stephen Smith's interpretation.

Traffic consultants engaged by the corporation projected 1.1 million visitors per year for the first year (averaging 3,000 per day and 7,000 to 8,000 on peak days), and 800,000 visitors thereafter—and, according to some, even these are grossly underestimated figures. The traffic consultants calculated that 70 percent of the visitors would arrive by car—adding 4,900 polluting cars to already choked and choking Harvard Square on peak days. I. M. Pei, the library architect, provided for on-site parking for 435 cars, while some in Cambridge opposed any on-site parking. At least one important official wanted any shuttle buses kept off lovely Memorial Drive—the road along the Charles River on which the Kennedy complex was designed to front—and perhaps out of Cambridge altogether.

At the June 1974 press conference, architect Pei admitted that, after eight years, the corporation had still not studied in detail the library's potential effect on pending development in the heart of Harvard Square or on existing business in the square.

Because the proposed size of the library-museum building was twice scaled down, the *Boston Globe* (whose able reporter Joe Pilati gave readers a running account of complex developments over a long period of time) foresaw serious problems in crowd control. The thousands of visitors each day journeying to Cambridge, many of them at great expense from the four corners of the earth, would have to be rushed through the museum exhibit in thirty-five minutes—with no indoors space provided for waiting when the weather outside was wet or stormy or just plain New England frigid. Crowd control, indeed.

Another consequence of the scaling down is that the museum's research center would be able to hold only 6 of the 22 million papers. The remaining 16 million would remain in Waltham, twenty miles away, to be provided to scholars on advance request.

With such transparently incomplete planning for so major a project, it was not surprising that a May 1974 poll found Cambridge residents divided on the desirability of the Kennedy memorial.

In a poll commissioned by the Kennedy Library Corporation, 48 percent favored construction on the proposed state-donated site; 42 percent opposed, and 10 percent had no opinion. The Kennedy Corporation's news release stressed the pollster's finding that about two thirds of "long-term" Cambridge residents (defined as residents for twenty years or more and presumably the more solid citizens) favored construction.

The pollsters also asked the sampling of five hundred registered voters their "generally favorable or unfavorable opinions" of five city councillors and two institutions directly related to the proposed library-museum. The Kennedy Corporation withheld the responses to those questions.

Ten days after the new library plans were unveiled, the Harvard Square Development Task Force, whose assigned duty is to monitor the environment in that area, said in a formal statement that it is "deeply concerned about the museum, and all it implies, in terms of competition between permanent residents and transients, the bus-auto and the pedestrian, and the square's traditional role as a people-oriented crossroads [rather than] . . . a tourist attraction."

To the Task Force, it was "reasonable to accommodate the predominantly scholarly activities that are part of this critical 12.2 acres"—that is, the archives and Harvard University facilities. But the museum, now projected as part of the same archives building, was not regarded as a reasonable use.

In a strong letter to the Task Force chairman, the Cambridge city manager wrote that "sensible public policy certainly argues for city intervention in instances where . . . development pressures are getting out of hand."

The city manager said:

> [A] Presidential Zoning District, which would have more universal applicability in the Commonwealth, might be what the situation demands. We cannot afford to sit idly by and tolerate the emergence of multiple fast-food franchises, souvenir shops, and similar enterprises which could . . . infringe seriously on the basic character of Harvard Square. A presidential district would be more restrictive in zoning.

The city-appointed Task Force had praise only for the "reduction in basic monumentality," the "understated exterior treatment," and "a greater emphasis on open areas and green spaces."

Besides neighborhood representation, the far-from-radical Task Force is composed of men and women from the banking, real estate and developer communities, a clergyman, a Harvard assistant vice-president, and others with "civic" backgrounds. In no other case of an institution v. a community that fears encroachment have I heard of the setting up of a citizens' committee to come to the defense of an unpopular institution. But less than a fortnight before embattled Stephen Smith and his chief archi-

218

tect met with the press, the JFK Library Committee sprang into being, specifically to support the Kennedy Corporation's proposals. The two chairpersons denied any direct ties to the corporation. But a Harvard Square clergyman and member of the Harvard Square Task Force, Rev. Richard Shmaruk of St. Paul's Church, charged the group with being politically motivated. He said its purpose was "to muffle any responsible criticism of the corporation's plans."

In their own "company town," the mighty Kennedy forces had come to this: an unrelenting and battering torrent of community criticism; a corporation wavering and a period of indecisiveness during which alternative museum sites were scouted; the felt need to set up a front committee to run interference; a retreat from $27 million to $15 million plans, and the partial concealing of the results of a public-opinion poll.

Much of the massive climb-down is directly attributable to the corporation's long track record of not deigning to answer challenges from the community. At bottom, when it comes to dealing with resistance by nearby peasants—even if some of the peasants live on Brattle Street and have Harvard degrees—sophisticated Stephen Smith is no different from Sister Cyprian Branco, the hawkish, hard-lining executive director of little backwater Columbus Hospital who refused even to meet with hospital tenants for one turbulent year. Like all good expansionist policymakers, they always assume that they can weather *any* storm just by sitting tight and saying nothing (Plan A).

But that assumption is increasingly risky. On February 6, 1975, the final humiliating climb-down came when the Kennedy Corporation made its bitter announcement: it was dropping all plans to set up shop at the Cambridge site.

219

Section V   Beacon Hill

The Boston Common and the Public Garden are the sole physical barriers between the proposed commercial Park Plaza area and quaint historic Beacon Hill. In 1972, the company that was officially designated to be the developer of the $266 million Park Plaza urban-renewal project wrote a letter to the *Boston Globe,* with an accompanying illustration which was designed to show that the proposed new forty-five-story skyscrapers would cast only a minimal shadow over the Common and the Garden for just a short part of the day.

Boston After Dark, a weekly counterculture paper, was suspicious of the self-serving letter and drawing. The staff went to a basic reference work, *Architectural Graphic Standards,* and boned up on what Euclid taught about shadow studies. With the help of several architects, *Boston After Dark* then produced nine drawings of its own. They accurately showed how very far indeed the shadows would fall across these two great oases of calm and charm—on different days and seasons of the year, and at different hours of the day.

The nine drawings and text refuting the developer made up a two-page spread that *Boston After Dark* published under the headline: "The Gentle Rape of the Swan Boats/A.K.A. [Also Known As] the *Boston Globe* Wears Blinders." Especially since the *Globe* was supporting the Park Plaza project, *BAD* felt the *Globe* should have felt a special journalistic duty to check on the authenticity of the developer's claim before publishing the misleading letter and illustration.

Because of the clear and present danger to their neighborhood, the 1,200-member Beacon Hill Civic Association has been exceptionally active among community groups opposing Park Plaza. The association goes back a half century, to the era when "the Hill" was synonymous with Boston Brahmins and the Late George Apley types.

Though its population as a whole is vastly changed today and is far more heterogeneous, the image or aura of wealth persists. "People don't want to acknowledge that there are problems," Bernard Borman, an attorney who is president of the Civic Association, says of the 12,000 people who inhabit the Hill's ninety acres.

Institutional pressures have made his community into an island, Borman argues:

> There's Storrow Drive [the expressway along the lovely Charles River], with the ever-increasing pressure to widen. It never even should have been built in the first place.
>
> Historic Bullfinch State House [atop the Hill] expands in unplanned fashion with an ever-growing bureaucracy scattered all over the area, and is now building another atrocity at Ashburton Place. The State House makes no effort to handle its traffic, and builds with no impact studies.

Borman accuses the City of Boston of letting universities expand in an uncontrolled fashion. Around the Hill's edges are Suffolk University, Emerson College, Government Center (where federal, state and municipal agencies converge), and an expansionist-minded Massachusetts General Hospital. And now, Borman says, "We are to be surrounded on our other flank by Park Plaza. The Boston Redevelopment Authority is the biggest blight of all. They are our biggest threat."

The Civic Association looks ahead twenty years and sees its blocks eliminated as a "viable residential area, unless negative trends can be held or reversed. To date, it has been the elderly on Beacon Hill who have been especially uprooted by the various random and unplanned expansions."

Although one might expect Beacon Hillers to get favored treatment in the halls of government, Borman does not find that to be the case. He has had his fill of "city officials who scorn suggestions of people living with problems. There is an affliction at City Hall. Almost all the people there think that, by virtue of their position, they have acquired some sort of omniscience about public problems."

Henry Lee of Beacon Hill, president of the Friends of the Public Garden, and Bernard Borman represented their groups on the runaway Park Plaza Civic Advisory Committee. All the committee members soon found that, to the Boston Redevelopment Authority which had appointed them, they were on the Committee to be window dressing. Their recommendations—on the environment, for example—were totally ignored. When BRA and the state decided on a fourth submission of the Park Plaza project, the Advisory Committee was not consulted.

To a slum dweller fighting to keep an Inner Belt out, or to keep a next-door university or an expanding medical center from demolishing his/her block or entire neighborhood, it may not be much consolation to know that expansionist institutions and their allies in government give short shrift even to upper-middle-class civic associations that refuse to accept the "progress" party line.

But if that same slum dweller is interested in analyzing why he/she has to fight, and why the impersonal enemy forces behave the way they do, it is important to know that the hustlers for the mix of money and power that we call expansionism are not necessarily racist or exclusively antiworking class in their motivation. They will trample on *anyone* and *any* community and *any* symbol in order to reach their goals. And they are stopped and routed and turned back and sent scurrying for cover when—and only when—they run into the barbed barricades and the stone walls of people united.

Section VI   Highways

Given our political system of deals, payoffs and big campaign contributions rather than of issues debated and decided on their merits, elected officials feel compelled to strike the true-blue, statesmanlike pose today, only to balance it off tomorrow, especially when campaign funds are short, by taking care of narrow, selfish interests.

Thinking back to November 1972, I don't recall anyone's confidently predicting that Governor Francis Sargent of Massachusetts would come out smelling sweet after a then impending showdown with the highway lobby. Earlier in that month, the *Boston Phoenix* headlined a story: "Will Sargent Bury Boston Under Highways?" From within his own administration, the governor was being pulled and pushed by his Secretary of Transportation, who wanted some new roads, and by his personal staff which, from a somewhat broader vision, did not.

Earlier in the decade, Sargent had scrapped the so-called Inner Belt. It would have run to Boston from Somerville and Cambridge, to hook up, in the city's Roxbury section, to the Southwest Highway. The designated route would have necessitated throwing people out of 2,600 homes, and the state bureaucracy had no means of fulfilling the legal requirements of relocation.

Thus on an issue so fraught with long-term and

223

nationwide implications, it was not impossible to hope that the governor of a traditionally trailblazing state might again take the heat and declare a moratorium on further expressway construction in and around Boston. Vast portions of the city had already been converted into strips of concrete. Nationally, 40 percent of our cities have been consigned to roads, to parking lots, to gasoline stations, to high-rise garages. A former mayor of Boston, John Collins, representing the Greater Boston Chamber of Commerce, was pressing for the building of a six-lane tunnel under Boston Harbor (tunnel Number 3), a six-lane highway from Boston north about twenty miles to Danvers, and a $500 million expressway along Boston's northwest corridor.

The president of the state senate predicted economic disaster for the Bay State unless the highways were built. A spokesman for the operating engineers union said that proposals for mass transit were "boondoggles," but that any new roads were vital links.

With an 8.3 percent state unemployment rate, a tempting billion dollars in federal monies was available for the taking on a 90/10 basis. Aside from the environmentalists, who don't command many votes, the only political clout against more road building came, almost unanimously, from inner-city groups of residents.

For years they had seen large chunks of Roxbury and Jamaica Plain lying vacant (and insanely non-tax-producing)—land that had been cleared of houses and people long before any imminent construction of the new roads. The fait accompli—that is, the fact that so much land had already been acquired by eminent domain—gave rise to the "logical" argument that ergo the roads should be built. The Greater Boston Committee on the

Transportation Crisis (GBC) countered with the alternative land-use plan that their different devastated communities had themselves devised. It was projected that the building of the Southwest road would preclude Boston from meeting federal air-quality standards. All experience showed that every new road generated extra traffic. East Bostonians vehemently rejected any third under-the-harbor tunnel, whether two-, four-, six-, or eight-lane, because it was seen as an automatic encouragement to further expansion of Logan Airport onto whose turf any new underwater tunnel from the Boston mainland would emerge.

When Francis Sargent did make his moratorium speech (November 1972), his discussion of transportation priorities attracted national attention, one year before the gasoline crisis. Looking back now on his decision, one can conclude that the spell-breaking ban on further mad construction—the tearing down of a city renowned for its grace and charms, in order to bring more cars in—was probably inevitable. Perhaps not on that precise day or in that same month but in the fullness of time. A year and a half later, the governor's Transportation Secretary, Alan Altshuler, said that the decisions to stop highway construction "were dictated by the citizenry, which rose up in opposition to all projects that would result in disruptive influences in the community." Quite a belated tribute to people power from an erstwhile tough and uncritical advocate of highway construction from Boston outward to infinity.

About the same time that Secretary Altshuler was publicly acknowledging that the worm does turn, Massachusetts in May 1974 received $665 million—the first transfer of federal highway funds to mass transit.

The money came from the three interstate highways—the Southwest Expressway, I-95 North, and the Inner Belt—which Governor Sargent had decided not to build.

At the State House, the governor called a jubilant press conference and reminded his 1972 critics of their prediction that "we would never get the funds transferred." The transfer was allowed under a 1973 compromise amendment to the U.S. Highway Trust Fund—an amendment that never would have been given serious consideration had not people in innumerable communities taken their save-our-houses, save-our-shops struggles to the streets and to the court of public opinion. Even for North Americans with our cultural impatience for immediate victories and immediate fruits of battle, these occasional dramatic triumphs—years later—show that, in one way or another, it *always* pays to fight the good fight: win, lose, or draw.

In that sense, the tenant, the homeowner, the small neighborhood merchant were way ahead of public officials—certainly in part because the people *collectively* are independent of improper and corrupting pressures from the highway lobby.

And since the better and the higher judges are au courant to some extent, the courts catch up too. Just as premature virtue was paying off in mass transit dollars for Massachusetts, a three-judge Appeals Court in Trenton was enjoining the building of a thirty-eight-mile, $325 million spur of the New Jersey Turnpike, because the Turnpike Authority had misled the public by proposing one route at a public hearing and then actually approving another route at a later date.

The court ruled that by "recommending a different alignment after a public hearing addressed to the other routes, the Turnpike Authority effectively shielded from public exposure areas of legitimate and reasonable concern."

The people of New Jersey are to the Turnpike Authority what the people who live near Logan Airport are to the Massachusetts Port Authority: the enemy to be lied to, the enemy to be tricked and bamboozled, the enemy to give the runaround to, the enemy to be feared above all.

In an effort to set precedents and to impose restrictions on the highway lobby's appetite, the Environmental Defense Fund takes various freeway, expressway, highway cases to a variety of state and federal courts.

In two related cases—Iowa's Century Freeway and a proposed Interstate Highway from southwestern Connecticut through western Massachusetts and Vermont —the fund hopes to obtain through the judicial process an overall, multisection environmental impact statement.

To the fund such a statement would, in its own words, be important for two reasons:

1. to establish a requirement that highway planners state their objectives, and assess environmental consequences, at an early stage, so that the citizenry, if it has objections, can make them known, and if appropriate, organize opposition. The usual practice is to make plans known only as to short segments and at the stage when these are virtually a fait accompli, and to fend off inquiries into long-range plans on the grounds that these are tentative and speculative;

2. to establish a requirement that where overall highway plans involve multistate projects, the responsibility for preparing the impact statements lies with the responsible *federal* officials, not with the applicants for federal aid—namely the state highway department. If established, this would be a highly significant reform, because it would take the statement-preparing function

from the people who are committed *only* to highway building [the state highway departments] and lodge it with people who can be expected to have a broader perspective [the U.S. Department of Transportation].

In an Iowa case, the State Highway Department sought to cut that part of the proposed highway then at issue into seven-mile segments for impact statement purposes. The court ruled that the impact statement be broadened to cover an additional twenty miles, extending it to what the court considered a "logical terminus."

Early in 1974, in another sign of the times, the University of Vermont hired as a research associate on a transportation study project a planner whom the governor had fired for refusing to cooperate with the Highway Department on the extension of Vermont's roads. Just as Daniel Ellsberg's decision of conscience to leak the Pentagon Papers was deeply rooted in the climate created by the mass antiwar movement, so the conscience of an unsung Vermont planner was quite possibly moved to action by the cumulative effect of "enough is enough" popular struggles. Everything is interrelated. In terms of consequences, nothing we do is really private; nothing is strictly local; no idea or lonely decision that seems to originate wholly within us can be separated from the enveloping climate and from the interacting people around us; everything we do is important.

In characteristic Boston fashion—where unswervable individuals have left their mark on history since colonial days, since Abolitionist days, and since the days of Emerson and Thoreau—two trailblazing crusaders, Jim Morey and Fred Salvucci, and a relatively small antipoverty agency, Urban Planning Aid (UPA), helped stall for years the proposed community-wrecking Inner Belt until enough political momentum was generated for the governor's all-embracing moratorium. Morey, a disenchanted Rand Corporation systems analyst, and Salvucci, an alumnus of Massachusetts Institute of Technology and a Fulbright scholar, talked the American Friends Service Committee into a $20,000 seed-money grant to launch UPA.

Staffed mostly by young college graduates and later funded (uncertainly, on a hand-to-mouth basis) by a skeptical, Nixonian Office of Economic Opportunity, UPA's research and publications departments—including a hard-hitting, easy-to-read monthly Community Press Service—became an invaluable technical resource for a wide variety of community groups in the fields of housing, occupational health and safety, transportation, prison reform, noise pollution, cable television, and rent control. UPA is living testimony to the possibility of effective, informed, sustained community self-defense—provided people are serious and eschew *all* jive—even though the overall system is flagrantly stacked against the helpless elements of society.

Even with a stacked deck political flukes do occur. On July 31, 1975, President Ford's new Secretary of Transportation, William T. Coleman, Jr., ruled against completion of the northern Virginia leg of Interstate Highway 66 into the nation's capital.

The New York Times reported the ruling as a "surprise" to supporters of the six-lane highway. As a "prudent alternative," Secretary Coleman suggested a $350 million spur of the Washington subway and rapid rail system that would serve the same corridor as the proposed highway.

Especially since President Ford had indicated he favored the road, the decision was an unexpected victory for a coalition of environmentalists, property owners

229

and residents who for five years had been in virtual hand-to-hand combat with proponents of the highway. Besides the White House, powerful supporters of the road included Virginia's governor, Mills E. Godwin, the Virginia Highway Commission, the state's General Assembly, and the area's Congressional delegation. But local authorities, including suburban Arlington and the District of Columbia government, disapproved the proposed roadway.

In 1970, the highway lobby everywhere was still riding high, and the Nixon administration had a projected life span of seven more years in power. The lonely ecologists and the homeowners had no possible way of foreseeing even the remote possibility of a sweeping ultimate victory in 1975 under a new Cabinet member. But even with a bleak prognosis, the Highway Action Coalition and others plunged into the fray, unaware—as we all are in such encounters—of the vast array of variables, including a change in the national climate toward mindless demolition and ugly concrete, that can turn the tide of a particular battle.

Section VII   McDonald's

Christian Science International Center . . . University of Massachusetts/Boston . . . Logan International Airport . . . Kennedy Library–Museum . . . institutional pressures on Beacon Hill . . . highways—to the Greater Boston community has come all this and more in its effort to keep itself together.

It certainly doesn't need any additional fronts to fight on. But McDonald's has come to the Central Square area of Cambridge, as to other communities across the country. In a growing number of places the battle has been joined with every weapon short of guns.

To a cohesive neighborhood the coming of a fast-food restaurant is almost always a symbol of creeping instability. The litter problem, the double parking, the noise, the all pervasive stench of fried food—they cannot help but jar old-time residents who take pride in their blocks. In July 1974, the village of Thomaston, New York, passed an ordinance banning fast-food restaurants within village limits. The mayor of the 2,700 residents on the Great Neck peninsula said the law was designed to "protect our business center from the honky-tonk atmosphere that goes with these in-and-out places. They are a nuisance to residential areas. They're noisy. There's a garbage problem."

Around Cambridge's Central Square, it wasn't as if a new McDonald's would stand in not-so-splendid isolation. Nineteen fast-food places were already there, including pizza shops, sandwich-stocked bars, a Brigham's ice cream shop, and a Jack-in-the-Box. The aggregate could only indicate that Central Square, long a poor and very unacademic cousin to Harvard Square a mile away, was on the skids.

The odds were never very favorable for the year-and-a-half-long struggle to keep the latest intruder out. The spirit of the people was strong. But under Cambridge's rent-control law, the threatened tenants were unable legalistically to block ultimate eviction after their landlord had sold the building with six tenants to McDonald's for $170,000 on March 22, 1974.

Yet the tenants and their loyal neighbors fought a tough, delaying battle. Delay is important in that, in some struggles, entirely unforeseeable events do arise, which enable people unexpectedly to remain in their

231

homes. Over a matter of months, among other developments, inflationary building costs can change the mind of a developer or of an expanding institution when a project can no longer be afforded. There can be changes in a zoning ordinance that put the offending project beyond the legal pale, and tenants-rights laws and regulations controlling evictions can be strengthened. Particularly in view of great economic uncertainty on all fronts, rearguard delaying actions and ploys are not to be dismissed out of hand as ineffective tactics when people's lives and happiness are at stake.

In Cambridge, there were public hearings, protests at City Hall, disputes over architecture, and injunctions. The issue was easy to publicize: housing, not hamburgers. Livable sixty-dollar-a-month housing that working-class people could afford. With a flair for the dramatic, the community got the City Council to declare unanimously that the 1849 Greek Revival building (the best example of that architecture in Cambridge) had historic value and was therefore eligible for a city takeover by eminent domain.

Armed with that resolution, the City of Cambridge, on behalf of the tenants, got a judge to enjoin the demolition of the building for a month, in order to give the state Historical Commission time to concur or dissent from the historic-value decision of the city Historical Commission. Just before the injunction became operative, McDonald's sullied its name forever by ripping off that part of the roof directly over the apartment of the one remaining tenant even as she sat inside. A suspicious fire in March had driven out the other tenants. In the dead of the winter, McDonald's had turned off all water, gas and electricity, in order to harass tenants into moving. The woman holdout got electricity via an extension cord

232

from sympathetic tenants in the next building. But she had to haul water from the outside on her own.

For six weeks after the antidemolition injunction expired on April 29, the Douglass Street Tenants organization was able to force McDonald's to negotiate with land architects, planners and neighborhood groups in an effort to retain housing on the upper floors. Eventually McDonald's construction superintendent said that the proposed renovations would cost $136,000 more than the total amount—$250,000—that the company had set aside for construction and furnishings for its restaurant. The superintendent's final comment summed up the thinking of all who put corporate interests—whether profit or "nonprofit"—before human needs: "We're simply not in the apartment business."

With that, demolition began on June 17, to make way for a single-story structure exclusively for use as a restaurant, in order that McDonald's can return a profit on its $170,000 purchase price and its $250,000 investment in construction costs. It will take the sale of a lot of hamburgers and French fries to pay the costs of uprooting six tenants and taking over a building that the Massachusetts Historical Commission ruled was "worthy of preservation." But the commission decided that this four-story brick example of Greek Revival architecture did not have "historical or antiquarian interest sufficient to justify taking by eminent domain."

Obviously, McDonald's computer projected that it all added up to a paying proposition. And just as obviously, because the weak and inadequate consumer movement and the much corrupted trade-union movement have no organic relationship with the narrowly focussed tenant movement, there was no prospect of organizing permanently an effective consumer boycott, cutting off

233

all deliveries and services through the Teamsters Union, and shutting the hamburger joint down.

Until there are such links and that kind of coordination between all fronts of the people's struggle for justice, the McDonalds's of this world and the other rapists will be in no serious danger of ultimate overthrow, despite a tenant victory here, a consumer victory there, and a worker victory elsewhere.

chapter 5
Protest Springs Eternal

"Do these hospital doctors who rip up neighborhoods to build empires fully grasp what they're doing?" I asked as, appropriately, we drove past Boston's famed Lahey Clinic.

"You're damn right they do," replied Donnell Boardman, a Quaker doctor affiliated with Massachusetts General Hospital.

In the early 1940's, Albert J. Fitzgerald, president of the United Electrical Workers and himself a Catholic, grew weary of the parade of tenacious realtors and other emissaries from the nearby New York Chancery Office. They were forever haunting his busy office at 11 East 51st Street, persistently wishing to buy the union property.

UE had bought the old Vanderbilt mansion, which is still today the national headquarters, and the officers and members were quite content with their midtown location near St. Patrick's Cathedral. Then, as now, the Archdiocese owned much of the property in the vicinity.

To put an end to the annoying visits, Fitzgerald

finally told one of the realtors: "Once and for all, we're not interested in selling. But if Cardinal Spellman ever decides to put the cathedral up for sale, let us know."

Given the sacrosanct attributes that our society bestows on a person's home-as-castle, one might assume that a firm "no sale" from property owners would always be sufficient, legally and practically, when confronting expanding institutions. But the culturally conditioned premise behind that unwarranted assumption is that churches, hospitals, universities, museums and even respectable businesses play by the rules of chivalry. In the New York regional office of the Department of Housing and Urban Development, an official told me of a hospital in a New Jersey town a few years ago that was determined to take over its entire block by wearing down homeowners who had no intention of selling. On the mother site, the friendly community hospital built new structures tall enough to blot out all sunlight. Extremely noisy garbage collections were scheduled at hours designed to awaken all neighbors. To create both an eyesore and a breeding ground for rats, uncovered garbage was left out on the sidewalk long before the collection trucks were scheduled to arrive. The book of dirty tricks was infinite. Sadly, over a period of time, it worked. One family after another decided they could take no more and surrendered to what loomed as indefinite harassment—unless, of course, the community fought back.

Had it been a working-class-conscious neighborhood with a tradition of fighting back, blow for blow, there might have been effective resistance through a direct confrontation. Persons who stoop to such methods are invariably cowards, and they panic at the mere physical approach of their victims.

But until times grow desperately hard economically, the middle class, as a class, is never renowned for picking up on even a lawless challenge from the powerful and the arrogant, except, by and large, on respectable ecological issues. Sometimes, outraged middle-class individuals rise magnificently to the occasion. As a rule, though, as long as one last rationalization for inaction can be dreamed up—as long as even one highly inconvenient alternative presents itself (such as chucking the issue at hand and moving on to a new "problem-free" home site)— those persons who stay and fight are the exception in the enervating aromas of cookouts and well-tended lawns.

On occasion, the lawlessness of the expansionist fraternity soars to levels of breathtaking audacity. In August 1974, as the Great and General Court (the official name, since colonial days, of the Massachusetts legislature) sped toward preelection adjournment, the *Boston Globe* reported the following brief item buried in a lengthy round-up story:

> One [last-minute bill], filed by Senate President Kevin Harrington, would make legal the taking of 4.9 acres for Route I-95 North in Newburyport.
> In 1971, the Department of Public Works took 11.9 rather than the authorized 7 acres.
> The bill had no public hearing.

With the Senate president covering up for the highway lobby and its partners in government, the legislature did not trouble itself with the question of how many families had lived on those "extra" 4.9 acres, or with the disruptive effects from this illegally invoked power of eminent domain.

If Massachusetts officials will grab land and property to which they haven't the slightest legal (not to mention moral) claim, it should not surprise even the most naïve that state officials there and elsewhere will brazenly lie and go back on their written word, as well as on "mere" oral commitments. On Christmas Eve in 1974, in an unusual "effective immediately" injunction, a judge in the borough of Queens ordered the New York City Off-Track Betting Corporation to halt all work, already begun, on a proposed betting parlor.

In the previous August, because of strong community opposition, OTB had signed a stipulation that it "does not intend to and will not open a branch office" at the Queens location. Residents had contended that a betting parlor would greatly increase traffic, would divert business from the adjacent shopping center, would be unduly close to several schools and places of worship, and would become a magnet for undesirable types. The local city councilman had worked out the stipulation between OTB and residents. It's a fair guess that the community then relaxed, never expecting to wake up one day and find the construction work well under way. Decades ago, New York's superexpansionist, Robert Moses, fathered this doctrine of the "stake in the ground"—or the fait accompli to which, sadly, most judges bow.

Originally, the Community Planning Board had approved the betting parlor site by a 9–5 vote. But after a public hearing the vote was reversed. The city councilman told the court that OTB was apparently rushing the construction of that and other parlors in Queens in an effort to open them before the state legislature could act on his home-rule bill, putting all OTB parlor locations under the jurisdiction of the local planning boards.

During that same pre-Christmas period, a Bedford, Massachusetts, manufacturer was telling the annual Greater Boston Chamber of Commerce economic-outlook

238

luncheon that no deep-water port exists on the East Coast for oil supertankers, and that "every effort to even plan for an oil refinery in Massachusetts has been scuttled." Bernard J. O'Keefe added that there was also a movement under way to block an addition to nuclear facilities in Plymouth.

"The examples I have given you are not examples of action taken by the Arabs, or the South Americans, or the Canadians, or the federal government, but they are taken locally by your elected representatives," the manufacturer told the luncheon audience in a back-handed tribute to the growing responsiveness of elected officials to popular resentment over community rape. In 1973, this trend was highlighted when a powerful New York legislative leader, Albert Blumenthal, while campaigning for mayor, joined our demonstration outside a religiously affiliated hospital. In a prepared statement of support, he declared:

Institutional expansionism is perhaps the logical outgrowth of a shadow government more concerned with bureaucratic self-preservation than with the needs of our city's neighborhoods. By continually expropriating land and resources, these giant corporations really aid no one but themselves. Decentralized, community-based health centers would provide a humane counterpoint to institutional behemoths such as Columbus. Our hospitals must finally learn that "big" does not invariably mean "better," and, in fact, usually signifies just the opposite.

A socially concerned Quaker, Dr. Donnell Boardman, recently elaborated on the same theme to a Boston University journalism class: "Our dying system of medical care is grasping for expansion as the essential for its survival. We are snuffing ourselves out by burning up everybody around us."

Statistics from Boston's own South End support Dr. Boardman's thesis. They clearly show that there is not necessarily any connection whatsoever between good health care in a particular community and a heavy concentration there of the most modern, expanded medical facilities. Poor neighborhoods in the South End, for the last reported year (1972), showed eight hundred new cases of tuberculosis (on a scale of 100,000 persons)—figures comparable to rates in Harlem, the South Bronx, and San Francisco's Chinatown. Massachusetts as a whole is close to the national average of "only" 13.5 cases per 100,000 population.

In a letter to the editor of the *Boston Phoenix*, the South End Interagency Council pointed out that many South Enders seldom see a physician, although there is an unparalleled patient ratio of seventeen residents to each M.D. because of the concentration of nearly 1,500 physicians at Tufts University, Boston City and Boston University hospitals. Over the last half decade, each of those institutions has been on an expansionist binge that has changed the face of their respective blocks and neighborhoods. Such hard statistics make plain that, in order to survive and thrive in the long run, a threatened community has no choice but to insist on controlling its own destiny.

Even in the face of public awareness of hospital neglect of routine primary care—not to mention specific failures to cope with serious communicable diseases of poverty—the hospital lobby plunges on, fighting what in the long run will be seen as its dying rearguard skirmishes. In December 1974, *The New York Times* editorially approved President Ford's policy of reducing and recalling unobligated Hill–Burton funds for hospital construction and expansion "where there is already an excess number of hospital beds." The New York State Hospital Association, with its three hundred member institutions, objected in a letter to the editor, which could easily beguile those unaware of the de-facto control still exercised in many states and communities by the hospitals themselves over reviews and controls of hospital expansionism:

"With all of the reviews and controls, there is little opportunity to build 'excess beds.'"

The Hospital Association letter professed to be particularly concerned about the impact of the Ford policy on inner-city hospitals "where the need for modernization is most pressing." Floating in space amidst real angels, the statement sounds solicitous, and the need for better hospitals does exist. But here on earth, because of the lobbying clout of the nonangelic voluntary hospitals, the municipal hospitals in the poor sections of inner cities invariably come out on the short end of public funds, while Bedpan Alleys in the private sector proliferate and wax ever more opulent. "Hospitals should be near more people, *not* near more hospitals" was one of our slogans in 1971 when we picketed outside Governor Rockefeller's Fifth Avenue apartment to protest the planned $39 million state expansion loan to Columbus Hospital.

While Columbus in Manhattan was busily competing with its three nearest neighbors for duplicating facilities and high-rise towers, 346-bed Lincoln Hospital, a sixty-five-year-old municipal institution serving the devastated South Bronx, was being stripped of its accreditation by the Joint Commission on Accreditation of Hospitals after staff testimony on patients dying because of inoperable elevators, insufficient quarantine space for isolating patients with tuberculosis, hepatitis and bacterial dysentery, a poorly equipped intensive-care unit with only seven beds for all services, and frequently broken cardiac monitors.

"In the end the gods take a hand in everything," says Antigone. "In the end, order takes things in hand," wrote French prodigy Raymond Radiguet in his classic novel *Devil in the Flesh*. Slowly but unmistakably, the chaos, the anarchy, and the life-and-death scandals inherent in unbridled institutional expansionism are beginning to register in the popular consciousness. "Flexing relatively new muscle," wrote the *Washington Star-News* in late 1974, "health planning groups in 39 states disapproved $200-million worth of hospital construction in nine months this year because they deemed the building unnecessary, according to a federal health official. . . .

"A check of some local and state health planners shows that [these] figures may be, as one said, 'extremely conservative'."

A 1972 amendment to the Social Security Act provides that hospitals constructed without governmental approval cannot get Medicaid and Medicare funds to help offset interest and depreciation costs.

"Mr. Rubel [the Health, Education and Welfare official quoted above] noted that the $200-million represented only 5 per cent of the $4.5 billion invested in hospital building this year. [No wonder it's called an industry!] He said he believed that, as local health planning agencies become more sophisticated, the percentage of rejected construction applications will grow."

In November 1974, by a vote of 65–18, the Senate passed and sent to the House a bill that would greatly increase that higher rejection possibility by providing new powers and increased funding for most local health-planning agencies. The bill would also end the twenty-eight-year-old Hill-Burton hospital building/expansion program.

As in Washington, so in many state capitals where certificate-of-need laws have recently multiplied. In other words, the hospitals have stepped so far out of line that it is becoming good politics to take them on and to stand up to the rest of the medical Establishment.

Though the signs are fewer and less clear, public and political pressures are also building to prune the perennial growth demands of the education industry, and to examine the true nature of today's universities. A Senate subcommittee headed by Senator Lee Metcalfe (Democrat, Montana) has been studying interlocking corporate directorships for possible antitrust violations. From the sub-committee's investigation into the spider-web concentration of Boston's considerable financial power, links to Boston's billion-dollar education industry have emerged. In a 1970 report, *The University and the Corporation*, Senator Metcalfe said:

"The universities as institutions—rather than as groups of students and faculty—are very much part of the corporate orbit today. Universities could provide monumental service . . . by redirection of the voting power of university stock in corporations."

From 1945 to 1972, U.S. education was a growth industry, "with more of everything in each successive year"—more students, teachers, buildings, money. As the 1973–74 academic year began, colleges found themselves face to face with the economic problem of a half million unfilled places. To match popular alienation from the mammoth, impersonal medical centers, an ever larger part of the student-age population is losing interest in what higher education presently has to offer.

"Will the universities, like the railroads, pursue a defeatist, obsolescent course until the Government at last tries to bail them out?" asks *The New York Times* education editor Fred Hechinger in a piece entitled "Campus Adrift."

Because easy-come, easy-go public funds were available for the taking, campus expansionism continued long after the postwar birth curve dictated a halt. As usual, our legislators and members of Congress who opened wide our state and federal treasuries lagged years behind what the demographic charts clearly spelled out.

Today, as enrollments tend downward, over-extended and less well-reputed colleges are closing their doors—and, presumably, defaulting on their state and federal expansion loans. Others are scuffling to make it—by cutting salaries, by raising tuition, and by introducing, as has Cazenovia College, for instance, such career-oriented courses as fashion design and equine studies. Cazenovia has also converted a surplus dormitory into a commercial conference center, has begun leasing classroom space to a local school district and, in the nonacademic words of the president, is "trying to keep one jump ahead of the competition [sic] in guessing on the careers students will be pursuing. Now we say: 'You tell us what you want, and we'll provide it.'"

Since Greater Boston and Massachusetts are traditional pacesetters in the field of education, it probably was a straw in the wind that, in 1975, the newly elected governor, Michael Dukakis, wanted to slash the higher-education budget from $231 million to $164 million, and to use existing space at private colleges and universities before expanding the state's public universities further.

In still another area—land conservation and land banking—uncontrolled and uncontrollable community forces are putting a crimp in the style of speculators and the growth brigades. All across Massachusetts, the significance of what is quietly happening is undeniable. Perhaps Texas will continue along with unplanned, unchecked growth. (When last there in 1972, I was astounded to be told that Houston has no zoning law. Anything can be built and put anywhere.) But in the long run anyway, the likelihood is that, as the Bay State goes, so will go the nation.

What's happening is that Massachusetts cities and towns are buying large tracts of land not only for conservation or parks, but also in pursuit of explicit no-growth, preserve-open-space policies. In some cases, as in Framingham and Peabody, communities are competing with powerful developers for land. Under new state and federal policies of the past decade, money is available to pay up to 75 percent of the acquisition costs of land to be used for parks and recreation. The state Department of Natural Resources has spent $6 million on the program, and to date no community has been turned down for funds.

"Once open space is acquired [banked], it's easier to decide what to do with it in the future. Once developed, it's forever lost," says a department spokesperson. Little by little, in pure self-defense against wild speculation, the old Native American (Indian) concept of land as a common trust is beginning to grab a trailblazing minority.

"Nothing moves in a straight line," says Betty Friedan. It would be misleading to leave any overall implication that well-organized antiexpansionist forces have seized the initiative and, from East to West, are mowing down divided and demoralized enemy troops. In our kind of crocodile society, as long as a single dollar and a single gram of "prestige" is lying around to tempt the conglomerates of headlong growth, the brigands will remain a threat to the distinctive character of livable communities and to individual lives within those communities. "Watergate in White" is how the Health-PAC Bulletin captioned this gem of expansionist rivalries.

In late August [1974], the owner, attorney and administrator of the Clinton Community Hospital in Prince George County, Maryland, were arrested for conspiring to bug and break into a local physician's office in an attempt to prevent the construction of another hospital he was setting up, reports the Washington Post.

The three had engaged the services of a private investigator to steal documents and gather information that might prevent the building of the new hospital.

The investigator arranged a job for his wife with the physician in question so that she might spy on him. The endeavor even included plans to crash-land a small plane on the hospital site to demonstrate that it lay dangerously close to the flight path of Andrews Air Force Base.

Later in that autumn, East Harlem suffered a long-pending defeat that, given a more dispersed and perhaps full-time grass-roots leadership, was definitely avoidable. As part of its massive rip-up and expansion program —which included one of those typical fires in buildings with recalcitrant tenants—Mount Sinai Hospital won final approval from the New York City Board of Standards and Appeals for a nine-story, exclusively-for-hospital-use, 590-car parking garage, on Park Avenue between 98th and 99th Streets. The garage had been opposed by Community Planning Board 11 and by poorly organized aggregates of residents, on grounds of the traffic problems and the environmental pollution it will create.

Involved here was a distinct political conflict

of interest for a member of Congress. The antigarage forces could never get Representative Herman Badillo, whose Bronx district dips down into East Harlem, to take a clear and unequivocal position on a long list of Mount Sinai nightmares. The conflict of interest was largely of Badillo's own making, in that it was more a psychological hang-up than a material matter of substance. As a Puerto Rican, Badillo seemed honored to be sitting on the board of a prestigious teaching hospital. Apparently he forgot the systematic harassment that hounded Puerto Rican and other tenants out of the buildings that Mount Sinai had bought and collected for its 590-car garage and for other planned facilities. From that low-income but quite livable corner of East Harlem, Mount Sinai "relocated" tenants to horror slums.

But that familiar old minority-group insecurity —that Stepin Fetchit gratification at "making it" into the larger WASP culture—paralyzed Badillo, and converted him into a useful institutional front man.

I do not mean to imply that the neighborhood should have put all their eggs in their Congressman's basket. To do that with any but the most highly principled politician is to ask to be left high and dry at some pivotal point. However, given the prestige and the publicity potential that elected officials do enjoy, strong support from Badillo could have helped to galvanize a genuine block-by-block resistance. I recall one offensively fence-sitting letter to a save-our-homes group from the Congressman, who was then in the midst of being all things to all men while campaigning to be mayor of New York. Despite its wishy-washy stance, the letter was not even signed.

One of the many ironies in institutional imperialism is the life-and-death attribute of what results when a healing institution (sometimes boasting that it has an inhalation-therapy unit) successfully schemes to substitute parking space for living space. Community Board 11 complained that the city's Traffic Department failed to give community leaders copies of the detailed study relating to the Mount Sinai parking facility. On a hospital's three-shift, around-the-clock schedule, the environmental impact on patients and on others of cars moving in and out of 590 parking spaces is hardly negligible. As Mount Sinai approached its moment of triumph over the neighborhood, the National Academy of Science estimated that up to 4,000 deaths each year in this country and 4 million sick days can be attributed to automobile emissions.

"The cunning of the fox is as violent [and as vile] as the murderousness of the wolf," said Tom Paine. Oppression refined remains oppression, said the eighteenth-century Quaker John Woolman. Perish the thought that the administrator of an expanding hospital or a university president or a museum director would ever personally threaten some benighted person standing in their publicly financed path to glory. But I perceive little substantive difference between their "refined" and foxy tactics, and the alleged threats in the spring of 1974 to "ruin my career" and to inflict bodily harm upon an environment consultant for Manhattan's West Side convention center.

According to the consultant, C. Michael Hogan, the threats came from the top and not from underlings: the center's executive vice-president and from two attorneys connected with the proposed $200 million project. One of the three men admitted applying pressure to get Hogan removed from the study. Hogan claimed they feared that his report might be negative. City officials took Hogan's charges seriously enough to withhold a decision on a construction permit until after a "thorough investigation."

Anyone who has waded into any bristling controversy where large amounts of money hang in the balance should not be surprised when the gloves come off and the going gets nasty. The fact that, by now, well over a half million dollars is tied up in my apartment building explains why a frustrated hospital periodically unsheathes its knives. Two years after Columbus supposedly settled its differences with us tenants, one of their attorneys, with fists drawn, leaned across a conference table and threatened tenant-representative Neal Hitzig for having challenged his veracity. "I'll have your eyes pulled out" was what the attorney spat out. The choice of language was of considerable interest to us.

Unless this country lapses into a U.S. version of right-wing totalitarianism, enough forces of dissent seem to be loose in the land to keep somewhat in check those expansionist elements that would like to rely on open threats and intimidation. Since that "scare 'em" (Plan C) mentality often goes hand in hand with organized corruption, we may even see a damper of sorts on both bullying tactics and the old-fashioned, almost openly displayed corruption that characterized a lot of expansion projects before the rise of consumerism and environmentalism. In Boston, at the end of 1974, "there were no eulogies," the *Boston Globe* reported, at the funeral of John A. Shea, old-line patronage dispenser until the mid-1960's for the State Public Works Department, for the Massachusetts Turnpike Authority, and for the sticky-fingered commissions that constructed the state office building and Boston's under-the-Common garage.

For twenty years, as those hundreds of millions

of dollars flowed without serious debate from the public treasury, changing forever the face of a lovely city and laying concrete over large sections of the state, John Shea was, in the *Globe*'s words, "one of the most powerful men behind the scenes of Massachusetts politics." In 1959, U.S. Attorney Elliot Richardson and Federal Judge Charles E. Wyzanski, Jr., teamed up to prove wholesale shakedowns involving the construction industry. Shea was among those indicted on conspiracy charges.

Shea's type is a dying breed, the *Globe* obituary correctly concluded. Those like him who linger on are probably baffled to see their wheeling-and-dealing power slipping through their fingers. In the mid-1970's, the no-growth, preserve-open-space conservationists, the antihighway groups and the we-won't-move forces would quickly have the scalp of a John A. Shea—especially if he compulsively kept dipping into the public cookie jar.

"It is impossible to patch up a crisis locally which is part of a world catastrophe," wrote Nobel Prize winner Albert Szent-Gyorgyi, M.D., in a Christmas 1974 letter to *The New York Times*. By every index of close kinship, the galloping crises in our health and educational systems are linked to Szent-Gyorgyi's larger picture. In his own way he appears to be saying that nothing will really change in a fundamental sense until everything changes. As I replay first the mental record of the 1968 Columbia University upheaval, then the Cambridge and campus cops out for student blood at Harvard in 1969, and finally our less dramatic but no less bitter confrontation with Columbus Hospital from 1970 to 1975—all with expansionist issues in the forefront—I latch onto a sentence by Eugène Ionesco in the December 1974 *Esquire:* "Ideologies and religions act as alibis; they are the alibis of the means."

The phrase brilliantly fits the moral and the mental makeup of all expansionists. Compulsively, institutionally, the godmother among the hospital nuns lies. Compulsively, institutionally, former President Pusey of Harvard lied. Compulsively, institutionally, former President Grayson Kirk of Columbia lied.

I would have more respect for a non-academic, non-medical rogue who would openly admit: "Yes, I'll hustle all the public funds I can lay my hands on, because that's what this institution of mine is all about. No, I care nothing about the patients, the students, our tenants, or those low-income neighbors just outside our gates. Yes, I know all about the private misery beneath and behind the glitter of my new publicly financed buildings.

"And, yes, I'll call in the cops and, if necessary, even the Mafia. Clear and simple, I'll tell them: If any student, any rent-striking tenant, any community resident sticks his head up above the crowd, smash it. I'm savage, and this institution is savage if you try to cross us."

Unfair and too strong, you say? Yet, do not the results of their remarkably similar policies all come down to that? On television, did not Senator Ervin remind the Watergate conspirators of the ancient legal adage that "Every man [every institution] is presumed to intend the natural consequences of his [its] acts"?

If the known natural consequences of tossing infirm elderly tenants out of their homes and out of similar surroundings are to precipitate their premature death, is murder not intended—whether by Harvard, by the Christian Science Center, or by Columbus Hospital?

If a natural and a known consequence of "relocating" families to unsafe slums is to add to the population of juvenile delinquents, is not increased crime in the streets intended—by a President Pusey in Cambridge, by a Mother Josephine in New York, or by some faceless leader of the Christian Science Mother Church in Boston's Back Bay?

But, you argue, do these men and women really and truly lie? Then hear this beginning of a 1970 *New England Journal of Medicine* article, "Aftermath of the Harvard Strike":

One of the student demands during their strike at Harvard in the spring of 1969 read as follows: "No evictions of 182 black and white families living in buildings Harvard is planning to tear down to expand its Medical School facilities in Boston."

On the evening of the University Hall takeover, before he called the police, President Nathan Pusey responded to this demand and to a demand concerning expansion in the University Road area of Cambridge: "There are no plans to tear down any apartments on University Road nor are any homes being torn down to make way for Harvard Medical School expansion."

If President Pusey had driven through the neighborhood surrounding the Medical School, he would have seen the rubble of houses owned by Harvard and torn down during the month preceding the University Hall takeover. In 1968, with a big splash in the Boston newspapers, Harvard publicized its plans for a new hospital complex to be built near the Medical School. Harvard's real-estate agent had already sent letters notifying residents that they would be vacated by 1971. Some houses had already been razed, and others had become vacant as tenants moved out.

On the day after the bust, Robert H. Ebert, dean of the Medical School, released a detailed statement of plans to tear down the housing in question.

Although this statement announced measures for relocation of tenants and offered an elaborate justification of the new hospital complex, it also verified that the student demand had a basis in fact.

Dean Ebert's announcement boldly contra-
dicted President Pusey's account of the Medical School's
expansion.

But, you further object, would a healing institution or one charged with tender loving care of the infirm
and the elderly really be allied with the underworld? In
late 1974, the Senate Subcommittee on Long-Term Care
and the Temporary New York State Commission on the
Economy and Cost of Living both thought so when they
announced joint public hearings into the murky, ever-
expanding nursing home industry, its underworld ties, and
its political connections. "An empire of pain and profit"
is how the Commission chairman summarized the shock-
ing care and the multimillion-dollar overcharges to the
government.

The names of Meyer Lansky, Joseph A. Colom-
bo, Sr., and financier Louis Wolfson have all come up as
men with investments in or links to the industry. In reporting the launching of the investigation, *The New York
Times* (December 21, 1974) added: "Law officials have
been alerted to possible links between the Mafia and
nursing homes since the Medicaid program began eight
years ago."

The *Times* referred to reports that underworld
interests use nursing homes to launder funds—an easy-to-
cover-up process that an East Side accountant has long
suspected is true of a particular expansion-minded hospital
in Manhattan's Bedpan Alley.

As a battle-scarred five-year veteran who early
resolved that Columbus Hospital would *never* convert our
building into a parking lot, I know we would have lost the
war (and maybe our heads) long ago if we hadn't taken
repeatedly to the streets and to the courts, if we hadn't

253

dreamed up a wide variety of imaginative tactics that brought protective publicity, and if we had neglected to draw constantly on support from the citywide tenant movement, loose though that force may be.

We've had our problems: money problems, lawyer problems, personality problems (though these have been held to an amazing minimum), up-and-down morale problems, and problems of politically underdeveloped tenants and neighbors. (In 1971, when "underdeveloped" neighbor Dick Flanagan, promotion manager of the *Wall Street Journal* and a tenant in another Columbus-owned building, decided to join our demonstration outside Governor Rockefeller's apartment, a whole new—and surprisingly joyous—world opened up for him. Like so many other novices, the thought of picketing had never before entered his mind. And, like other novices, he may well have worried in advance about being seen by respectable friends and business associates.)

But all those obstacles seem as nothing when stacked against the overriding hurdle of a brilliantly structured, profit-oriented institutional system that is implicitly-explicitly, subtly-grossly, peacefully-violently anti-people to its roots. In order for us the people to win, that system has to be turned inside out, made public, and made responsive/responsible to a local, decentralized constituency. As Health-PAC points out, it's not enough for the financing to come from public sources and to be funneled through the secret and fly-papered labyrinths of the "voluntary," expansion-minded hospitals. To a large extent, that is already the case. By 1971, 60 percent of their operating costs came from Medicaid and Medicare. Yet they very much remain closed, private, guarded empires.

With such obvious civil-liberties exceptions as private medical records, just about everything in institutional life—and especially *all* financial records and transactions—must be made regularly subject to full and immediate disclosure. (The word "immediate" is crucial. In 1974, when the expansionist Port of New York Authority scratched the back of its executive director and voted him an inordinately high raise, that little item was discreetly omitted from the minutes of their closed meeting. The hope and plan was that neither the governors of New York and New Jersey, with their veto power, nor the public would learn about it for a good long time. By then, the sting would have gone out of the issue.) Only by full and immediate disclosure can the corruption and the de facto profits be taken out of health, educational and other institutions that are robbing us blind under one halo or another.

The secrecy of universities, the stealth of life-and-death hospitals is self-condemning. It makes a mockery out of the U. S. self-image of an open society. Slow though it may be, the trend is definitely away from the arcane and the secretive, as more and more laws force more and more information out into the open. The laws, of course, are a response to popular pressures and to pressures from other entrepreneurs upset that so much of the goodies have been going to the "nonprofit" sector. In less than a decade, we've reached the point where hardly any politician or any serious molder of public opinion would dare to challenge the concept of community involvement in educational, health-care and other institutional policy-making. Today, public hearings are routine on a wide range of issues that, as recently as the Kennedy years, were still decided far from the public gaze.

Hospitals will continue to be pressured to decentralize and to experiment—just as cottage hospitals are being tested out today under England's wholly different (but also troubled) structure of health care. Were universities to stand pat and still, their enrollments would drop even further. For higher education as presently structured has already lost much of its hitherto automatic appeal for young North Americans. Field work and community service—which create no rationales for expensive, tuition-raising expansionist policies—will be even more in vogue, especially in a period of deep national distress. And nursing homes will be under more and more constraint to accept, at lower cost to Medicaid, elderly patients who can sleep at home in their own beds at night, but who require some daytime supervision and company. The heat is on. None of these institutions will be permitted to remain static and frozen.

Before this decade runs its painful course, I would expect to see linkage of tenant and community groups across the country that will exchange valuable specific experiences in coping with encroaching institutions. David Dellinger and other seasoned activists are responding to a movement-public communication gap by initiating a national newsweekly magazine, *Sevendays*. Still others are mapping plans for an openly revolutionary labor or socialist party, which will be designed to pull together under one ideological umbrella those tens (or possibly hundreds) of thousands who are toiling in ever more vibrant movement vineyards.

Just as workers' education is a staple in the better and more democratic trade union, so will there be workshops and weekend institutes and summer conferences—some financed out of the participant's own pockets; some operating with foundation/church/individual grants —to train a whole new generation of organizers to function efficiently and effectively in housing, health and other fields. In the fall of 1974, for example, in both Brooklyn

256

and Manhattan, there was a School for Organizers, sponsored by the Brooklyn Tenants Union and the East Side Tenants Union, in cooperation with the Student Bar Association of Brooklyn Law School and the Lenox Hill Neighborhood Association. Included in the curriculum were courses on Affirmative Action in the Housing Court, The Heat Crisis and Your Landlord, Paper Expenses and Hidden Profits, and All About Rent Control. Tuition was free.

In Bedpan Alley (the one in Manhattan that might be covetously eyeing Peter Stuyvesant Park for a tiny corner here and a little piece there were it not for coordinated neighborhood protection of that turf), we veterans of four separate hospital wars are well aware of the limited impact we have had. For half a decade, we've been chopping away at the four nearest tentacles of an octopus that reaches out to Chile and environs south of our borders, to Greece, Italy, Portugal and every other troubled country in the Old World, to the Middle East and Indo-China, to the Philippines and to neocolonized Africa. It is, as Dr. Albert Szent-Gyorgyi put it in his letter to the *Times,* "the conspiracy of the few against the many." Our globe, he maintains, "has shrunk too much to have politics [concentrated economics] based on 'dog eats dog' instead of 'man helps man'."

That unloving system with which we've been doing battle is far from dead. Having had to dissect its workings in order to hold our own, we've gotten to know it far better than we did on May 15, 1970, when Columbus Hospital's get-out-and-get-lost notices arrived in the mail via Urban Relocation enforcers. Not from any elitist bias, but rather because I'd never before shared one trench with so many for so protracted a war, I did not viscerally feel five years ago Jefferson's abiding trust in the wisdom

257

of ordinary people when they are fully informed and when they are unburdened by manipulative leaders. Today, in my guts, I do:

> There is no safe depository of the ultimate powers of society, but the people themselves. . . . If we think them not enlightened enough to exercise their control with a wholesome discretion, the remedy is not to take it from them, but to inform their discretion by education.

In any definitive sense, we haven't won—nor will we for a good long time to come, unless the brotherhood of man is much closer than any of us realizes. We too have pushed the system to the limit, but nowhere is that limit good enough. Visitors to these shores tell us that the United States is the most politically underdeveloped "advanced" country on the face of the earth. Despite this, people can and will become educated—sometimes overnight as the result of a personal or economic trauma—once the system in which they have had implicit faith fails them in more ways than they can possibly deny.

Every green tenant committee that comes looking for advice and counsel has to learn quickly that it's not necessary to reinvent the wheel. Book shelves and file cabinets are brimming with accumulated experience. For whatever they are worth, as distilled in the pages of this book, our diaries, our records, our files, the prized scalps hanging from our belts quite properly belong in the public domain—as does our collective destiny in the institutional wars that rage on.

Appendix A
How to Do It

If by dawn tomorrow the will to build institutional empires were to evaporate, every victim could turn in joy to life's more fulfilling demands.

Faced as we are with nuclear survival issues, no one should have to be preoccupied with rescue operations on the reformist level described in this book. In most instances, the expansionist mystique is so inherently irrational and indefensible that individual manifestations of it should fall of their own weight. Indeed, one day they will all fall. Unfortunately, in our present real world, one of the tales told by an idiot is institutional encroachment on people, on the ecology, on such urban amenities as lifting up our eyes to marvels of nature—like the two trees on East 19th Street that the Columbus Hospital construction bosses impatiently buzz-sawed out of their way.

And so there's no choice but to be trained in the arts of community survival while simultaneously building the social and moral climate where unhealthy institutional drives will indeed wither or evaporate. Like everything else of a why-does-it-happen-to-me? variety that looms up as burdensome and wearying and arduous, the difficulty of learning those arts is largely in our minds. When the resolve is there—and that comes from an almost spiritual awareness of what the destruction of communities really signifies—mastering them is not all that irksome or time consuming.

On one unenchanting evening in June 1972, my fellow tenants and I saw the block-busting mentality—condensed, crystallized and horribly naked—in the session with the Columbus Hospital nuns. We were told we'd all live happily ever after if we would trust the untrustworthy, would quit our homes on virtually no notice ("Sign in thirty-six hours, or we'll sell the building"), and would unlearn all that we had so painfully learned about them.

The $168,000 in bribes was available that Orwellian evening because of the cumulative impact of

1. our publicity;
2. our legal techniques;
3. our political activity;
4. our broad community support;
5. our painstaking research;
6. our action in the streets, up to and including arrests.

All of which, in turn, stemmed from

a. our durability;
b. our hard-nosed, no-nonsense determination to stay put in our apartments;
c. our readiness to pass through the fires of harassment;
d. our almost teeth-gritting enjoyment that comes from puncturing pretense, deflating pomposity, and exposing what we saw as common fraud in high institutional guise.

In it all, the secret of ultimate success lies in an

ever-shifting balanced program and in a schedule of collectively decided activity.

Under 1., perhaps the most important factors are the cultivation of a sense of pacing (a time to be noisy and a time to be quiet), the down-playing of any cult of personality (the public and editors have a sixth sense for ego trips), and the development of a reputation for accuracy (which is a major weapon against quaking institutional liars).

Raised as I was by parents who themselves were constantly into civic and antidiscriminatory battles, I've always remembered my mother's admonition to avoid even the appearance of being a sorehead. If that abrasive quality creeps into a group's image, the public soon turns off, however valid the grievances. Hence the not-without-laughter admonition, even in the thick of combat.

Under 2., what legal tactics one seeks to learn and to utilize depends, of course, on the particular situation. It may require mastering the procedures of an administrative agency, or becoming knowledgeable in complex zoning laws, or getting to know the rules of a housing court, or pressing for remedial legislation.

Also essential is a clear understanding, from the beginning, with a group's attorney that he/she has been retained to represent collective decisions—and *not* his/her notion of what's best for a group of lay persons. To get this point across belatedly to our own tenant lawyer, I cited an imaginary case of a middle-class union attorney who might sincerely believe, from his perspective, that the members he represents need, above all, longer annual vacations from the tedium of an assembly line. But during collective bargaining sessions it would be highly unprofessional for him to impose that view if the workers wish to give priority to in-plant safety demands.

Under 3., it's very important to take a broad

definition of the word "political," in order not to wind up one day in the tightly sewn vest pocket of some unreliable politician. The range of political activity is only as narrow as the group's own horizon, and there should be no feeling of undue gratitude toward an official whose help is no more than a proper part of his job.

A group's enduring muscle comes from the cultivation of 4. The ground rules here are obvious: mutual aid, constant communication, total honesty, broad democratic involvement in decision-making.

Realistically, not everyone is equipped to take on 5. But even in a poor Appalachian belt of high illiteracy, there would almost always be someone with the potential, if cultivated, to dig up the relevant information. Talent abounds in the unlikeliest places, and learning to tap it is the beginning both of organizational wisdom and also of a leader's faith and trust in people. In addition, the recognition that skill is widely dispersed, if often hidden, helps avoid the obnoxious savior complex.

6. can be strong and useful wine when taken in proper intervals and in restrained amounts. Addiction becomes counterproductive. Of all courses open to a group at a particular strategic moment, direct action is the one that warrants the most careful consideration. So long as the action is well thought out and effective, the sight of the resisting "hordes" out in the street—or, worse, marching onto an institution's premises—triggers the greatest panic ("Oh, God, here *they* come"—the ones we've been abusing).

For protest demonstrations mean that the victims of rape are not relying solely on publicity, or solely on a two-strikes-against-them legal system, or solely on the weight of researched evidence, or solely on a one-hand-tied-behind-our-backs political process that, especially after

262

Watergate, is perceived as not quite for real. Direct action signifies also that community support has been mobilized and yanked out of polite and decorous channels. (We glimpsed that at the 1972 demonstration led by Dan Berrigan outside Columbus Hospital when a sympathetic and very supportive foundation executive who lives a block away got so carried away by the spirit of the day that he grabbed a picket sign and joined the march.)

"Nobody Knows the Trouble I've Seen" could be the theme song of everyone who has had to confront encroaching institutions. They are truly incorrigible. Their ambitions burn with an unquenchable white heat, turning some otherwise decent individuals into ogres. They halt their depredations when—and only when—they are unable to mow down a superior massed force.

Never would I have chosen, of my own free and informed will, to tie myself down for half a decade over a microscopic community battlefront. (When you run into friends you haven't seen for a long time and who know nothing about the institutional expansionism issue, it's incredibly difficult, in a brief conversation, to account for those "lost" years.) But aside from helping to save the roof over my own head, the satisfaction from playing a part in keeping elderly fellow tenants in a sound building at rents they can afford makes every difficult moment and every gray hair and all lost income entirely worth it.

Appendix B
How to Get Publicity

> If you don't know where you're going, any road will get you there.
> —PROFESSOR N. CHATERJEE, Antioch College

One basic rule: assume nothing. Without follow-up phone calls, don't assume that the U. S. Post Office has delivered your releases. Don't assume that the desk person or reporter is aware of such issues as hospital expansionism, etc. Watch your calendar carefully, and don't assume that a particular Sunday is just like any other when you're planning an event or press conference. Sunday morning, April 11, can turn out to be Easter, and all the TV crews may be out covering the big parade.

The date for a release may be determined by your would-be target audience. For example, in New York I have a strong preference for the *Times* as the newspaper of record, with TV as a close second. Traditionally, but not invariably, the easiest days to get stories into the papers are Monday (because of relatively little news breaking on Sunday) and Sunday (because of the larger number of pages devoted to news, and because Saturday too tends to be a light news-breaking day).

If you're aiming for repetitive radio news coverage, then Saturday and Sunday are usually good for twenty-four-hour-news radio stations. The disadvantage of weekends is the reduced number of TV crews on duty, especially with the recent economy cutbacks. But if the story is sufficiently serious and important, and if the TV assignment editors have been given adequate advance notice wherever feasible (adequate meaning by Thursday), you can usually get TV coverage.

Releases should be as short as possible, but adequate to tell the story, should conform to all the stylistic rules (double- or even triple-spaced; wide margins at top and bottom and sides) and be neatly typed. The person sending out a release should ask himself or herself: If I were on the city desk and knew absolutely nothing about the subject matter, would this release tell me enough to judge the importance of the story? Be sure there are up top at least two phone numbers (not perpetually busy) where during daytime, evening, or weekend hours, the newsperson could call and be filled in. Try to design an imaginative and distinctive letterhead for news releases that will stick in the memory of persons on news desks. This can include the use of soft, not garish, colored paper (canary yellow, light blue, or green). Then, if your releases are few and far between, you won't be a new (i.e., a forgotten) group each time whose bona fides must be established afresh.

Editors and assignment desks are extremely susceptible to trends. If the competition is showing an interest in a continuing story, they're much more likely to be interested, even if the thrust of the story goes against the political grain of the paper or news agency. Therefore it pays to send one or two previously printed press clippings of the same general story as background material.

Always mail releases at a post office—preferably your town's main post office. Almost never rely on the corner mailbox, no matter how many collections are listed. I for one am not so irrational as to spend hours on a release and then be unwilling to spend an extra half hour to deposit the envelopes at a post office.

With regard to newspapers, a general rule is to send the first release to the news director, local desk. "Local" unless there is clearly a broader regional or foreign angle. Thus if Dr. Spock were to participate in some fairly dramatic housing action, or if elected officials (such as a Julian Bond) were going to be sitting in at a hearing held by New York City councilmen, then the release should also go to the national desk. And if Bernadette Devlin were to help lead a squat-in in Chinatown, then the release should go in separate envelopes to the local, national and foreign desks. When appropriate, a release should go in separate envelopes to the photo editor (dailies, AP, UPI, etc.). Also, don't neglect or forget your neighborhood, local college, local church, ethnic and racial minority publications. They reach a great many people.

If you're trying to get coverage of a press conference or an event, a second or reminder release should go to the assignment editor, local desk, or to the weekend assignment editor if the event is on a weekend. A final reminder can be by phone twenty-four or thirty-six hours in advance of the event.

Over and above the basic mailing to the key decision-making persons (news directors, assignment editors), there can and should be a mailing of copies of the release to reporters or desk persons whom you know to be honest, fair-minded, sympathetic, or familiar with the subject matter. Sometimes they are in a position to get an otherwise uninterested assignment editor to see the importance of an upcoming event or story.

It's important never to rely solely in your mailings on such individuals. They may be ill, on assignment, on vacation, etc. Remember, too, that they're usually off two days a week in succession, so last-minute mailings to them can be futile.

With limited manpower and resources, hand-delivery of releases to widely scattered addresses is not an economical utilization of man hours. Use the mails whenever possible, but hand-deliver if there's any serious question of delivery in time. Sometimes, for the most important agencies, I invest an extra sixty cents, in addition to first-class postage, for special-delivery service. But to those agencies I also send duplicate copies by regular mail, as a double check.

In New York City there are one or more outfits with direct teletype lines into the main news agencies. If you're pushing, say, a 3 P.M. deadline for a story for the following morning's paper, you can, for a fee (used to be $25.00—probably more now) phone in your story to one of these outfits (I'd feel safer, in terms of accuracy, hand-delivering it, or having a messenger or their messenger pick it up and deliver it). They'll get it right out on their wires to AP, UPI, the *Times*, the TV stations, etc.

I believe that most members of morning newspaper staffs come to work in midmorning (10 to 11 A.M.) and that only a skeleton crew is on duty until then. Therefore, there are few reporters to be sent out on early-morning assignments—a factor to be kept in mind in planning any event or press conference that could be set at a later hour. Especially in big cities, be extremely wary of calling press conferences unless the issue is genuinely hot, or unless you have a "name" person who is almost certain to guarantee coverage. A group can become demoralized if no reporters show up. The staff of an afternoon paper begins arriving at work about 1 A.M., so their desk people and reporters are usually available in full numbers in the postsunrise hours. Thus an 11 A.M. press conference or event may be a good hour for morning and afternoon papers and for the evening TV newscasts.

If aiming to make the early evening TV newscasts with pictorial coverage, try to give the camera crews an hour to return (in traffic) to their studios with their film, and three-four-five additional hours for developing, editing and fitting into a news show. Obviously, if the news should be earth-shattering and the desk is awaiting the arrival of certain film, less time for processing would be required.

On the phone or face to face, especially if a reporter or desk person is at all sympathetic or just fair-minded, always try to get his or her name, telephone number and extension. Make an index card noting the occasion and date you were in touch with him, his degree of knowledge and sophistication, and his seeming viewpoint (friendly, hostile, neutral). On any follow-up or for some future event, you can ask for a specific person and thus save minutes of backgrounding whoever happens to answer the phone.

If something is confidential and can't be revealed, don't try to be coy or evasive. Just tell any reporter or desk person frankly that it's a matter that you're not authorized or in a position to discuss at this time.

Though a reporter, not necessarily out of ill will, may try repeatedly to coax you into predicting the expected turnout at a meeting or a demonstration, you should practically never give out figures. It is adequate and

268

reasonable to reply that the coming event has been widely publicized. But given the uncertain weather factor, people's busy schedules, and their competing commitments, as well as other events on the community calendar, there is no realistic way of knowing how many people will be on hand.

In their enthusiasm, activists are nearly always way off in the accuracy of their predictions. A group may be acutely and needlessly embarrassed if one inexperienced spokesperson has confidently prophesied a crowd of a thousand, and then "only a hundred" actually appear. Ironically, without an exaggerated prediction, the target institution or government agency may be greatly shaken if a mere dozen or two community residents—in good spirits and with high morale—turn up on a picket line. (In the early days of protest over Vietnam, antiwar groups rejoiced if fifty people joined a carefully planned demonstration.)

For any future rush releases, you can save a half hour or so by always having several sets of press envelopes already typed up and stamped (for mailing) or unstamped (for hand-delivery). Also, there's less chance of typographical errors if the material is not typed under pressure.

Index

270

Brown, Sam, 61-62
Bruzelius, Nils, 160, 161

C. E. Maguire, Inc. (consulting
    firm), 201, 214-215
Cabrini, Mother Frances, 74, 76, 92,
    102, 122, 124, 125, 133
Cabrini Health Center, 146
Cabrini Towers, 104, 105
Cambridge, Massachusetts, 29, 213-
    219, 230-234
Cambridge Civic Association, 216
Campbell, Robert, 59
Campus by the Sea (brochure), 193
Carr, Bernard F., 170
Cassidy, Father, 139, 141
Catholic Archdiocese of New York,
    138-139
Catholic Charities, 101, 138-139, 141
Cazenovia College, 244
Cedars of Lebanon Hospital, 36-37,
    57, 173
    bankruptcy scandal, 165-169
Certificates of eviction, 81, 154
Chase Manhattan Bank, 132
Chemical Bank, 50
Chicago Daily News, 166
Christian   Science   International
    Church Center, 177-191, 230,
    251
    community resistance to, 185, 187-
    188
Christian Science Monitor, 180-182,
    184, 203
Christian Science Mother Church,
    177-191, 252
    expansion program, 178, 181-182,
    186-187
Church Park I, 183, 184, 187
Church Park II, 187
Churchill, Sir Winston, 147
Citadel   Management   Corporation,
    70, 77, 109
Citizens League Against the Sonic
    Boom, 205
Clark, Monsignor Eugene V., 139,
    142, 143, 145
Clingan, Eldon, 71, 91, 95, 99, 123,
    129
Clinton Community Hospital, 246
Coffin, Frank M., 189
Coleman, William T., Jr., 229
Collins, John, 224
Colombo, Joseph A., Sr., 253
Columbia Point, Massachusetts, 191-
    198

housing project, 192, 195-198
racial prejudice, 192
student housing, 195-198
Columbia University, 49, 251
Columbia-Presbyterian Medical
    Center, 26
Columbus Hospital, 33, 42, 47, 70,
    72-151, 174, 219, 239, 241, 249,
    250-253, 257, 259, 260, 263
adverse publicity for, 85, 86, 91,
    99, 100-103, 104, 126, 145-146
Cabrini Towers and, 104, 105
certificates of eviction, 81
compared to Bellevue, 74
damage suit filed against, 96-97
dedication of Cabrini Health
    Center, 132-147
expansion plans of, 75, 93-94, 104
files countersuit, 123
medical reputation of, 74-75
Mother Cabrini's feast day, 122,
    126
political ploy, 118
state mortgage loan, 95-98
Urban Relocation Company and,
    77-91, 98-100
ColumbuScope (house organ), 146
Committee for Economic Develop-
    ment, 64
Commonweal, 58
Community Development Revenue
    Sharing (CDRS), 60
Community groups
educating organizers, 256-257
guide for organizing, 259-263
legal tactics for, 260, 261
national linking of, 256
political activity, 260, 261-262
publicity for, 260-261, 264-269
research required, 260, 262
street action by, 260, 262
support for, 260, 262
Community Planning Board 6, 89,
    94
Community   Planning   Board   11,
    246-248
Comprehensive   Health   Planning
    Council of Florida, 167
Concorde (SST), 205, 206
Connecticut River, 54
Connolly, Mother Irene, 75, 92
Cooke, Terence Cardinal, 133, 146
CORE (Congress of Racial Equal-
    ity), 31

Davis, Alton, 185

271

Interstate Highway, 227, 228
Interstate Highway 66, 229
Iowa's Century Freeway, 227, 228
New Jersey Turnpike, 226
Southwest Expressway, 226
state government resistance to, 223-224
University of Vermont's resistance to, 228
Hill-Burton Hospital Construction Act (1947), 155, 240, 243
Hilton Hotel Corporation, 57
Hitzig, Neal, 71, 95, 105, 107, 114, 119, 136, 141, 142, 249
Hogan, C. Michael, 248
Hospital for Special Surgery, 175
Hospital Workers Union, 73
Hospitals
curbs on expansion, 239-243
decentralization of, 225-226
expansion programs, 153-158
experimentation by, 225-226
health planning groups and, 242
increase in costs, 155-156
increase in expenditures, 36
state regulation of, 173-174

Iannuzzi, John Nicholas, 70, 107, 108, 113, 126, 127, 131-143, 147, 148-150
Iannuzzi, Nicholas, 70, 107, 108
Innocent, Mother, 100, 141, 142
Institutional coercion, 33-34
The Master Plan, 33-34, 71
Instrument Landing System (ILS), 212
Internal Revenue Service, 165
Ionesco, Eugène, 250
ITT (International Telephone & Telegraph Corporation), 153

Jackson Memorial Hospital, 167
Jefferson, Thomas, 257-258
Jersey City, New Jersey, 46
JFK Library Committee, 219
John, DeWitt, 180-181
John Hancock Mutual Life Insurance Company, 158, 193
Johnson, Eric, 155
Johnson, Karla, 185
Johnston, William, 176
Joint Commission on Accreditation of Hospitals, 241
Jones, Hubie, 197, 198

Kee, Jed, 118

Kennedy, Edward M., 205-206
Kennedy, John F., 30
Kennedy Library Corporation, 213-219
Kennedy Library Museum, 29-30, 213-219, 230
community resistance to, 213-219
initial cost of, 214
Kennedy School of Government, 214
Key Biscayne Bank, 166
Killay, Dr. William H., 171
King, Edward J., 200, 202, 203, 210
King, Will, 23
Kirk, Grayson, 251
Klein, Bertram, 76
Klein, Mayer and Korn, 76-77, 109
Knights of Columbus, community resistance to, 66-69
Koch, Edward, 81, 129

Land conservation (banking), 244-245
Lansky, Meyer, 253
Le Blanc, Nancy, 150
Lee, Bobby, 144, 187
Lee, Henry, 222
Lefkowitz, Louis, 78
Lennox, California, 209
Lenox Hill Neighborhood Association, 257
Levitt, Arthur, 38-39
Lewiston, Maine, 47
Lincoln Center, 37, 41, 42, 78
Lincoln Hospital (South Bronx), 241-242
Lindsay, John, 81, 133, 152
Logan International Airport, 191, 198-213, 227, 230
community resistance to, 198-199, 202, 204-205, 208
suburban resistance to, 210-213
Logue, Edward J., 186, 193
London *Times,* 200
Los Angeles International Airport, 209
Lovejoy, Samuel H., 53-56
Lyons, Richard D., 65, 169, 170

McCue, Wood C., 168-169
McDonald's, community resistance to, 230-234
Mancini, Charlie, 104, 134, 136, 140-142
Manhattan Convention Center, 59, 248
Marpaul Corporation, 77

273

274